Groups in Process

An Introduction to Small Group Communication

SIXTH EDITION

Larry L. Barker

Professor Emeritus Auburn University

Kathy J. Wahlers

Barry University

Kittie W. Watson

Tulane University

Allyn and Bacon

Boston • London • Toronto • Sydney • Tokyo • Singapore

Editor-in-chief: *Karen Hanson*
Series Editor: *Karon Bowers*
Series editorial assistant: *Jennifer Becker*
Marketing Manager: *Jacqueline Aaron*
Composition and prepress buyer: *Linda Cox*
Manufacturing Buyer: *Megan Cochran*
Cover Administrator: *Linda Knowles*
Editorial-production service: *Shepherd, Inc.*
Electronic composition: *Shepherd, Inc.*

Library of Congress Cataloging-in-Publication Data

Barker, Larry Lee, 1941-
    Groups in process : an introduction to small group communication / Larry L.
Barker,
    Kathy J. Wahlers, Kittie W. Watson.—6th ed.
      p.   cm.
    Includes bibliographical references and index.
    ISBN 0-205-32850-4
    1. Small groups. 2. Communication in small groups. 3. Group decision making. I.
Wahlers, Kathy J. II. Watson, Kittie W. III. Title

HM736.B37 2000
302.3'4—dc21   00-061854

Printed in the United States of America
10 9 8 7 6 5 4 3 2 1 05 04 03 02 01 00

Photo Credits: Chapter 1: Courtesy of Barry University; Chapter 2: Courtesy
of Barry University; Chapter 3: Will Hart; Chapter 4: Courtesy of Barry Univeristy;
Chapter 5: Robert Harbison; Chapter 6: Courtesy of Barry University; Chapter 7: Will
Hart; Chapter 8: Courtesy of Barry University; Chapter 9: Ron Edmonds/AP/
Wide World; Chapter 10: Courtesy of Barry University; Chapter 11: Will Faller

Contents

5 *Listening and Feedback in Small Groups*   68

6 *Problem Solving*   92

8 *Leadership in Small Groups*   *141*

9 *Conflict Management and Resolution in Small Groups*   *160*

10 *Special Forms and Techniques for Small Group Communication*   *179*

11   *Planning and Conducting Meetings*   214

Preface

The sixth edition of this book went into production as we changed from the twentieth to the twenty-first century. Twenty-five years have lapsed since the idea for this text was conceived by a small group of communication teachers, researchers, and authors. Our basic premise was that a group should be able to write a more complete, relevant, and accurate text than any one of us could write alone.

Our small group had several goals. One goal was to write a student friendly text. We think we have accomplished that goal as each chapter begins with study questions, includes principles that act as internal summaries of important points, and ends with ideas for discussion, selected projects and activities, and annotated suggested readings.

A second goal was to bridge the gap between traditional group discussion books and the newer approaches to small group communication texts. While the reader might have made other choices in attempting to balance these two approaches, our group is comfortable with the compromises that we have made and think that each edition has come closer to this goal as well.

The thought that the members of our team would change over time never occurred to us twenty-five years ago. While the untimely death of our friend and colleague Bob Kibler stunned us, we still feel his presence through the contributions that have been carried over into each new edition. Kittie Watson joined the team, developed some of the ideas of Don Cegala (a contributor to the first two editions), and provided the applied material in meeting management. Larry Barker took early retirement from Auburn University a couple of years ago to devote more time to consulting. Even the editorial team changed as the first four editions were published by Prentice Hall and editions five and six have been published by Allyn and Bacon. Although some of the members have changed, the group spirit remains.

We can never fully acknowledge the suggestions of all our students, friends, colleagues, and reviewers over the years. Special thanks goes to Bonnie Gabel of DePaul University and Rebecca Litke of California State University at Northridge. for their suggestions for this edition. We also want to acknowledge the contributions of Lisa Darnell who became a "temporary" team member on this edition. Thank you as well to Barry University for contributing photographs to this edition and to the entire editorial and production team at Allyn and Bacon.

As always, we welcome your comments and suggestions for future editions.

Introduction

Study Questions _____

After reading this chapter, you should be able to answer the following questions completely and accurately:

1. What are nine basic levels of communication?
2. What are three distinctions between small group communication and dyadic communication?
3. What is the definition of a small group?
4. What is the definition of small group communication?
5. What is the relationship between small group performance and individual performance?
6. Who requires less time to complete a task—individuals or small groups?
7. To what does the term *process* refer in the study of small groups?

No interaction

In any given day, many of us interact with small groups: our family unit at breakfast, our colleagues at the office, the aerobics class at the gym, the league softball team. Most of us don't actually stop to think about all of the groups with which we are involved. Some of us are involved with many groups; some of us are members of only a few. How are the groups in which you are involved alike? How are they different?

When several students took time to list the number of groups in which they participate, most of them found that they were a part of twenty to thirty small groups. Some of the groups were not continuing ones (such as group projects in biology lab), while others have existed for years and would probably continue indefinitely (such as civic, social, or religious organizations). The students also noticed differences in the way they reacted in different groups, differences in their own reactions versus those of others in their groups, and differences in decision-making strategies used in the various small groups.

This book will help sharpen your personal awareness of communication behavior in small groups and will provide principles to improve your ability to contribute in small group interactions. It assumes that you have had experiences in small group communication and that you will have an opportunity to apply some of the principles and concepts presented in this book in real-life situations.

Small groups are important to you not only in interpersonal relationships but also in such areas as education, politics, business, industry, and religion. Although you may not be a direct participant in many such groups, they often have a direct bearing on your future and your happiness. For example, most businesses and government agencies use committees to make recommendations and decisions, and most committees use the principles of group dynamics in their interactions. This book should help you understand some of the ways in which decisions are made in groups and some of the forces that shape and modify small group communication.

The subtitle of this book, "An Introduction to Small Group Communication," indicates that two primary concepts will be discussed: small groups and communication. Although communication may be discussed without reference to a given level (e.g., interpersonal, mass, cultural), and small groups may be discussed without reference to communication (e.g., primary groups, social reference groups), the combination of the concepts results in a unique interrelationship. Consequently, in this book, communication will be discussed primarily as it relates to small groups, and small groups will be examined from a communication viewpoint, as opposed to a sociological or psychological viewpoint.

By way of definition, a *sociological* approach to a small group interaction would emphasize the role of small groups in establishing and maintaining social order. The emphasis would also be on pressures provided by small groups to conform to social norms. In addition, a sociologist would be concerned with the function small groups serve to help link the individual to society as a whole.

The *psychological* approach to small group behavior focuses on the role that groups play in helping people adjust to their world and its problems. Group therapy is used by clinical psychologists and psychiatrists to help individual members feel accepted and secure; T groups and sensitivity groups are also tools of psychologists and social psychologists. Some of these concepts are discussed briefly in this book, but the primary focus is on the broader area of small group behavior—that which takes place on a daily basis in education, business, government, civic organizations, and social settings.

This approach focuses on a *process* or *systems* view of small group communication. However, the text includes elements from all approaches and attempts to provide both traditional and contemporary approaches to the study of small group communication. The following section identifies the interrelationships among levels of communication with special emphasis on the relative status of small group communication.

Levels of Communication

Several communication scholars (Ruesch and Bateson, 1951; Barker, 2001) have attempted to develop a hierarchy of communication levels, proceeding from the simple to the complex. The levels are identified in Figure 1.1. Note that small group communication is a subclass of interpersonal communication near the middle hierarchy of levels in terms of perceived complexity. The diagram suggests that intrapersonal communication and

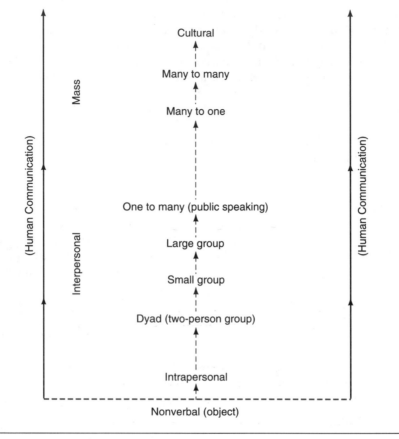

FIGURE 1.1 *Levels of Communication*

dyadic communication skills may precede or be combined with small group communication skills.[1] In essence, small group communication may be viewed as a level of interpersonal communication that incorporates intrapersonal and dyadic (verbal and nonverbal) elements, but that differs as the number of potential interactions increases.

In addition to the increased possibility for interaction inherent in small groups, there are other important distinctions between small group communication and other levels, particularly the dyad (two-person) groups. Although some scholars identify dyads as small groups, this text does not, because there are several important differences between the two. Perhaps the most important distinction is in the potential for information sharing and

[1]Of course, the nonverbal (object) level also may interact with small group communication. Examples of such interaction might be the environment in which a small group communicates, the physical arrangement of chairs in the room, or music in the room.

Dyads → Two people groups
Small Group → Three or more people

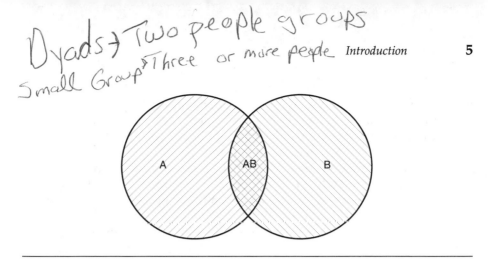

FIGURE 1.2 *Dyad (One Combination)*

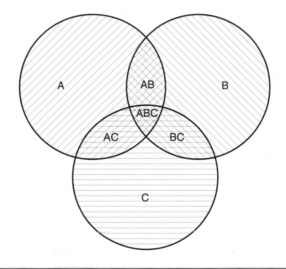

FIGURE 1.3 *Basic Small Group (Three-person, Four Combinations)*

exchange. Figures 1.2 and 1.3 illustrate differences in the number of original combinations of ideas possible between a dyad and a three-person group. The different shadings represent areas in which new combinations of ideas are possible by putting members with original ideas together and allowing them to interact.

What this means in real-life discussion groups is that if member A has an idea that is not fully developed, it is possible that member B might be able to provide some insight on the basis of previous training or experience. However, by adding the background and experience of both member B and member C (see Figure 1.3), the possibilities of adding valuable information increase *four* times. As group members are added, the potential for new combinations of ideas among members increases geometrically (i.e., increases several times

the actual number of members added). Of course, there is a point of dimin-
ishing returns (at about fifteen participants), in which adding other members
is of little (or negative) value, because possibilities for interaction are limited.
It is at this point that the group no longer has a basic quality of the *small* group:
potential for interaction with every member of the group.

Another difference between the small group and the dyad is the presence of an observer or audience. In a two-person group, there is only a speaker
and a listener—no one else. In a small group (three or more), there is always
someone else present, usually observing or listening, while the other two people are interacting. This quality of a group is often termed the *quality of co-
action*. The presence of the observer does affect group interaction—sometimes
positively and sometimes negatively, depending on the topic and the composition of the group, among other factors.

Another critical difference between the dyad and the small group is the
potential for a majority (and a consequent minority) to occur in the small
group. In the dyad, if there are differing views, no majority can form. If participants disagree on an issue, there is an even split of views. In a small
group, a majority coalition can form, creating sensitive or disruptive relationships within the group. Persuasion can be used in both dyads and small
groups, but in the dyad it is the only available tool for opinion change. Voting (by majority rule) is possible in the small group. Consequently, in small
groups, the number of members present (to outvote the opposition) may be
more important than logical arguments or evidence.

Differences between small group communication and higher levels,
such as public speaking, mass communication, and cultural communication,
are probably obvious. Perhaps the differences between small group communication and communication in larger groups are not so apparent. The following section defines the concepts "group" and "small group" and will
help clarify the differences between these two subclasses of interpersonal
communication.

Principles

1. There are at least three important distinctions between small group
   communication and dyadic communication.
   a. The potential for information sharing is greater in the small group.
   b. There is always an observer or audience present in the small group.
   c. There is a potential for a majority to occur in the small group.

Small Group Communication Defined

Before determining the working definitions of small group communication,
we should first agree on an acceptable definition of the term *group*. In the
broadest sense, a group may be defined merely as a collection of individu-

als. However, this broad definition does not discriminate between random aggregates of individuals and collections of people who meet for a purpose. Although more specific definitions of a group have been proposed, most include some important qualifications of a broad definition developed by an early sociologist nearly a century ago:

> The term "group" serves as a convenient sociological designation for any number of people, large or small, between whom such relations are discovered that they must be thought of together . . . a number of persons whose relations to each other are sufficiently impressive to demand attention. [Small, 1905, p. 495]

Small's definition helps distinguish between a *group* and what some sociologists and communication scholars term an *aggregate* or *class*. The latter terms simply refer to any collection of individuals (i.e., our initial broad definition).

The term *small group* has special meaning to sociologists, social psychologists, and communication scholars. The qualifier *small* refers to more variables than just size. The following definition suggests dimensions of a small group that are generally associated with the term. *A small group is a collection of individuals, from three to fifteen in number, who meet in face-to-face interaction over a period of time, generally with an assigned or assumed leader, who possess at least one common characteristic, and who meet with a purpose in mind.* Let's discuss each of the elements in the definition separately. (For other definitions and discussions, see Barker and Gaut, 2001, and Cragen and Wright, 1999).

Group Size

Scholars of small groups often debate the absolute size of a small group. The fewest number, three, is generally agreed upon (although some scholars do not distinguish between the dyad, two, and a group of three or more). This book differentiates between the dyad and the three-person group, because the purposes and interaction patterns of each differ significantly. In most groups, the upper limit will be about fifteen, yet in some groups it may be only seven. Still other groups may exceed twenty. The maximum size depends on the maturity of the group, the style of leadership, the personalities of group members, and a variety of other variables. When the potential for face-to-face interaction ceases among all group members, then the size of the group has exceeded the upper limit for a small group.

Face-to-Face Interaction

Some critics may question the face-to-face element in the previous definition of a small group. However, because the focus of this book is on small group communication, groups that do not meet for face-to-face interactions are not a primary concern. In addition, small groups that do not meet in face-to-face interaction often possess characteristics of larger groups, not those generally associated with the small group.[2]

Time Period

Groups that meet over a period of time have somewhat different characteristics from those meeting only once. Although this quality of continuation may not apply to all groups that are composed of relatively few individuals, it is usually included in the general connotation of the term *small group*. Several examples in this book refer to temporary groups. In addition, much research cited later is based on experiments employing groups formed solely for the purpose of the experiment. The inclusion of this ongoing quality in the general definition is based on the fact that groups that meet over a period of time gain maturity and communication skills difficult to obtain in a temporary group. Thus, from the viewpoint of a small group communication framework, this ongoing quality is an important aspect of most small groups.

Leadership

Writers of textbooks on small group communication widely discuss the role of leadership in groups. Many writers insist that a designated leader must be present in order for a group to function effectively. However, the view of this text is that whether or not a leader is designated, one or more people in a group generally will assume leadership duties. Thus, the definition of *small group* presented in this text acknowledges the potential for leadership but does not restrict the description of small groups to those with only assigned or elected leaders.

Shared Characteristic

The presence of a common (i.e., shared) characteristic helps distinguish the small group from the small aggregate. Shared characteristics may range from having similar religious beliefs to sharing common goals for a class project. Such additional variables as ethnic background, race, geographic location, social class, economic level, lifestyle, and education level often create common bonds among people in small groups. The common characteristic must exist whether it is assigned, assumed, or self-identified.

Common Purpose

Finally, the presence of a common purpose or goal, whether it is specific or very broad, binds the small group together and gives it a basic level of cohe-

---

[2]Media-assisted groups (see Chapter Ten) were not included in the discussion of face-to-face interaction, although they are fast becoming an alternative to actual in-person discussions. Media-assisted groups include teleconferencing and computer-mediated communication.

siveness (see Chapter Four). You will find that groups formed with no concrete goal in mind generally break up or gradually disintegrate. Goal-directed behavior holds group members together, and the more relevant the goal is to the group members, the more motivation they will have to maintain the group and their identity in it.

This definition of *small group* provides a basis for defining the phrase *small group communication*. To form the definition, the emphasis is simply changed from the structure of a group to the communication process involved. Therefore, *small group communication is the process of verbal and nonverbal face-to-face interaction in a small group*.[3]

Principles

1. A small group is a collection of individuals from three to fifteen in number, who meet in face-to-face interaction over a period of time, generally with an assigned or assumed leader, who possess at least one common characteristic, and who meet with a purpose in mind.
2. Small group communication may be defined as the process of verbal and nonverbal face-to-face interaction in a small group.

An Overview of Efficiency and Other Considerations in the Small Group

Time management became a buzzword in the early 1970s, and many people today routinely attend time-management seminars to try to squeeze more work into their days. Rather than trying to increase the amount of time spent on tasks, using the time we do have more efficiently might be the key. Sometimes working in small groups may increase our individual efficiency. Research concerning the efficiency of the group versus the efficiency of the individual has been confined to two areas—performance and use of time. Groups tend to be more efficient than individuals in some conditions but less efficient in others.

Performance

Studies of group performance have produced both interesting and conflicting findings. One group of studies suggests that groups may not be effective in solving problems under certain conditions.

> Problem solving implies the possibility of change and the exploration of alternatives to the status quo. Because of this point of potential discomfort, groups

---

[3]This definition reflects an emphasis on private (not public) small group communication. The definition is concerned with intragroup communication, *not* communicating via the group to an audience or to outside agencies.

can compound the difficulties of problem solving beyond those resulting from the volatility created by a roomful of different personalities with all of their individual needs, biases, and personal agendas. [Napier and Greshenfeld, 1999]

Considering the foregoing statement, it may seem counterproductive to use groups at all. In fact, there is considerable evidence that group performance is sometimes inferior to the performance of individuals (Shaw, 1981). However, other researchers highly recommend the use of groups over individuals in selected settings for the following reasons (adapted from Napier and Greshenfeld, 1999):

1. The participants in a problem-solving group will achieve a common understanding and an information base through the act of working together. Such involvement inevitably results in a greater understanding of the complexities of the problem and provides the substance for the group's acceptance of the eventual solution.

2. Each participant will enter the process with his or her own individual needs, biases, and perspectives. A group setting provides an environment that legitimizes a variety of viewpoints. Provided that good information is translated in an intelligent manner, and assuming that a climate exists in which individuals are not compelled to defend their positions, a group will move toward the best ideas.

3. Given even a minimal level of trust and goodwill, a group is capable of producing a greater quantity and variety of ideas than the average individual.

4. A good experience in a group can generate enthusiasm. A commitment to eventual action can be born of teamwork, arguing, building alternatives, and movement toward choice. Individuals can feel good about their contributions and relationships to the group.

5. The give-and-take of open and free discussion in a group can bring new ideas into play that may never have been considered by an individual. Open discussion enables group members to be irreverent, to question even the unquestionable, and to push against old absolutes. This process can tap the group's natural creativity.

Time

The amount of time a group uses to complete a task is one of the weaknesses of the group process. Your own experience has probably taught you that working in a group takes a lot of time. Group effort is not the most efficient way to achieve a goal when a measure of minutes per person is used as a criterion. There is some evidence that although groups take less time than individuals to achieve learning and to make simple decisions, this superiority disappears or is even reversed on problem-solving tasks (Bradford, 1978).

An example of how learning occurs in a group will help clarify the point. Assume that your history teacher has divided the class into small groups, and each group is responsible for completing a specific task related to the assigned reading. Your group is required to list the ten major causes of the United States' entry into World War I. The causes are all listed and discussed in the assigned reading material. Given that all or most of you have read the assignment containing the information, it is a reasonable guess that the group would complete the task in a little less time than it would take an individual. This is true because many of the strengths of group behavior can be used efficiently (e.g., information from several people can be pooled, members can check one another for consistency and accuracy, and division of labor is possible). The group's major task is to find or remember the content from the readings. However, on a test of mastery of the content, the group might not perform much differently from students who completed the task on an individual basis. This is the pattern revealed by some of the research on learning groups.

The decision to work as groups or as individuals may be partially the function of the relationship between errors and time. If you have a simple task to perform, one for which an early response is required, you should probably use the group rather than an individual to complete it. You will also want to use a group over an individual when an early response is needed on tasks involving learning or simple judgments. If a complex task, such as problem solving, is demanded and an early response is a priority, you should consider using individuals rather than a group. The use of individuals over a group, however, will probably decrease the accuracy and increase the errors in judgment. So, if errors are costly relative to success and an individual's time is cheap, the decision may be to form a group.

Other Considerations

The decision to group or not to group should not be based solely on the consideration of efficiency. Working in groups produces at least three additional advantages over working as individuals (Bradford, 1978).

First, groups should be used for decision making when they can contribute to the solution of the problem. A group may be used effectively for decision making when the type of decision to be reached is one in which there is a quantitative need for various opinions and points of view.

People tend to carry out decisions if they shared in the decision-making process. In addition, if the group is to be directly affected by a decision, the group should help make it. This does not mean, however, that there are not many instances when, due to the pressure of time, type of decision, or deferred area of responsibility, an individual may most appropriately make a decision.

Second, group decision making can be valuable if the group members have learned to work together effectively. One of the major reasons for ineffective group decision making is that the group members have not learned to work together efficiently as a unit. If this is the case, the leader might want to spend some time on improving the efficiency of the work group rather than making hasty decisions. A group may need to deal with some of the emotional problems of its members' interpersonal relationships before it can reach decisions effectively. Decision making, at its best, depends on the kind of working relationship in which disagreement, creativity, and shared responsibility can flourish.

Finally, group decision making is most appropriate when shared leadership is practiced. A group of persons brought together in a decision-making situation will not function at maximum efficiency if its members are "rubber-stamp" or "yes" people for an administrator or leader. If the leader of a group is interested both in assuming responsibility as chair in the decision-making process and in developing the membership of the group so that the functions of leadership are shared, leader attitude will go a long way toward achieving effective decision making.

Principles

1. There are several advantages of using groups over individuals for decision making:
   a. Participants will achieve a common understanding and information base.
   b. A group setting provides an environment that legitimizes a variety of viewpoints.
   c. A group is capable of producing a greater quantity and variety of ideas than an individual.
   d. A commitment to action can be born of teamwork, arguing, building of alternatives, and movement toward choice.
   e. The give-and-take of open discussion can tap the group's natural creativity.
2. Individuals are generally superior to groups in terms of the amount of time required for completion of the task.
3. There are at least three advantages of groups over individuals in addition to the performance advantage.
   a. Groups should be used when they can contribute to solving the problem.
   b. Group decision making can be valuable if the group members have learned to work together effectively.
   c. Group decision making is most appropriate when shared leadership is practiced.

Groups as Process

The definition given for the terms *group, small group,* and *small group communication* might appear to describe an entity that has a specific location in time and space. While theoretically this may be true, in reality, groups are dynamic structures and, as such, are constantly involved in change.

The term *process* is generally used to refer to the dynamics of small group communication. This term suggests the changing nature of the individual and intragroup interactions. As individuals modify their own ideas through external stimulation and interaction, they tend to alter ideas and even the personalities of those group members with whom they interact. Consequently, a description of a group at one point in time may be misleading because the group changes from moment to moment. Chapter Two describes the process nature of groups more completely. At this point, keep in mind that although groups may be referred to as static entities, you should mentally perceive them as constantly in process.

Summary

This chapter established a framework for examining and understanding small group communication. Small group communication was identified as a level of interpersonal communication and differentiated from dyadic communication on the basis of (1) greater information sharing, (2) the presence of an audience, and (3) the potential for majorities to form in small groups.

A small group was defined as a collection of individuals, from three to fifteen in number, who meet in face-to-face interaction over a period of time, generally with an assigned or assumed leader, who possess at least one common characteristic, and who meet with a purpose in mind. Small group communication was defined as the process of verbal and nonverbal interaction in a small group.

Groups are formed in order to investigate problems and to devise, propose, and implement solutions. There are factors that recommend the use of groups over individuals, but groups require more time to complete a task. Advantages to working in groups include the use of decision-making groups to carry out the decision and the opportunity for members to work effectively as a unit and to share leadership. Groups should be understood and studied as dynamic entities.

Ideas for Discussion _____

1. What relationships exist among different levels of communication in addition to those mentioned in this chapter? Discuss particularly (1) verbal versus non-verbal differences, (2) formality and informality, (3) purposes and goals, and (4) efficiency of decision making.

2. What would be an example of a situation in which a leaderless group might be more effective than a group in which a leader was appointed? What would be an example of the reverse situation?

3. What role does individual motivation play in group formation?

4. What variables, in addition to those mentioned in this chapter, tend to make groups dissolve quickly? What variables tend to make groups stay together for a long period of time?

Suggested Projects and Activities

1. To understand the role of groups in your life, make a list of all of the small groups to which you belong. Then rank them (1) in order of their importance to you, (2) according to the length of time you have been associated with each, and (3) in terms of the degree of formality and informality of each.

2. Using the reasons for group formation suggested in this chapter as a starting place, elect three groups of which you are currently a member and write a brief paragraph about the history of each group's formation.

3. Using other textbooks as your sources of information, locate as many different definitions of *group, small group,* and *small group communication* as you can. Then prepare a chart illustrating similarities and differences among the definitions. With which definition do you most agree? Why?

References

Barker, L. L., and D. A. Gaut. *Communication,* 8th ed. Boston: Allyn & Bacon, 2001.

Bradford, L. P. *Group development,* 2nd ed. La Jolla, Calif.: University Associates, 1978.

Cragen, J. F., and D. W. Wright. *Communication in small groups,* 5th ed. St. Paul: West Publishing Company, 1999.

Napier, R. W., and M. K. Gershenfeld. *Groups: theory and experience,* 6th ed. Boston: Houghton-Mifflin, 1999.

Ruesch, J., and G. Bateson. *Communication: the social matrix of psychiatry.* New York: W. W. Norton & Co., 1968.

Shaw, M. E. *Group dynamics: the psychology of small group behavior,* 3rd ed. New York: McGraw-Hill, 1981.

Small, A. W. *General sociology.* Chicago: University of Chicago Press, 1905.

Suggested Readings

Johannesen, R. L. *Ethics in human communication,* 4th ed. Prospect Heights, IL: Waveland Press, 1996. Chapter 1 discusses ethics and communication in general while Chapter 8 focuses specifically on ethics in interpersonal and small group communication.

Napier, R. W., and M. K. Gershenfeld. *Groups: Theory and experience,* 6th ed. Boston: Houghton-Mifflin, 1999. Chapter 1, "Perception and Communication," discusses factors that influence group communication. Chapter 2, "Membership," explores reasons why people join groups, differences among types of group membership, and factors that affect attractiveness to the group.

Shockley-Zalabak, P. *Fundamentals of organizational communication: Knowledge, sensitivity, skills, values,* 4th ed. New York: Longman, 1999. Chapter 6, "Groups in Organizations," identifies some of the types of groups common to organizations and includes general guidelines for effective group participation in self-managing groups. Chapter 12, "Organizational Communication: Values and Ethical Communication Behaviors," discusses organizational and individual values and ethical dilemmas in organizations. The chapter also includes an exercise for self-assessment of personal values and a set of guidelines for evaluating ethical behavior.

Wood, J. T. *Communication in our lives,* 2nd ed. Belmont, CA: Wadsworth, 2000. Chapter 10, "Foundations of Group and Team Communication," identifies characteristics of small groups as well as their strengths and limitations. Chapter 4, "Communication and Cultures," discusses ethnocentrism and judgment as two dangers to effective communication in a multicultural society.

A Systems Approach
to Small Group
Communication

Study Questions

After reading this chapter, you should be able to answer the following questions completely and accurately:

1. What are the differences among primary, social, educational, encounter, and problem-solving groups?
2. Why is a group dynamic, and why does it have no beginning or end?
3. What is the definition of a system?
4. What are the distinctions between open and closed systems?
5. How does interdependence operate within a small group system?
6. What is the hierarchy of the small group system?
7. What is cybernetics?
8. What is the difference between an input and an output?
9. What is the importance of balance in the small group system?
10. What is equifinality?
11. What are interacts?
12. What four phases do decision-making groups follow?
13. What is field theory?
14. What is lifespace?
15. What is the theory of syntality?

Groups in Process

As was mentioned in Chapter One, most of us are members of at least ten to twenty different groups. Our involvement in each of these groups differs based on how many people are present, who is in charge, and why we are meeting. As we meet with a group of people, the group is in a constant state of change. For example, individual group members might lean forward to signal interest, doodle in notebooks, ask clarification questions, respond to feedback, get into heated disputes, and offer advice. How one person responds in a given situation influences how others will respond to him or her. In fact, second meetings are often influenced by what has happened at the meeting before. For example, when Sarah's group met with her professor to discuss their class project, she couldn't get there on time. At their next meeting, the other group members didn't accept her apology, ignored her suggestions, and gave her tasks they didn't want to do themselves. Finally, feeling as though she couldn't work with the other members, Sarah asked to be assigned to another group.

As you can see, a person who feels frustrated, unappreciated, or left out is more likely to quit or seek alternative groups in which to participate. You, too, can probably think of a time that you changed work or social groups because of what another person said or did. The actions of one member affect every other member of the group. Thus, when a group gets together to solve problems, share information, or plan activities, the group consists of interrelated elements working together to achieve a goal.

As children mature, they develop social skills. In turn, the number of groups to which children belong and the frequency of their participation increases as they get older. Because you spend much of your time participating in groups, it is important to understand how group goals differ from one group to another. The following section discusses five types of groups in which you participate: primary, social, educational or learning, encounter, and problem-solving (or work) groups (Tubbs and Moss, 2000).

Primary groups are the most basic and long-lasting groups, as they are composed of family members or close friends. You get a sense of belonging and support from your primary group memberships. Unlike many other groups that meet on a one-time or short-term basis, a primary group meets on a long-term basis.

Social group members exchange ideas and conversation. These groups form for social proposes rather than for task purposes. For example, neighbors who get together for a monthly barbecue, employees who take breaks at work, or friends who get together daily are considered casual groups.

An *educational* or *learning group* is formed to provide members with some type of instruction. An aerobics class, a lecture about this chapter, a photography club, a training seminar, and a study group are all forms of educational groups.

In addition to primary, social, and educational groups, we also participate in *encounter* or *therapy groups*. These groups are designed to help members make changes in their interpersonal relationships. For example, if you were a recently divorced single parent, you might join a Parents without Partners group or attend "coping with divorce" counseling sessions.

The type of group with which this book will be dealing most directly is the *problem-solving* (or *work*) *group*. Problem-solving or work groups usually have specific goals to achieve. They may be assigned some sort of task, such as gathering information, evaluating problems and solutions, and/or implementing policies. These groups are concerned with accomplishing their task goals and objectives. Even so, a group can satisfy more than one group goal. To illustrate, a person who joins Parents without Partners for the therapeutic benefits might also form social groups of friends who begin having potluck dinners once a month, participate in educational seminar groups sponsored by the organization, and work in a problem-solving committee.

Fundamental System Concepts

As you can see, the communication that takes place within small groups is *dynamic:* It changes constantly to meet the needs and goals of the group. The process of group communication also has *no beginning or end.* As members form a group, each person brings unique, individual life experiences to it. In the same way, even if a group of which you have been a member is dissolved, how you participated and what happened during the time you were a part of that group continues to influence you as you join and interact in other groups. Thus group members in one group or system also influence group members in other groups or systems. You are both a part of and influenced by the groups to which you belong. For this reason, it is important to study the system of group processes. First the elements involved in a system will be studied, and then how those elements work together and are affected by one another will be discussed.

Definition of a System

Mr. and Mrs. Grayson were eager to take their newborn daughter home from the hospital. Checkout was scheduled for 10:00 A.M., but the billing office had not received the insurance forms from the admitting office or the delivery room charges. Finally, in the early afternoon, the records were located. Unfortunately, however, by this time a number of people had been inconvenienced, including the hospital staff, the parents, and relatives waiting at the Graysons' home. In this example, the actions of one person in the billing office caused a chain reaction that affected other persons as well.

In this example, the parents were included in at least two different groups or systems—first as a family and second as a group within the hospital environment. According to general systems theory (Bettalanffy, 1968), a system—or, in this case, a group—functions as a set of interdependent parts or elements that form a whole. Within this system, communication is what links the parts or elements of the system together.

To remedy breakdowns in communication processes such as this one, organizations train their employees to work more effectively in teams (see Chapter Ten). Groups of employees, whose work tasks influence other work tasks, meet together to analyze work systems and processes. Since the key to what links the employees together is communication, poor communication almost always contributes to poor customer service, misunderstanding, and inefficiency in products/services.

Closed and Open Systems

Systems are viewed as either *closed* or *open*. A *closed* system restricts the flow of communication with the environment. A closed system is completely isolated from its environment. It does not accept information or input from the outside world. Unfortunately, a system or group cannot survive without input from the outside. Think what it would have been like for you if your parents had never allowed you to have friends, attend school, go outside, watch television, or read newspapers or books. What would have happened to you? If you are like most people, the isolation would have retarded your social, psychological, and intellectual development. The same isolation often occurs when businesses fail to adapt to their environment. Think of the number of companies that have lost business and have had to declare bankruptcy because the owners failed to listen to customer complaints, employee suggestions, or stockholder warnings.

An *open* system, on the other hand, is one that communicates and exchanges information freely with its environment. It openly receives matter and energy and has the potential for life and growth. Unlike a closed system, an open system takes information it receives from its environment and then sends the finished product back to the environment. For example, a group of reporters saw a need and decided to write an article about methods of overcoming stage fright or speech anxiety. After brainstorming among themselves, they decided to consult experts and interviewed performers, speech trainers, presentation-skill consultants, and professional speakers. A newspaper published the article, and the reporters mailed reprints to all the people they interviewed. As you can see, in this situation the reporters as a group first received information from the environment (perceived a need outside their group and consulted experts) and then sent the final product (the article) back to the environment (subscribers and experts).

Principles

1. Group goals differ from group to group.
   a. Primary groups, composed of family members or close friends, provide a sense of belonging and support.
   b. Social groups exchange ideas and conversation.
   c. Educational or learning groups are formed to provide knowledge and instruction.
   d. Encounter or therapy groups help members adjust or make changes in their interpersonal relationships.
   e. Problem-solving or work groups are concerned with accomplishing goals and objectives.
2. Small groups are dynamic and have no beginning or end.
3. Group membership influences how a person behaves in other groups.
4. A system is composed of a set of interdependent parts linked together by communication.
5. A closed system is completely isolated from its environment.
6. An open system exchanges information freely with its environment.

Small Groups as Open Systems

Based on the principles identified here, you should see the value of viewing group interaction as an open system. Within these small group systems, group members are the elements of the system. The following section will provide a better understanding of the systems approach to small group communication by explaining common qualities of systems (Buckley, 1968; Hall and Fagen, 1968; Littlejohn, 1999; Eisenberg and Goodall, 1997).

Interdependence

The systems approach is based on the concept of interdependence. The system as a whole is constituted of integrated parts or elements. These elements interrelate and affect one another. When something changes in one part of the system, eventually all other parts of the system will also change. You have probably experienced the effects of interdependency in your family group. It is not unusual to hear parents, for example, say, "How do you think it would make us look if we allowed you to go out of the house looking like that?" "We didn't get to sleep last night until we heard you come in," or "How can you say, 'That's *my* business' when everything you do in this house affects us?" These statements suggest that what a child does as an element of the system affects the family or whole system.

Hierarchy

Within each system there are a series of subsystems. These subsystems, which are all parts of the whole, form a hierarchy of increasing levels of complexity. For a moment, picture yourself as a salesclerk for a retail chain. Let's say that you work in the small appliances department. Your department may be a subsystem of the store, which is a subsystem of the retail chain, which is a subsystem of the conglomerate. Even so, you may be a member of an even smaller subsystem of part-time or night-shift workers in your department. In addition, within your work groups or systems there is also a hierarchy based on factors such as position, seniority, or age. Perhaps, for example, the "supervisors" get together for lunch or breaks.

Self-Regulation and Control

Systems operate and are controlled by the goals and aims of their elements or members. As a group member of a system, you find that your behavior is governed by both stated and implied rules. For example, a fraternal organization may have a written rule that fines members after two absences and unwritten rules about how to behave during meetings. An unwritten rule may require members to raise their hands before speaking. If a member speaks out without using the ritual of raising his or her hand, other members may give nonverbal feedback, such as not acknowledging the person, frowning, or looking disgusted as a means of letting the person know that he or she was out of order.

An important aspect of self-regulation and control involves how the system adapts to the environment based on feedback. This feedback is known as *cybernetics,* or the process of adjusting to feedback about outputs. For example, before a meeting Stan called to make room reservations, ordered refreshments, collated materials, set up the chairs, and arranged for necessary audio-visual equipment. During the meeting, other members commented on what a good job Stan had done in planning for the meeting. Stan felt reinforced and volunteered to plan the next meeting as well. Now, if, on the other hand, Stan had failed to make the necessary arrangements and the group members had verbalized their disappointment, Stan might have responded quite differently. He could have, for example, tried harder to please everyone the next time, or he might not have volunteered to serve again. During your own group meetings, for example, notice how members constantly adjust to new information and responses/reactions from others. (Feedback will be discussed in greater detail in Chapter Five.)

Interchange with Environment

An open group system is also characterized by its interchange with the environment. The interchange takes place though a series of *inputs* and *outputs.* Inputs are the energies that keep a group functioning and on track. If a group is trying to develop a better teacher evaluation form, for example, the members will need input from sources other than members of the group. Perhaps members will need to conduct research about what forms have been used in the past, determine a method of evaluating their effectiveness, get samples for forms used at other universities, and/or get suggestions from both student and faculty groups.

The outputs are the products, information, and/or services that the system or group sends to its environment. For example, outputs may include bird feeders sold by a junior achievement group, the request to place warning labels on chewing tobacco pouches by a concerned consumer group, or a local church group's reading for the blind. Usually groups have more time, energy, and resources available than they actually share with their environment. For example, a civic group may have a project to send entertainers to five children's hospital wards once a week, even though they have resources available to send entertainers to six hospitals twice a week. Groups usually protect their resources so that if, for example, there is an entertainer shortage one week, the group will still have enough performers to make the scheduled visits.

Balance

Another important quality of an open group system is balance. Balance ensures that the group has more inputs than outputs. With this in mind, balance does not suggest that a group does not change. In fact, balance implies a constant state of change as the system or group adapts to inputs from its environment. For example, a group was required to turn in an agenda before presenting a group project. The teacher returned the agenda with a number of questions and comments. Instead of ignoring the comments, the group members conducted further research to justify sticking with the agenda they had outlined. Likewise, organizational groups continue to exist only if balance is maintained and they continue to receive inputs. Without inputs, the group is no longer necessary. For example, one company that stopped receiving orders for typewriters phased out a department that employed fifty people and hired additional personnel for its computer department.

Equifinality

Finally, systems or groups have a goal or objective they are trying to achieve. The concept of *equifinality* suggests that the final state or goal can be reached by using different starting points and methods. Your college or university, for example, may offer several sections of a small group communication course using different instructors. One instructor may lecture 90 percent of the time, another may use discussion with 10 percent lecture, and another may divide the class into groups and get the groups to present the lecture material. Even though different instructors use different teaching methods, students should learn the same basic information.

At times, it may be difficult for group members to accept the principle of equifinality. Especially when we are convinced that our plan or strategy is best, we are likely to oppose or object to another point of view or alternative. At those times, try to remember that the same goal can be achieved from different starting points and by using different methods.

Small Group Systems at Work

Now you should have a better understanding about qualities of the systems process. Examine how these qualities function together as a system by observing what takes place in the following group situation: A representative in the state legislature decided to run for mayor of a large city and called a meeting of his local supporters. Obviously, his primary goal was to get elected. About fifty people arrived to plan his campaign strategy. A hierarchy immediately developed as the candidate introduced his campaign manager and top staff. After the introductions, the campaign manager established an agenda for the meeting. After she spoke, others in the room raised their hands to offer suggestions about how to garner both financial support and votes. Several participants got into a heated discussion that could have led the meeting in a different direction. At that moment, the people in charge began to adjust to the feedback they were receiving and began to regulate the discussion. In so doing, they were operating as an open system.

To make the best use of the group's energy and ideas, the moderator divided the larger group into smaller groups of five to seven members. (See Chapter Ten for specific discussion-leader techniques.) The smaller groups were given fifteen minutes to come up with ideas and methods for raising support in the community. Some small groups appointed a leader, while others just started throwing out ideas, and others thought silently for a while before offering suggestions. When the time was up, a spokesperson from each group presented the group's ideas. Several groups had similar ideas, such as setting up telephone banks, canvassing neighborhoods, and scheduling fund-raising dinners. In addition, some groups came up with slogans and invitations for speaking engagements. Balance from the system's viewpoint was achieved, as the groups generated more inputs than outputs. In addition, the candidate's goal for the evening was achieved, even with the smaller groups starting at differing points and using different methods to get there.

As you can see, groups function as systems. Qualities of the system process include interdependence, hierarchy, self-regulation and control, interchange with the environment, balance, and equifinality.

Principles
1. Interdependence suggests that elements of the system interrelate and affect individual elements and the system as a whole.
2. Within each system there are hierarchies of increasing levels of complexity.
3. Systems operate and are controlled by the goals and aims of their members.
4. The process of adjusting to feedback about outputs is known as *cybernetics*.
5. An open system is characterized by its interchange with its environment.
   a. Inputs are the energies that keep a group functioning and on track.
   b. Outputs are the products, information, and/or services that a system or group sends to its environment.
6. Balance ensures that the system has more inputs than outputs.
7. *Equifinality* suggests that the same goal can be reached by using differing starting points and by using different methods.

Small Group Communication System Perspectives

You should now be able to identify qualities that are inherent in small group systems. With these qualities in mind, it is time to see how these elements can be studied within the small group context. The next section explains how several system theories relate to small group communication. The *interact system model, field theory,* and the *theory of syntality* will also be discussed.

Interact System Model

Fischer and Hawes (1971) developed the interact system model for the study of communication or *interacts* within small groups. An interact is a verbal or nonverbal act of another person. For example, if one member were to say, "We've got so much to do . . . I think we need to meet on Saturday night," other group members may respond by rolling their eyes, shaking their heads or saying, "You've got to be kidding. There is no way I'm going to give up going to the ball game for a class project." As you can see, as one member makes a contribution, he or she influences the reactions that other members and the group make as a whole.

By observing interacts using this system model, we can better understand how groups function, how individual members interact, how decisions are made, and how groups develop or disintegrate over time. One systematic method of observing interacts is by watching the group process in action. As decision-making groups interact, they typically follow four stages of development (Fisher, 1970): *orientation, conflict, emergence,* and *reinforcement.* During the orientation phase, group members get to know one another, try to avoid conflict, and begin to express tentative points of view.

After members have expressed themselves and begin to feel more secure, conflict usually occurs. During this phase, group members begin to take sides, find allies, and form coalitions. In addition, members begin arguing in support of their points of view and try to persuade other members to agree with them. It is at this point that we begin to notice system qualities, such as self-regulation and control, with group members adapting to feedback from others.

In the third stage, emergence, coalitions lose their strength. During emergence, group members finally begin to cooperate and make compromises. Again, as in the orientation phase, however, members often make statements tentatively in an attempt to establish agreement. During this stage, you will begin to hear more positive responses and comments during discussion. As members reach this stage, they seek a state of balance or equilibrium as the group adapts to input from inside and outside the group.

Finally, during the last phase, reinforcement, group members achieve consensus. When decisions are made, group members develop unity of purpose and become committed to their decisions. As the group progresses through the stages of decision making, the interrelated small-group system experiences constant states of change. As a group receives new input, it adapts to changes in individuals and in the group. Phases of the group process are often repeated when a solution has been implemented and a new problem is introduced. By examining and adapting to individual communication patterns between and among group members, you are in a better position to ensure successful group outcomes and products.

Field Theory

Whereas the interact system model examines individual interacts that affect the group system, Kurt Lewin's *field theory* (1948) provides an overall description of group behavior. His theory supports the open system, applies to all types of groups, and suggests that group behavior is the product of various positive and negative forces inside and outside the group. These forces affect individual members and the group as a whole. For example, a manager who calls a staff meeting immediately after hearing bad news will influence the group differently from the way he or she would if good news had been received.

An important element of Lewin's theory is the concept of *lifespace*, or the physical space in which a person has activity. A person's lifespace involves his or her subjective perceptions about the people and events in his or her surroundings. You are a member of many groups at once, so your lifespace changes as others enter and leave your presence. For example, think of the different roles you assume when visiting with your parents and grandparents, with close friends, or with work associates. In addition to the people you are with, the environment or places you meet also affect your lifespace and interaction in groups. As an illustration, think of a time in which it was difficult for you to listen during a group meeting. What caused you to daydream or stay out of the conversation? Perhaps you were distracted by a telephone ringing, other people, or a television. On the other hand, you may have been uncomfortable because the room was too crowded, the temperature was too cold, or you were too far away from the moderator to hear what was said. As you can see, no matter what the environment is like, it has an affect on your lifespace. For this reason, it is important to meet in private, quiet places that are as free of distractions as possible.

According to Lewin, a group is "a 'dynamical whole'; this means that a change in the state of any subpart changes the state of any other subpart. The degree of interdependence of the subparts of members of the group varies all the way from loose mass to a compact unit" (p. 94). Just as with hierarchies, group members are influenced by personal needs as well as by group standards. Because of personal needs, some groups give no freedom to their members; others provide complete freedom. When groups are too restraining, individual members may, for example, rebel by staying out after curfews, canceling scheduled meetings, or moving church memberships. Likewise, if a group is weak and shows no real direction or purpose, members are likely to show a lack of commitment by, for example, coming to meetings late or scheduling other activities during scheduled meeting times. For instance, draw the word "trust" on one end of a continuum and the word "mistrust" on the other. Next consider five families with which you are most familiar. Using the continuum, place the family's name on the continuum as to how they treat their children. Families who monitor all their children's actions may fall on the far end of the mistrust, while others may appear on the opposite end of trust. As group members, we are constantly adjusting to our individual needs and our group's expectations.

Therefore, it is important to assess how people's lifespace affects them during each new meeting. If it is assumed that individuals don't change, then it is assumed that events cannot alter behavior. Take a look at your own behavior for a moment. Are you in the same mood day in and day out? It is highly unlikely that your moods remain constant, especially during times of stress. For instance, Ellen, who is usually highly participative and insightful, is acting withdrawn during a planning meeting. Unknown to the group, prior to the meeting she received news that her father had been hospitalized with chest pains. If group members were to make assumptions about Ellen's interest and involvement in their group project during this meeting, they would probably get the wrong impression.

Since individual contributions are important, some groups plan ways to assess group members' states of mind before discussing meeting issues by using warm-up activities and/or icebreakers. For example, a human resource manager might start all staff meetings with the PIT exercise. PIT stands for personal (P), interpersonal (I), and task (T). Starting with a different group member each time, individuals share what is going on with them personally, interpersonally with other group members, and with tasks on which they are working. After the exercise, group members generally relate to each other and focus on meeting issues more effectively.

Theory of Syntality

Raymond Cattel's theory of group syntality (1948) is related to Lewin's field theory and emphasizes the importance of interrelationships within groups. He suggests that groups have three interdependent characteristics that distinguish them from other groups. These group sets, or panels, are labeled *population traits, internal structure,* and *syntality.*

The term *population traits* refers to member characteristics, such as their ages, education levels, incomes, values, attitudes, and motivations. A group's internal structure includes such aspects as its size, member roles, leadership styles, seating arrangements, and interaction patterns. Finally, groups have syntality. Syntality, the group's personality or the effect that the group has as a totality, helps us predict patterns of group behavior and determine the group's chances for success. Based on the syntality or personality, a group may be characterized as efficient, argumentative, energetic, friendly, or dependable. As you might guess, there is a parallel between the personality traits of the group members and the syntality traits of the group. Keep in mind, however, that the group syntality is greater than the sum of its parts. In other words, the personality of each group is unique because of the unique combination of the individual group members. Collectively, groups have a mind of their own. What one person may not try alone, he or she may try in a group. For example, one student usually does not make a complaint to a department head about poor teaching by one instructor; however, if several students in the class got together and discussed the poor teaching, they might approach the head of the department together.

According to Cattel, syntality is the most important element of the three panels. Syntality is composed of *synergy,* or the total amount of energy available to a group to perform group activities. The interrelated or combined energies of group members are determined by (1) the total number of members, (2) the attitudes of the members present, (3) the individual abilities and resources of the group members, and (4) reasons why the group was formed. If a group is formed voluntarily and is highly motivated toward achieving a goal, the group system will have greater syntality or energy to expend. However, group energy is often expended on things unrelated to group goals. Group synergy used for establishing rapport, overcoming conflict, controlling disruptive participants, or maintaining relationships is known as *maintenance synergy.* This energy expenditure is necessary, but it does take energy that could be better used to help the group achieve its goals and tasks. Yet, action synergy or *effective synergy* is used only after the group is working harmoniously. It allows the group to meet its goals and objectives. Obviously, groups that use less synergy dealing with interpersonal issues are likely to be more successful at achieving their goals.

This section has identified three system theories and has explained how they relate to small group communication. Each theory presents different ideas by focusing on such elements as interacts, fields, and syntality, but each has key elements or qualities of systems theory in common. It would be a good idea to keep these theories in mind as you plan for and participate in small groups. If you do, you will have a better understanding of what is happening in your groups, and how you can make the best use of your individual group memberships.

Principles
1. The interact system model studies interacts within small groups.
    a. An interact is a verbal or nonverbal act of one person followed by a verbal or nonverbal act of another person.
    b. Using interacts, decision-making groups typically follow four stages of development.
        1. Group members get to know one another during the orientation phase.
        2. Conflict usually occurs after members have expressed themselves and have begun to feel more secure.
        3. During emergence, group members begin to cooperate and make compromises.
        4. Group members achieve consensus during reinforcement phase.

2. Field theory provides an overall description of group behavior by examining forces inside and outside the group.
   a. Lifespace, or the physical space in which a group member has activity, is a key concept of field theory.
   b. Although groups vary in degrees of freedom and constraint, group members maintain some degree of interdependency.
3. The theory of group syntality emphasizes the importance of interrelationships within groups.
   a. Population traits are member characteristics, such as ages, education levels, income, values, attitudes, and motivations.
   b. A group's internal structure includes aspects such as group size, member roles, leadership styles, seating arrangements, and interaction patterns.
   c. Syntality is the group's personality or the group's effect as a totality.
   d. Synergy is the total amount of energy available to a group to perform its activities.
      1. Maintenance synergy is used to establish rapport, overcome conflict, control disruptive participants, and maintain relationships.
      2. Effective synergy or action synergy is used to help the group achieve its goals.
      3. Whenever maintenance synergy is used, it takes away energy that could be better used to help the group achieve its goals. Therefore, less effective synergy is available to the group.

Summary

This chapter discussed a systems approach to small group communication. Initially, the chapter examined five types of groups: primary, social, educational or learning, encounter, and problem-solving. The discussion explained how group goals and membership influence how a person behaves or participates in groups.

Groups were described as dynamic systems without a clear beginning or end. Each small group system is composed of a set of interdependent parts linked together by communication. These systems are either closed or open. A closed system is completely isolated from its environment; an open system exchanges information freely with its environment.

Qualities of the systems process include interdependence, hierarchy, self-regulation and control, interchange with the environment, balance, and equifinality. Interdependence suggests that elements of a system affect other individual elements and the system as a whole. Hierarchies include the increasing levels of difficulty within the small group system. The process of adjusting to feedback is known as cybernetics, or regulation and control. An open system is characterized by its interchange, or inputs and outputs, with its environment. Balance ensures that a system has more inputs than outputs. Finally, equifinality suggests that the same goal can be reached by using differing starting points and by using different methods.

Finally, the chapter explained how three system theories relate to small group communication. The interact system model studies the effects of interacts within small groups. These interacts, verbal and nonverbal acts of one person followed by verbal and nonverbal acts of another person, are observable in the orientation, conflict, emergence, and reinforcement stages of development in decision-making groups. Field theory describes group behavior by examining the effects of various positive and negative forces inside and outside the group. A person's lifespace, or physical space in which he or she has activity, changes as the people and events in his or her surroundings change. The theory of syntality emphasizes the importance of interrelationships within groups. Each group has three panels or interdependent characteristics which distinguish that group from other groups. These panels are population traits, internal structure, and syntality. The most important panel is syntality, which is composed of synergy, or the total amount of energy available to the group to perform its activities.

Ideas for Discussion

1. What is the value of studying small groups from a systems perspective?

2. Explain how qualities of the systems process work together as a whole.

3. How do elements of the small group system differ based on the goals (social, educational, encounter, etc.) of the group?

4. What are the primary distinctions among the interact system model, field theory, and the theory of syntality?

5. Which systems theory would you select to analyze a small group discussion? Why?

Suggested Projects and Activities

1. Divide the class into groups and have each group come up with examples of open system groups. Then have each group select one open system group situation and explain how the group functions as a system.

2. Observe a discussion in a group of which you are not a member. Select one of the system theories discussed in this chapter and analyze the group process using their theory systematically. Explain the advantages and disadvantages of using the theory you selected.

3. Observe a real-life problem-solving group. Using the four phases of small group decision making, listen carefully for statements or interacts which suggest that the group has moved from one phase to another. Record statements

as examples of each phase. Compare your statements with those of other members of the class.

4. Divide the class into five groups. Assign each group to observe another group with different group goals. One group should observe a primary group, another a social group, another an educational group, and so on. Observers should look for signs of the systems process at work. Have each group identify specific examples and illustrations. Discuss the differences based on differences in group goals.

References _____

Bettalanffy, L. *General system theory: foundations, development, applications.* New York: Braziller, 1968.

Buckley, W. Society as a complex adaptive system. In W. Buckley, ed. *Modern systems research for the behavioral scientist.* Chicago: Aldine, 1968, 490–513.

Cattel, R. Concepts and methods in the measurement of group syntality. *Psychological review,* 1948, *55,* 48–63.

Eisenberg, E. M., and H. L. Goodall, Jr. *Organizational communication: balancing creativity and constraint,* 2nd ed. New York: St. Martin's Press, 1997.

Fisher, B. A. Decision emergence: phases in group decision making. *Speech monographs,* 1970, *37,* 53–66.

Fisher, B. A., and L. Hawes. An interact system model: generating a grounded theory of small groups. *Quarterly journal of speech,* 1971, *57,* 444–453.

Hall, A. D., and R. E. Fagen. Definition of system. In W. Buckley, ed. *Modern systems research for the behavioral scientist,* Chicago: Aldine, 1968, 81–92.

Lewin, K. *Resolving social conflicts: selected papers on group dynamics.* New York: Harper & Row, 1948.

Littlejohn, S. W. *Theories of human communication,* 6th ed. Belmont, Calif.: Wadsworth, 1999.

Tubbs, S. L., and S. Moss. *Human communication,* 8th ed. New York: McGraw-Hill, 2000.

Suggested Readings _____

Eisenberg, E. M., and H. L. Goodall, Jr. *Organizational communication: Balancing creativity and constraint,* 2nd ed. New York: St. Martin's Press, 1997. Chapter 4, "The Systems Perspective on Organizations and Communication," examines similarities and differences between biological systems and organizational communication systems as well as the appeal of systems theory for organizational communication.

Littlejoin, S. W. *Theories of human communication,* 6th ed. Belmont, CA: Wadsworth, 1999. Chapter 3, "System Theory," presents an excellent overview of systems theory. Chapter 13, "Communication in Group Decision Making," and Chapter 14, "Communication and Organizational Networks," explain how systems theory works within group and organizational contexts.

Neher, W. W. *Organizational communication: Challenges of change, diversity and continuity.* Boston: Allyn & Bacon, 1997. Chapter 6, "System and Contingency Theories of Organizations," not only discusses systems theory but also communication implications of systems theory. Chapter 8, "Channels, Media, and Communication Systems in Organizations," includes a discussion of network roles as well as characteristics of communication networks.

Rogers, E. M. *Intercultural communication.* Prospect Heights, IL: Waveland Press, 1999. One characteristic of a group that should be considered in a system analysis is culture and this text provides a good overview of intercultural communication.

3

Goals and Roles in Small Groups

Study Questions

After reading this chapter, you should be able to answer the following questions completely and accurately:

1. What is a general definition of the term *goal?*
2. What is a task as it relates to the goals of the small group?
3. What are the definitions of *personal goal, conscious personal goal,* and *unconscious personal goal?*
4. What are the two major types of group goals? How do you define each? What are some examples of each?
5. What should participants expect to happen if the personal goals of members conflict with the goals of the group?
6. What are some problems participants might expect to encounter when working on achievement goals for the group? What are some behaviors that might reduce the magnitude of these problems?
7. What problems are likely to occur when working on the group's maintenance goals, and what are some behaviors that might curtail such problems?
8. What is the interrelationship between achievement goals and group maintenance goals? What can members do to help provide the optimal balance between the two types of goals?
9. What does the term role mean as it is applied to groups?
10. What are the three general sets of roles?
11. What are three types of role problems that can develop in groups?
12. What are five bases of power in groups?
13. What is the effect of status on power and influence in small groups?

Several members of the student-faculty Committee on Students with Disabilities have attended their first meeting. For more than an hour they have floundered aimlessly from topic to topic. One member has expressed a willingness to go along with whatever the group decides; another has been sharing personal experiences; while a third member has been telling political jokes. At the request of one of the members, the chairperson has again read the committee's charge and statement of responsibilities. Each person seems to have his or her own reasons for being there and also appears to have different expectations than the other members. The discussion appears to be going nowhere when one of the participants says, "I guess we'd better figure out why we're here and what we intend to get done on this committee." Then the members begin to list some possible goals.

Does this sound familiar? Most of us have been in a similar situation at one time or another—bored or frustrated with a group's lack of direction or maybe even entertained by the antics of other group members. This chapter will first focus on how goals provide direction for a group. Next it examines some different types of goals. Finally, the roles group members take on as they interact to achieve goals and the effect of role status on power and influence will be discussed. You should apply the concepts and principles discussed in this chapter to your small group interactions.

An Overview of Goals and Tasks in Small Groups

Suppose you just started a weight-training program, and a friend asks you what you are aiming to accomplish. Or, perhaps you are taking your first photography course, and your instructor questions, "What effect are you trying to achieve?" Whether you are "aiming" or attempting to achieve an effect, you are setting goals and will have to accomplish certain tasks (i.e., selecting and composing objects for a photograph) in order to achieve those goals. However, first it is important to understand exactly what a goal is, how goals differ from tasks, and how personal goals relate to group goals.

A General Definition of Goal

A *goal* is defined as the objective, or result, that a group or an individual seeks to achieve. As such, it refers to the target or end product that is sought. A goal is also a state of affairs that people value and toward which they work (Johnson and Johnson, 2000). Theoretically, a small group's major reason for existence is the achievement of its goal.

You can undoubtedly recall several small groups in which you have participated recently. Further reflection on the goals of these groups probably will reveal to you that they varied widely. You may have met with a regularly scheduled small group *to learn desktop publishing.* In a meditation group, you may have attempted *to gain a better understanding of yourself* through your interaction with others. You may have met with a small group of close friends for lunch at the arboretum or a coffee shop *to enjoy the pleasure of one another's company and/or to share experiences.* The italicized portions of the previous examples reveal that groups and individuals usually, but not always, have goals—however vague—and that these goals vary across groups. Goals may vary considerably depending on the nature of the group, the physical environment and social climate in which the group functions, the personal needs of individual members, and a multitude of other factors.

Relationship of Goals and Tasks

Sometimes the terms *goal* and *task* are used interchangeably and almost synonymously in the literature on small group research. *Task* may be defined as an act, or its result, that a small group is required, either by someone or by itself, to perform. A task is thus viewed as what people do, what they produce, or that on which they work in small groups. Tasks are performed by the group to accomplish goals. Generally we think of members of small groups as working on the task to achieve the goal, but sometimes the goal is to complete the task satisfactorily (in other words, "to get the job done"). When the latter occurs, there is considerable overlap in usage of the two terms. As a general rule, however, the task is usually the work done by the group to achieve the goal.

Suppose that a goal of the Intercultural Center on your campus was to show a series of movies reflecting lifestyles in other countries. Among the tasks the group might perform to accomplish this goal are the following: gather information of available films, select and prioritize those films that the group wishes to show, obtain funds for or otherwise determine how the movie rentals will be funded, schedule a place for showing the movies, obtain the equipment and personnel to show the movies, and so on. It might be necessary to complete all these and other tasks in order to accomplish the group's one goal.

To the extent possible, tasks should be stated in behavioral terms (statements of what people will do when performing the task). For example, "send a check to David Brightbill for $50 for his services as a projectionist to show the movie *The Cultures of Southeast Asia,* scheduled for Ace Hall on November 10, from 8:00 to 10:00 P.M." Such specific wording of tasks avoids ambiguity in interpretations and directs the effects of the group in a precise manner. These specific statements of tasks may be viewed as subordinate tasks for the major goals set for the group. Finally, brief descriptions should be written concerning how each task is to be completed, who is responsible for its completion, the date by which it is to be completed, and how its completion will be evaluated by the group.

Goals or aims may be expressed by individuals or by groups. The next section examines both individual personal goals as well as several types of group goals.

Principles

1. *Goal* is a term that refers to the objective or end result that a group or an individual seeks to achieve; it is a state of affairs that one or more people value and toward which they work.
2. *Task* is a term that refers to an act, or its result, that a small group is required, either by itself or someone else, to perform; one performs tasks to accomplish goals.
3. You should select the group's tasks with other members after you have selected and prioritized the goals of that group.
4. You should arrange sequentially, in concert with other group members, the series of tasks required to accomplish a given goal.
5. Where possible, you and other members of the group should state in behavioral terms both the goals and, particularly, the tasks for the group.

Personal Goals

A *personal goal* is an objective or end result that an individual attempts to achieve. The emphasis in this definition is on determining and defining the end result that a person seeks as an individual—that objective which he or she desires to achieve. Each of us has our own set of personal goals to balance with group goals.

Conscious Personal Goals.   If personal goals we have are considered at a *conscious level,* there is an awareness of the goal to satisfy a need. We typically have thought about our goals to some extent, are cognizant of them, and have made a deliberate decision about them. Once we determine conscious goals, we pursue them with varying degrees of intensity, depending on the level of commitment to their achievement. Examples of personal goals that might be determined consciously include: to work out three times a week, to stop drinking beer, or to tell a roommate what you think of sloppiness. It is unlikely that anyone would pursue such goals without some degree of awareness.

Unconscious Personal Goals.   When we seemingly just try to achieve personal goals out of habit, without much awareness that we even seek an objective, we are considering the goal at an *unconscious level.* Unconscious personal goals may have been pursued consciously at one time, but our awareness of them may subside over time. The following are examples of unconscious personal goals: to smile when meeting people, to open doors for older people, to avoid burping in public, or to "save face" during conflict. Behavior related to our unconscious goals is frequently the most difficult to control and regulate. Even so, it is important to determine personal unconscious goals and evaluate those that may place constraints on our effectiveness in group situations.

As group members, we seldom make our goals public. Sometimes we don't announce them because they are unconscious, and we don't know what we want. Sometimes we don't speak of them, because we fear personal rejection if we make them public. These unrevealed goals (Napier and Gershenfeld, 1999) are sometimes referred to as *hidden agendas.*

Relationship between Personal Goals and Group Goals

When you enter a group, you are asked to determine, accept, and/or agree upon a group's goals. Can you do it? Most of us cannot without some degree of difficulty. What we have is a person out doing his or her "thing" and pursuing his or her own interests; then, that person is confronted with whether or not he or she can accept the goals of a group of other people who have been pursuing their "things" and their interests. Gouran (1982) terms this condition a *mixed motive situation.* A mixed motive situation occurs when group members have to make choices between their own needs and what appear to be the divergent needs of the group. Is it any wonder that so many of us find it difficult to join and participate in groups? How do we cope with this problem and what procedures are involved?

We acknowledge throughout this book that groups may be capable of performing functions and achieving goals to which individuals can only aspire. One of the first assumptions you must accept as an individual is that a group may be able to produce results that you are unlikely to achieve alone. You might be required to compromise or modify your commitment to your individual goals in order to achieve group results.

At this point you still have considerable choice, and no one is forcing you to conform against your will. You might decide that the group holds limited potential for you to achieve results or goals that you hold in high priority, or you might determine that the members of the group share objectives that are compatible with your own. Still, the choice is yours, and you must make the determination. No one forces you to compromise concerning your personal commitments and goals even though the group may exert social pressure. But if you elect to join the group and to pursue the goals determined, accepted, or assigned by or to the group, then you must agree to play by the rules the group chooses.

Principles

1. A *personal goal* refers to the objective or end result that an individual attempts to achieve.
2. *Conscious personal goal* is a term that refers to an awareness of the goal to satisfy a need.
3. Because conscious personal goals will guide your behavior in a small group and influence the responses of other members to you, you should continually evaluate them and be aware that they may influence the work of the group either negatively or positively.
4. *Unconscious personal goal* is a term that refers to a goal pursued without much awareness.
5. *Hidden agenda* is a term that may be used to refer to unrevealed goals.
6. A *mixed motive situation* occurs when group members have to make choices between their own needs and the needs of the group. Because a group's goals are rarely 100 percent compatible with the personal goals of individual group members, you should be prepared to compromise *if* you decide to participate in the group.

Two General Types of Group Goals

A *group goal* is the objective, or end result, that a group seeks to achieve. Logic suggests little reason for groups to exist without goals, whether they are vaguely or specifically defined, apparent or unapparent to members, or accepted or unaccepted by members. There are rare exceptions when groups seem to survive and perhaps continue to meet over time with little effort devoted to determining or achieving goals. But even in such groups, it is likely that a careful analysis of the needs of individual members might provide insight into some possible goals for these groups.

Two general types of group goals have emerged from earlier literature on small groups (Cartwright and Zander, 1968). One type of group goal is an *achievement goal*, which usually refers to the major outcome or product that the group intends to produce. The second major type of goal for groups is a *group maintenance goal*, which refers to the maintenance or strengthening of the group itself. The achievement goal is generally considered at the highest level of priority. But as we shall see, it is easier in theory than in practice to accept the priority levels for the two kinds of goals. Sometimes the establishment and maintenance of a group's structure may be necessary before any serious consideration of achievement goals is introduced.

Achievement Goals

Suppose you were appointed to the Student-Faculty Advisory Committee in the School of Arts and Sciences. An achievement goal of the committee might be "to recommend faculty members for promotion and to present the list to the Dean of the School." The terminal product sought by this group is *the list of names of faculty members recommended for promotion*. Members of the committee would probably seek to achieve this goal by engaging in decision-making and/or problem-solving activities to derive their final list of names from among all the names submitted.

At this point you might be wondering what you could do to help the Advisory Committee achieve its goal. While there are many behaviors that help groups attain achievement goals (Cartwright and Zander, 1968; Zander, 1994), the following examples are presented for clarification. Additional examples will be given later in the chapter as we discuss roles.

1. You might clearly define the group's goal and report on progress toward the goal. Group members frequently have a difficult time keeping their thoughts and interactions focused on their goal and its achievement. Reminding the members what the goal is or pointing out that the group has strayed from its target helps the group by redirecting the attention of the members to the goal.

2. You also might summarize and restate the salient points concerning the issue. Sometimes you will encounter a group situation in which the members appear unclear about an issue. When this happens, you might state the points that seemed to be understood and then develop those ideas that were unclear.

3. Another way of helping the group is to contribute a procedural plan to achieve the goal. You might do this in combination with other members, or you might present an entire plan to the group members for their reactions. Efficient group procedures are important to the success of a group.

There are many other behaviors that help group members reach their achievement goals. One of these behaviors is getting and giving information. When you possess information needed or that could be used by the group, you have an obligation to contribute it. This is particularly so if you have some personal expertise on the problem or have collected pertinent information from experts. There are other times when you will need to get or elicit information from individuals in the group, perhaps by asking either open or direct questions of specific members.

The extent to which members attain their achievement goals for the group will depend substantially on their ability to pool their ideas freely, make significant contributions willingly, reconstruct and summarize their ideas effectively, and accept compromise objectively. Additional skills needed by groups if they are to accomplish their achievement goals are discussed in greater depth in Chapter Eight, including leadership skills in groups.

Group Maintenance Goals

When you work alone on a task, your entire attention can be directed toward achieving the goal. This is not the case when you work in groups. Working on an achievement goal in the presence of other people requires attention to interpersonal obstacles that are a function of both the goal and the presence of others. Not only do you have to focus on the achievement goal, but you must also attend to maintaining the group at a satisfactory level of cooperation.

Maintenance goals have been related to the "climate" of the group and refer to the kind of relationships that exist among the various members of the group. The most common kind of group maintenance goal is *to keep the group together*. When you are in a group that does not achieve this goal to at least a minimal degree, you can expect your group to experience difficulties, if not failure, in its efforts to master the achievement goal.

Another kind of maintenance goal is *to ensure the continued existence of the group itself*. Just as your group must maintain itself to function effectively and efficiently, so must the group continue its existence if it is to function at all.

The third and final kind of common maintenance goal is *to strengthen the group*. The emphasis in this goal is on *upgrading* the current level of the group's *existing state*. With this goal, we seek to achieve more effective interpersonal relations, greater cooperation, and a higher level of cohesiveness (Johnson and Johnson, 2000).

As with achievement goals, there are many helpful behaviors that help groups to attain group maintenance goals (Cartwright and Zander, 1968; Zander, 1994). The following examples will help clarify these behaviors.

1. You might spend more time in the group encouraging or reinforcing the behavior of other members. Particularly, you could reward the contributions of any participant who gets involved in the group's activity but had not been involved previously. Compliment the idea presented and make a reference to it the next time you speak.

2. Similarly, you might work to establish more pleasant interpersonal relations among members of the group by limiting the number of critical comments made about other members' ideas and by avoiding direct personal criticism of fellow participants.

3. You might even find it useful to help arbitrate disputes. This could be done by first trying to find common points of agreement and then moving the discussion progressively toward points on which there is greater disagreement. Be sure that the minority is given a chance to be heard. It is difficult to keep people involved in a group if they feel that what they say has no possibility of influencing the group.

4. A final example of members' functional behaviors that contribute to the achievement of group maintenance goals is an effort to increase the interdependence among you and your fellow members. Such behaviors reinforce the common fate of the group, the feelings of "we," and the commitment to "together as a group."

Relationship between Achievement Goals and Group Maintenance Goals

We approach ideal conditions in groups when achievement goals are accomplished effectively while group maintenance goals are achieved satisfactorily. Unfortunately, the nature of human behavior in groups seldom permits such ideal relationships to emerge smoothly. Obstacles to the attainment of achievement goals or obstacles to satisfactory interpersonal relations among the group's members may result in the failure of the group.

The key to this apparent problem is balance between the two kinds of goals. The conditions of the group will determine the emphasis given to each type of goal. When the group is moving smoothly toward its achievement goal and interpersonal relations are favorable, primary attention may be devoted to the achievement goal. This is so because you can use interpersonal rewards among members to support the attainment of the achievement goal.

Under other circumstances, it may be necessary to shift the emphasis of the group to the attainment of group maintenance goals. For example, if the group's structure is deteriorating, but the group members are making reasonable progress toward the achievement goal, you would need to shift the emphasis to group maintenance goals. Sometimes you might envision these two kinds of goals as competing against each other for members' time. Other times the two goals may be worked on harmoniously and simultaneously by members. However, there is usually a continual fluctuation of the priority of each kind of goal. Your responsibility as a member of a group is to determine when to weigh the priorities in favor of one kind of goal over the other and then to shift the attention of your fellow members to the appropriate kind of goal. In the next section we will examine roles that group members enact and alternatives for balancing achievement and maintenance goals.

Principles

1. *Achievement goal* is a term that refers to the major outcome or product that the group intends to produce or seeks to achieve.
2. *Group maintenance goal* is a term that refers to a goal designed to maintain, strengthen, or ensure the continued existence of the group itself.
3. There are a number of behaviors that you can employ to improve the efficiency of the group in accomplishing achievement goals. Some of these behaviors include:
   a. Clearly defining the group's goal and reporting on progress toward the goal.
   b. Summarizing and restating salient points concerning an issue.
   c. Contributing a procedural plan to achieve the goal.
4. Because a group's cohesiveness, morale, unity, solidarity, and cooperation among its members contribute to or at least mobilize the potential of the group's productivity, you should be aware of problems in the group relevant to these factors and establish through consensus the necessary goals to maintain the group when appropriate.
5. There are a number of behaviors you can employ to help the group attain group maintenance goals. Some of these behaviors include:
   a. Encouraging or reinforcing the behavior of other members.
   b. Limiting the number of critical comments made about other members' ideas and avoiding direct personal criticism of fellow participants.
   c. Helping to arbitrate disputes.
   d. Increasing the "we" feeling of a group.
6. It may be necessary to balance achievement and maintenance goals in order to ensure the survival of a group.

Roles in Small Groups

The behavior displayed by a group member through interaction with others has been referred to as a *role* (Forsyth, 1999). Borrowed from the theatre, the term *role* refers to a "part" or a set of behaviors that is expected of and/or displayed by a group member.

Perhaps the concept of role may be understood best through the example of the structure of a university. President, dean, professor, and student are positions in the university. Specific behaviors are expected of each person in each of these positions: for example, rarely does the president of a large university attend classes.

Similarly, there is a tendency for various degrees of specialization to occur among members of discussion groups. For example, you may prefer to help the group with the achievement goal by gathering information about the group problem. Another member may prefer to promote group harmony (maintenance goal) by telling funny stories at particularly tense moments. When you are more likely to perform some behaviors (e.g., going to classes or giving information) than other behaviors (e.g., teaching classes or promoting harmony), you have assumed a role.

Several individuals may perform the same role in different ways. One of the variables influencing an individual's performance of a role is role skill. *Role skills* are the characteristics an individual possesses that enable him or her to effectively enact a role. Role skills include variables such as aptitude, appropriate experience, and specific training. For example, you may recall a group member (perhaps yourself) who was especially skilled in leadership. This individual was probably influential in the group and may have had considerable experience as a leader. In a similar manner, not every individual possesses the skills necessary to effectively take notes. Difficulties with spelling or grammar, for example, cause some members to decline the role of recorder or secretary. Obviously, not all groups are highly structured with roles such as leader and recorder. Even in informal groups, however, members expect certain behaviors from individuals, and those individuals possess a variety of skills for the roles they accept.

This section of the chapter will first present the *general roles* that individuals enact during a discussion. The enactment of each role will affect the group as a system. Problems sometimes arise when individuals enact roles, and we will discuss three of these *role problems*. Finally we will look at the effect *role status* has on power and influence in small groups.

General Roles

In the late 1940s and the early 1950s, social scientists began to identify different roles people play in small groups.[1] One of the earliest but more useful classifications of role types was developed by Benne and Sheats (1948), who divided roles into three broad sets: group task roles, group building and maintenance roles, and self-centered roles.

Group task roles are those behaviors related to the accomplishment of the group's task or achievement goal. Frequently an individual who enacts group task roles is referred to as a *task specialist*. Group task roles include the following:

> *Initiator-contributor*—offers new ideas to be considered by the group or states old ideas in a novel fashion. ("Let's consider the financial aspect of this problem.")

---

[1] It should be remembered that one individual frequently exhibits the characteristics of several different roles throughout the discussion.

Information seeker—asks for clarification of ideas or requests evidence and facts. ("Does anyone have information regarding the cost of this survey?")

Opinion seeker—asks for agreement or disagreement with ideas/proposals under consideration. ("I would like to know how the rest of the group members feel about conducting a survey.")

Information giver—contributes relevant information. ("Dan can have the survey duplicated for two cents per page.")

Opinion giver—offers own opinion. ("I'm in favor of a fund-raising project.")

Elaborator—clarifies and further explains another member's ideas. ("Perhaps Cindy is thinking that having the bake sale downtown would provide a new market.")

Coordinator—shows relationships among statements of fact or opinion from group members. ("The statistics from the Registrar's Office certainly seem to support the dean's opinion.")

Orienter—guides the discussion by keeping the group on track and moving the discussion along. ("Let's go back to our criteria.")

Evaluator-critic—evaluates the adequacy of the group's information and accomplishments according to some set of standards. ("That would be a good suggestion if we had enough money in our budget, but it doesn't seem to be feasible with our limited finances.")

Energizer—prods the members to action. ("Who would like to help me with the survey analysis?")

Procedural technician—handles routine tasks such as seating arrangements and handouts. ("I've placed a packet of information for each of you on the table.")

Recorder—keeps track of the group's progress or takes minutes. ("According to my notes, we agreed to limit this meeting to one hour.")

Group building and maintenance roles are behaviors that contribute to the functioning of the group by striving to maintain constructive interpersonal relations (maintenance goal). An individual who enacts group building and maintenance roles frequently is referred to as the social-emotional leader. Group building and maintenance roles include the following:

Encourager—provides support or shows acceptance of another member's idea or statement. ("That's a good idea, Michael. I'll help.")

Harmonizer—resolves conflict and reduces tension, frequently with humor. ("Since we're all friends again, let's agree to bring squirt guns to our meetings so we can have *real* battles.")

Compromiser—attempts to come up with an idea that will please every-one. ("Even though I'd rather have the bake sale on campus, maybe we would have time to do both—we could have the bake sale in town this Friday and on campus the following Friday.")

Gatekeeper—opens the channels of communication and promotes even-ness of participation. ("Just a minute, Sam. Sue, what were you starting to say?")

Standard—Expresses standards for the group to achieve or applies stan-dards in evaluating the group's progress. ("Why don't we try to reach a workable decision in forty-five minutes? Then this will be our short-est meeting!")

Group observer—evaluates the mood of the group. ("It seems as though group consensus has been reached.")

Follower—accepts ideas of others and goes along with the group trends. ("If everyone is going this Saturday, I'll go too.")

Self-centered roles are behaviors that satisfy personal needs rather than group goals. These behaviors tend to be either unrelated or negatively related to group goals and may operate at the conscious or unconscious level (see p. 36). Self-centered roles include the following:

Aggressor—attacks other members in an effort to promote own status. ("Bake sales are immature and a pretty dumb idea. My suggestion has class.")

Blocker—opposes all ideas and refuses to cooperate. ("I don't think a good idea has been suggested by this group yet!")

Recognition seeker—boasts about past accomplishments (frequently irrelevant), usually in an attempt to gain sympathy. ("Last year's fund-raising project was my idea, and it was successful, too. I think the group should reconsider their thoughts about my idea for having a car-nival this year.")

Self-confessor—engages in irrelevant discussion to work out personal mistakes and feelings. ("Last night I had this sudden insight into why I can't study. It all goes back to my fourth-grade teacher . . .")

Playboy—displays a lack of involvement in the group through inappro-priate humor or horseplay. ("Let's go to the beach instead.")

Dominator—embarks on long monologues and tries to monopolize the group's time. ("I guess what I have been trying to say for the past ten minutes is . . .")

Help seeker—attempts to gain sympathy from other group members through expressions of insecurity or inadequacy. ("I really don't think

I should be responsible for the survey analysis. I've never been very good in math, and I'd probably lose the results, too.")

Special-interest pleader—brings in irrelevant information and argues incessantly from own point of view. ("Tuesday is still a better day for a bake sale because it's the day after a 'blue Monday.' ")[2]

As you read the classification of role types developed by Benne and Sheats, you might have been able to identify one or more of these general interaction roles that you usually assume. Or, perhaps you recognized roles that other group members play. Identifying characteristics of roles that you and others assume may help you to understand the function of roles in small groups. Be careful of stereotyping, however. Rigidly held role expectations that lead to stereotyping can "lock" members into roles. Allow a member to be task oriented during one meeting and to be a "supporter" during another meeting. Group members may assume several of these general interaction roles during the life of a small group.

Principles
1. A role is a set of behaviors that is expected of and/or displayed by the individual who occupies a particular position in a group's structure.
2. Role skills are the characteristics that enable an individual to effectively enact a role.
3. The three general sets of interaction roles that a group member may enact are group task roles, group building and maintenance roles, and self-centered roles.
4. Group members also assume specific formal role positions.

Role Problems

Suppose you just received a letter from home reminding you that your little sister's school play is this weekend, and she is eagerly awaiting your attendance. As you finish reading the letter, the phone rings. A good friend excitedly tells you she has just managed to get two tickets to the regional baseball playoffs on Saturday. Your parents and little sister expect you to come home, and your friend expects you to go with her to the ballgame. These expectations to perform certain tasks, in a certain manner and at a certain time, are generally perceived as role pressures.

Role pressures can give rise to problems of role ambiguity, role conflict, and role overload (McGrath, 1984). *Role ambiguity* exists when some of the messages group members send about how the role should be enacted are

---

[2]Based in part on Benne and Sheats (1948), with permission.

unclear. Group members, for example, may not have made it clear to the chairperson that he is expected to arrange for audio-visual equipment to be used by a guest speaker at a meeting. *Role conflict* exists when some of the role messages imply different and even mutually conflicting actions. Examples of role conflict may be found in hierarchical organizations. A low-level manager may feel conflict between expectations of the work group to represent their point of view to management and management's expectations to support its viewpoint to the workers. *Role overload* exists when the role expectations exceed the capabilities of the role incumbent. Perhaps the group's secretary has so many other previous commitments that he can't remain for the entire meeting. Many role problems that groups experience are examples of these three types of role problems.

Groups attempting to resolve role problems may find it necessary to discuss role expectations. When discussing role expectations, members can clarify what is expected of them. Feelings of frustration resulting from excessive demands on their energy or from role conflict may lead to defensive communication, which is to be discussed in the next chapter. If a group member prefers to resign a specific role position, group members should be supportive and not pressure the reluctant group member. Members who fulfill role positions "in name only" generally do little to enhance group effort.

Role Status, Power, and Influence

At the beginning of this chapter we mentioned a student-faculty Committee on Students with Disabilities. Suppose you are attending this committee's first meeting and recognize most of the members—editor of the student newspaper, a faculty member from the Foreign Language Department, vice-president of the student government who is also a member of the Intercultural Center, a computer science major who is also president of the Jamaican Students Organization, and the chair of the Department of Communication. You don't recognize the sixth committee member, but her appearance suggests she also is a member of the faculty. Although committee membership appears to be evenly divided between students and faculty, your first guess is that power will rest with the faculty, because faculty members have higher status than students.

To help explain how power operates, let's briefly examine five bases of power noted by French and Raven (1968).

1. *Reward power* is the ability to provide others with something they want or need. Rewards might include promotions, good grades, or just a "pat on the back" for a job well done. Generally, the more group members value the reward and perceive another member's ability to dispense or withhold the reward, the greater the power.

2. *Coercive power* is based on the fear that another member holds the power to punish. Obvious examples of punishment include demotions, suspension, or withholding graduation. Coercive power, however, can be more subtle and can take the form of criticism or personal rejection.

3. *Legitimate power* generally occurs when group members willingly accept another's authority. Most students give legitimate power to their teachers in the classroom, while most employees give supervisors legitimate power in the work environment.

4. *Referent power* occurs when group members do what another member desires because they like him or her. People we like, admire, or identify with generally have greater influence over us than people we dislike.

5. *Expert power* refers to the influence that results when group members perceive another member to have specialized knowledge, information, or skills. Most of us will readily seek needed advice from physicians, electricians, or attorneys, for example. We give them power over us because we perceive them to have specialized expertise.

The first three bases of power—reward, coercive, and legitimate—tend to reside in a role position (e.g., chairperson or faculty member). Expert and referent power, on the other hand, tend to reside in the personal characteristics of a group member.

Most of your groups will have both high-status and low-status group members with varying degrees of power.[3] Since research (e.g., Kashyap, 1982) has found that a group member who is perceived to be either wealthy or an expert on some topic exerts more influence in changing others' opinions, let's return to the example of the faculty-student Committee on Students with Disabilities and see who is doing the influencing.

The committee's first meeting was unproductive. The committee members lacked clarity about their goals, and the student members participated minimally. The students seemed to accept faculty authority (legitimate power) and were concerned about the impressions that the faculty would form of them (perception of reward and/or coercive power). Understanding that forced participation would not further group goals, the chairperson adjourned the meeting. The chairperson began the second meeting by discussing the history of the committee. She emphasized that the students had been selected for the committee because each had an area of expertise not shared by the faculty (expert power) and sincerely communicated the faculty's esteem and respect for each of them (referent power). The student

---

[3]See Shaw (1981) for a summary of research concerning the effect of status differences in small groups.

members participated more readily at successive meetings, and the mutual influence necessary for successful goal accomplishment was achieved.

Members of successful groups generally do not ignore or deny power. They are aware of power and accept responsibility for its use. High-status individuals are sensitive to the potential to ignore or reject ideas from persons of low status. Low-status individuals are aware of their tendency to accept without logical criticism the ideas of higher status persons. Group members who are aware of power know that attraction to the group is generally greater when all members have had their say and are potentially able to influence others.

Principles

1. Role pressures can give rise to three types of role problems: role ambiguity, role conflict, and role overload.
2. Five bases of power in small groups include reward power, coercive power, legitimate power, referent power, and expert power.
3. Reward, coercive, and legitimate power tend to reside in a role position, while expert and referent power tend to reside in the personal characteristics of a group member.
4. High-status group members often have more power and influence than low-status group members.
5. Group members who are aware of power know that attraction to the group is generally greater when all members have had their say and are potentially able to influence others.

Summary

This chapter examined both the nature of goals and the roles group members may enact while attaining these goals. The chapter began by providing an overview of the general concepts of goals and tasks in small groups. A *goal* was defined as the result that a group or an individual seeks to achieve. A *task* was defined as an act, or its result, that a small group is required to perform. *Personal goals* were defined as the objectives that an individual seeks to achieve. Conscious and unconscious personal goals were discussed with the degree of awareness acting as the basis for distinguishing between the two types. The implications and consequences of trying to make personal goals compatible with the group's goals were stressed.

Two principle types of goals were discussed: *achievement goals* and *group maintenance goals*. The former refers to the major outcome or product that the group intends to produce; the latter refers to those goals designed to maintain, strengthen, and/or ensure the continued existence of the group. The relationship between achievement goals and maintenance goals was also examined.

This chapter also discussed the roles that group members enact during a discussion. Role problems and the resulting pressures that they place on group members were noted. Role status, power, and influence were examined, and five bases of power in small groups were discussed. In your systems analysis, you should identify the roles played by the members of your group and analyze how they affect interaction and attainment of the group's goals.

Ideas for Discussion

1. What are the important distinctions and relationships between goals and tasks? Why is it important to make them?

2. What are some of the implications of conscious and unconscious personal goals for small group behavior? How can culture affect personal goals?

3. How can you maintain a balance between the group's need to accomplish achievement goals and maintenance goals?

4. How would you attempt to deal with the following situations in a group: members seem unclear about an issue; participants are not focusing on the goal; the topic is not related to the goal; and the group is bogged down and not moving toward achievement of the goal.

5. What are some personal goals you have that would not permit you to accept conflicting group goals *under any circumstance*?

6. How might group members with differing personality characteristics (e.g., self-confidence, aggressiveness) affect the enactment of the same role in a small group?

Suggested Projects and Activities

1. List three groups to which you belong. Identify the goals of the three groups, listing achievement and maintenance goals separately. Finally, determine which tasks are used to accomplish those goals.

2. Using the same three groups, list your personal goals for the group. In a brief essay, discuss how your personal goals are or are not satisfied by your group memberships.

3. Over a period of two weeks, observe your own goals in three groups in which you participate. Write a paragraph describing your assumed role in each group. Discuss briefly the reasons that your roles differ across the different groups.

4. Compare and contrast the bases of power in two groups. Does member status affect communication? Group outcome? Attraction to the group?

References

Benne, K. D, and P. Sheats. Functional roles of group members. *Journal of social issues*, 1948, 4, 41–49.
Cartwright, D., and A. Zander, eds. *Group dynamics*, 3rd ed. New York: Harper & Row, 1968.
Forsyth, D. R. *Group dynamics*. Monterey, Calif.: Brooks Cole, 3rd ed. 1999.

French, J. R. P., Jr., and B. H. Raven. The bases of social power. In D. Cartwright and A. Zander, eds. *Group dynamics: research and theory. New York: Harper & Row, 1968, 259–269.*

Gouran, D. S. *Making decisions in groups.* Glenview, Ill.: Scott, Foresman, 1982.

Johnson, D. W., and F. P. Johnson. *Joining together: group theory and group skills,* 7th ed. Boston: Allyn & Bacon, 2000.

Kashyap, A. Differential efficacy of power base in opinion change in group discussion. *Journal of psychological research, 1982, 26,* 9–12.

McGrath, J. E. *Groups: interaction and performance.* Englewood Cliffs, N.J.: Prentice-Hall, 1984.

Napier, R. W., and M. K. Gershenfeld. *Groups: theory and experience,* 6th ed. Boston: Houghton Mifflin, 1999.

Shaw, M. E. *Group dynamics: the psychology of small group behavior,* 3rd ed. New York: McGraw-Hill, 1981.

Zander, A. *Making groups effective,* 2nd ed. San Francisco: Jossey-Bass, 1994.

Suggested Readings

Canary, D. J., M. J. Cody, and V. L. Manusov. *Interpersonal communication: A goals-based approach,* 2nd ed. Boston: Bedford / St. Martin's, 2000. Chapter 1, "The Importance of Interpersonal Communication in Achieving Personal Goals," distinguishes among three general types of interpersonal goals: self-presentation goals, relational goals, and instrumental goals. Although instrumental goals may be most important to North Americans, self-presentation goals may be most important to group members from other cultures (e.g., Southeast Asian countries).

Frey, L. R. Individuals in groups. In L. R. Frey and J. K. Barge, eds. *Managing group life: Communicating in decision-making groups.* Boston: Houghton Mifflin, 1997, 52–79. Each group member comes to the group with a personal history and this chapter discusses the effects of social characteristics, abilities, and personality and communication traits on the group.

Hackman, M. Z., and C. E. Johnson. *Leadership: A communication perspectives,* 3rd ed. Prospect Heights, IL: Waveland Press, 2000. Chapter 4, "Leadership and Power," explores the relationship between power and leadership including the cost/benefit ratios for the different types of power and the effect of language on power.

Haslett, B. B., and J. Ruebush. What differences do individual differences in groups make? In L. R. Frey *The Handbook of group communication theory and research.* Thousand Oaks, CA: Sage, 1999. This chapter in a research oriented text focuses on individual differences in characteristics such as perception, cognitive style, gender and culture.

Johnson, D. W., and F. P. Johnson. *Joining together: Group theory and group skills,* 7th ed. Boston: Allyn & Bacon, 2000. Chapter 3 Group Goals and Social Interdependence, "Group Goals includes discussion and exercises to increase understanding of the definitions, skills, structure, and types of goals. Chapter 9, "The Use of Power," includes discussion and exercises to increase understanding of power and influence in small groups.

4

Communicating Effectively in the Small Group

Study Questions

After reading this chapter, you should be able to answer the following questions completely and accurately:

1. What are the primary characteristics of a desirable discussion attitude?
2. What are three major differences between defensive and supportive communication?
3. What are six suggestions for asking questions in a positive, supportive communication climate?
4. What does the term *group cohesiveness* mean?
5. What are four major consequences of group cohesiveness?
6. What does the term *communication network* mean?
7. What are communication channels?
8. How does a central position in a communication network differ from a less central position?
9. What are two reasons that groups exhibit different communication structures?
10. What are two potential effects of group structure for the individual group member?
11. What is *subgrouping?*
12. What are nine suggestions for communicating effectively in the small group?

The very existence of a group depends on communication, whether verbal or nonverbal. Through communication group members reach some level of understanding, build trust, set goals, divide tasks, and conduct all group activity. Indeed, effective communication is a prerequisite to a productive and harmonious group.

How do you tell when communication is effective and when it's not? This chapter will first look at discussion attitude and the relationship between attitude and defensive communication. Next, it will examine group cohesiveness, one of the benefits of effective communication. Finally, this chapter will look at some networks of communication interaction and then provide you with some practical suggestions for communicating effectively in the small group.

Parts of this chapter may appear overly simplistic, and you may say, "I know that." But the value of this chapter depends on your ability to understand attitudes, develop skills, and apply the information to your real-life small groups. It is especially important that you remember to do a systems analysis and to take into account differences in settings as you apply this material.

Discussion Attitude

We often hear someone exclaim, "What an attitude!" Sometimes this expression refers to someone who is different from others, perhaps disagreeable, uncooperative, or even a "show off." This attitude can affect other individuals. For our small group purposes, we will consider *discussion attitude* to be mental predispositions toward (1) the topic or problem, (2) yourself, and (3) the other participants. Objectivity and open-mindedness form the basis of a desirable discussion attitude.

Attitude toward the Problem

Some individuals adhere to their views so strongly that they often refuse to undertake anything that is different, innovative, or new. Such individuals believe very strongly in one "right" and several "wrong" ways to accomplish any task. Zanjonc (1965) may have described it best when he said, "We may not know what we like, but we like what we know." It's probably easier to dismiss the new and unfamiliar than it is to work to understand it.

Attitude toward Self

Our self-worth is concerned with attachment to beliefs and ideas. If you contradict another group member's statement, for example, the contradiction may be perceived as dislike. Or perhaps several group members vote against your proposal. Do you wonder if "they're out to get you"? Such message distortion may be the result of your attitude toward yourself—your self-concept.

Your attitude toward yourself affects not only how you perceive others, but also how you behave. For example, one participant who feels self-conscious may say very little, while another may try to impress people by over-responding. Self-concept may explain a variety of "attitudes" we see displayed in our daily interactions.

Our perceptions of ourselves are a result of years of conditioning by significant others and are difficult to change quickly. While there is no miracle "cure" for low self-esteem, the more you try to be objective toward yourself and are generally self-accepting, the more you are approaching a desirable attitude toward yourself.

Attitude toward Other Participants

Within a few seconds of meeting, most people form impressions of or general attitudes about each other. Frequently based on stereotypes, the impressions may be favorable, neutral, or unfavorable. Often the responses are guided by a person's dress, facial expressions, and the like (see Chapter Seven), or are merely guided by the notion that the person "reminds me of someone I know." In other words, positive or negative reaction is based on attitudes rather than on facts.

Sometimes group members like or dislike other members to the extent that they fail to be objective. One inherent danger when this happens is that participants may agree with what their friends say and disagree with what the people whom they dislike say. A second and similar danger is that participants may perceive that individuals whom they like will be in agreement and individuals whom they dislike will be in disagreement.

Awareness of these dangers should help group members to remain objective about other members and their points of view. It is difficult to like everyone, but most people should be able to work together to accomplish a task even if they do not like or agree with other group members. In the next section, you will see how attitudes toward the problem, self, and other participants can affect small group communication.

Defensive and Supportive Communication

A closed-minded attitude toward other members' ideas, low self-esteem, and/or lack of objectivity toward other participants often results in *defensive communication.* After an eight-year study of communication behavior in groups, social psychologist Jack Gibb (1961) concluded that defensive communication is counterproductive because it interferes with speaking and listening abilities. People who behave defensively, for example, tend to put more energy into how they can win, dominate, or impress than into the task itself. Defensiveness not only makes it difficult to convey ideas clearly, it also prevents the listener from concentrating on the message. *Supportive communication,* on the other hand, usually occurs when group members are more accepting of the opinions of others and are more willing to listen openly to them. Because listeners generally find it easier to concentrate on the message, supportive communication tends to enhance listening abilities. Often it's not so much *what* the person says (the words) but *how* it is said (tone of voice, facial expression, and so on). The distinction will become clearer as we look at some of the differences between defensive and supportive communication, as outlined by Gibb, and then examine their role in a positive communication climate.

Evaluation versus Description

Suppose that you are attending a meeting for a community service organization to which you belong. The conversation turns to fundraising, and you offer a suggestion. Another participant turns and says, "Really, I thought that attending college meant that you were smart. That will *never* work!" How would you feel? A victim of another's "put down" attitude, you may be defensive. On the other hand, suppose the member instead had said, "I'm having a hard time projecting revenue. Do we have an idea of how much money that would bring in?" Now how do you feel? Maybe the group hasn't supported your idea, but at least you haven't been put down.

These comments illustrate the difference between evaluative and descriptive communication. The first comment is *evaluation,* because it is directed toward another's worth. It is based on "you" language. The second comment, however, is *description*. Based on "I" language, it describes the speaker's thoughts and feelings about the idea. Evaluation generally creates defensiveness, while description can promote interpersonal trust and group cohesiveness.

Control versus Problem Orientation

One of the symptoms of the difficult teenage years is parent-child disagreements. Teenagers often complain, "I'm tired of my parents telling me what to do." While control issues may be more apparent in families, communication aimed at *controlling* the behavior of others may also occur in small groups. Whether in families or other small groups, the "I know what's good for you" attitude toward other individuals usually produces defensiveness.

In contrast to control, *problem orientation* is communication that avoids manipulation and focuses on issues. Perception is important. A group member may think that she is issue oriented, but if the group perceives manipulation, defensiveness is likely to develop. A perception of problem orientation is desirable, however, because it can increase cohesiveness and group productivity.

Certainty versus Provisionalism

Closely related to control is *certainty*. Controlling people often display an attitude of certainty, and they appear to view their ideas as "truth" and anyone with different ideas must be "wrong." Just as a student may try to prove a teacher wrong, so also may group participants become defensive.

If attitudes toward the problem appear to be held *provisionally*, on the other hand, small group communication is more likely to be effective. In comparison to world knowledge, the human brain actually can store very little. Opening to new information, being flexible, and sincerely committing to solving problems can all help to reduce defensive communication.

Asking Questions

The degree to which group members are supportive or defensive creates the communication climate. When group members share ideas openly, listen to each other, and ask questions in ways that tend to be supportive, the communication climate is positive or open. Respect for one another is at the heart of a positive or open communication climate. Before focusing on the ways that group members listen (or don't listen)[1] to the ideas shared in the group, we will first look at the effect of questioning on the communication climate.

---

[1]Chapter five, the next chapter, focuses on listening and feedback.

You probably have realized that not only do listeners respond to the way questions are worded, they also respond to the manner or way questions are asked. A parent, for example, can ask "Where did you go last night?" in a way that indicates objective inquiry. However, the same question can be asked in a manner that implies distrust and an attempt to control. As in families, group members who perceive that they have been challenged may become defensive, may withdraw, or may refuse to cooperate.

The following guidelines are intended to help you ask questions that promote a positive, supportive communication climate.

1. Be tactful and kind. Avoid questions that evaluate or "put down" the ideas others, or that appear to be manipulative or to have ulterior motives.
2. Focus on issues; ask questions that clarify or analyze information.
3. Ask questions that demonstrate flexibility and openness to new information.
4. Be specific and clear in questioning. Avoid vague and unclear questions.
5. Paraphrase a speakers's point before asking a question. This is helpful when a speaker might misinterpret the question and think that the listener was not listening.
6. Just as turns are taken in speaking, take turns in questioning.

The way in which members of a group interact can affect the outcome of a group. If communication in the group is generally supportive, cohesiveness and group productivity can increase. Defensive communication, on the other hand, generally adversely affects group cohesiveness and productivity. Cohesiveness and productivity are very important to small groups and are discussed in the next section.

Principles

1. Objectivity and open-mindedness toward the problem, yourself, and other group members characterize a desirable discussion attitude.
2. A closed-minded attitude toward other members' ideas, low self-esteem, and/or lack of objectivity toward other participants may result in defensive communication.
3. Supportive communication usually occurs when group members are more accepting of the opinions of others and are more willing to listen openly to them.
4. Defensive and supportive communication differ on the following qualities.
   a. Evaluation versus Description
   b. Control versus Problem orientation
   c. Certainty versus Provisionalism
5. When group members interact in a supportive manner, the communication climate is open.

6. There are six guidelines for asking questions to promote a positive or supportive communication climate.
   a. Be tactful and kind.
   b. Focus on issues.
   c. Ask questions that demostrate flexibility and openness.
   d. Be specific and clear.
   e. Paraphrase a speaker's point of view before asking a question.
   f. Take turns in asking questions.

Group Cohesiveness

Why do individuals in some groups have warmer interpersonal relationships than individuals in other groups? Why are individuals in some groups more involved with the group than individuals in other groups? Explaining differences in "groupness" can be difficult. Many researchers in small group communication say that the answers to these questions lie with a concept called *group cohesiveness.*[2] Although variously defined over the years,[3] *cohesiveness* is generally regarded as the complex of forces that bind members of a group to one another and to the group as a whole. In other words, cohesiveness may be thought of as the emerging sense of "we-ness" rather than "I-ness."

The concept of group cohesion appears to be multidimensional. Tziner (1982), for example, suggests that there are two types of group cohesiveness. The first type is socio-emotional, or interpersonal, cohesiveness and is based on interpersonal attraction among group members. Emotional satisfaction provided by participation in the group is emphasized. The second type of cohesiveness is instrumental, or task, cohesiveness. Members of groups with this type of cohesiveness put more energy into working for the group (Prapavessis and Carron, 1997) and are more likely to remain group members until completion of the task (Spink and Carron, 1994). Although researchers have not reached consensus on a definition of group cohesiveness, some studies (e.g., Zaccaro and McCoy, 1988) indicate that both high task and high interpersonal cohesiveness are necessary for group success. Other studies (e.g., Littlepage et al., 1989) suggest that cohesion and performance are often, but not always, related.

Earlier we stated that groups need to balance task needs and maintenance (socio-emotional) needs. Think back to some of the groups to which you have belonged. Perhaps some of those groups were satisfying because of the harmonious interpersonal relationships. Others may have been satisfying because of successful goal attainment. Perhaps many of those groups were satisfying

---

[2]See Bettenhausen (1991), Shaw (1981), and McGrath and Altman (1966) for a discussion of research in the area of group cohesiveness.

[3]See Mudrack (1989) for a discussion of the confusion regarding a definition of group cohesiveness.

because they effectively balanced both of these two types of needs. This next section will look at some of the consequences of group cohesiveness.

Consequences of Group Cohesiveness

Because it is unlikely that group members who are repelled from one another will stay together, cohesiveness may be thought of as a continuum ranging from low to high. Increasing cohesiveness from low to high positively affects communication, and this, in turn, affects other aspects of groups. Shaw (1981) notes four major consequences of group cohesiveness: Group productivity, satisfaction, social influence, and interaction. A brief explanation of each of them follows.

Group Productivity. At the beginning of our discussion of cohesiveness, we noted that there are two types of cohesiveness and that cohesion and performance are often, but not always, related. If group norms emphasize emotional satisfaction, for example, it seems reasonable that productivity might be lower. Suppose that two highly cohesive groups meet each week for the stated purpose of improving conditions at the local animal shelter. One group appears to have an implied purpose of reinforcing group friendship. The accepted ways of behaving at the group meetings include drinking coffee and sharing the past week's experiences and rumors. The other group also values friendship. The members stop for coffee after the meetings to socialize as friends, but the conversation always seems to drift back to organizing the fundraiser for the animal shelter. Thus, it seems that a highly cohesive group would be productive if group value were placed on accomplishing the group task (Goodman et al., 1987) and if the task requires joint performance of its members (Gully et al., 1995; Langfred, 1998).

Satisfaction. We are usually attracted to groups that we perceive are meeting our needs and are beneficial for us. For example, if an individual participates in a group and the group's efforts are a success, participation becomes a reinforcing experience, and personal attraction to the group is increased (Elias et al., 1989). Because even limited success may increase satisfaction and attraction to the group, the tasks initially do not necessarily even have to be directly related to the group goal. In addition, remember that it is possible for members to be dissatisfied with the group as a whole yet still be satisfied with the group's progress toward the goal.

Social Influence. Communication in highly cohesive groups tends to be more supportive. That is, members are generally more willing to listen to others and are more accepting of the opinions of others. Imagine, for example, that you have been elected to a group that is trying to reduce the amount of paper waste generated on your campus. You don't agree with a solution proposed by one of the group's members which was that the group should place recycling bins in the dormitories. You listen and finally suggest that the university really needs a "waste reduction" program rather than just a "recycling" plan. The group votes, and the majority of the group votes for recycling only. Your solution was rejected, but you conform and agree to help place recycling bins around campus.

Although you attempted to influence others, you were eventually persuaded. This tendency of individual group members to influence (persuade) and to be influenced (persuaded) is greater in highly cohesive groups.

Interaction.   Communication is the vehicle through which group members interact and influence one another. As a result of taking a course in small group communication, for example, you may interact with people you had not previously known. You may notice that as your interaction increases, you become more cooperative and friendly, and in general behave in ways that promote group interaction. These qualities are characteristic of groups high in cohesiveness (Elias et al., 1989). Members of low cohesive groups, however, interact less frequently and behave more independently.

You are probably now beginning to understand how important effective communication is to small groups. Ideally, rewarding interactions increase the probability that group members are able to mutually influence one another and work together to accomplish the task (assuming that the group values task accomplishment). Individual commitment to the group would tend to increase as group members become more satisfied with group membership. In other words, the group is developing a sense of "we-ness" and is becoming cohesive. This attraction to the group may also be affected by the group's network of interactions, which is the subject of the next section.

Principles
1. Group cohesiveness is generally regarded as the complex of forces binding group members to one another and to the group as a whole.
2. Two types of cohesiveness include socio-emotional (interpersonal) cohesiveness and instrumental (task) cohesiveness.
3. Increasing group cohesiveness affects productivity, satisfaction, social influence, and interaction.

Communication Networks

You have probably heard the expression "Three's a crowd." Why is it that the addition of just one person can significantly change the interaction between two people? An example may help explain. The simplest communication pattern exists in a two-person group, or dyad. Suppose that Ann and Bob are interacting. Ann may send a message to Bob and/or Bob may send a message to Ann. If Charlie joins Ann and Bob, however, the communication pattern becomes more complex. The interaction possibilities in a triad, or three-person group, are listed and illustrate that the system changes with just one new person.

Ann to Bob	Bob to Ann	Charlie to Bob
Ann to Charlie	Bob to Charlie	Charlie to Ann
Ann to Bob and Charlie	Charlie to Ann and Bob	Bob to Ann and Charlie

This pattern of "linkages" (or who talks to whom) is the structural aspect of a group called the *communication network*. Since the late 1940s social scientists have focused on communication networks in a considerable number of laboratory studies (e.g., Bavelas, 1948; Gilchrist et al., 1954; Shaw, 1954). The research has primarily been concerned with types of communication networks, the reasons groups become structured, and the effects of group structure.

Types of Communication Networks

Scientists who study communication structure usually specify communication channels. Between any two positions (individuals), there may be a two-way channel, a one-way channel, or no channel at all. In a two-way channel, Ann and Bob may send messages to each other. In a one-way channel, however, Ann may send a message to Bob but Bob may not send a message to Ann (or vice versa). Note the networks in Figure 4.1. In the *wheel network*, Bob, Charlie, Diane, and Ed may send and receive messages from Ann, although they may neither send nor receive messages from one another. The *chain network* allows the sending and receiving of messages from the posi-

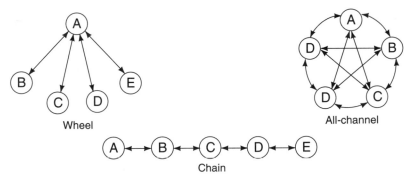

Wheel

All-channel

Chain

In each structure the circles represent individuals and the lines indicate communication channels.

FIGURE 4.1 *Examples of Communication Networks Frequently Employed in Experimental Studies*

tions to either the right or left, except for the two end positions, where messages may be sent and received from only one position. For example, Ann may send a message only to Bob, and Ed may send a message only to Diane. In the *all-channel network,* all positions may send and receive messages from all other positions; Ann, Bob, Charlie, Diane, and Ed may interact freely with one another. Thus, the type of network restricts the communication interaction.

Reasons Groups Become Structured

Research in the area of group structure has produced several possible reasons that groups form differing communication patterns and, therefore, exhibit differing structures (Shaw, 1981). Two of several possible reasons that groups exhibit differing structures are (1) requirements for efficient group performance and (2) different abilities and motivations of different individuals.

Efficient Group Performance.   You may recall being in a small group that was organizing a party or some other similar social function. The group probably agreed to divide the responsibility for entertainment, decorations, refreshments, admissions, and so on among the individuals in the group. The decision to divide the responsibility was probably reached with little disagreement; most individuals who participate in a group task find that a group is more efficient if it specializes the tasks (e.g., responsibility for entertainment). Suppose, for example, that Ann is responsible for entertainment for a social function. For the sake of efficiency, she assigns to each member of her subgroup a different band and asks them to determine the cost of having that group entertain at their social function. Each individual reports back to Ann and does not find it necessary to communicate with the other members of the subgroup. Thus, the group exhibited the characteristics of the wheel network (Figure 4.1), because the members determined that an efficient way to complete the group task was to assign each member a part of the task and to have each member report directly to Ann, the leader.

Abilities and Motivations of Individuals.   Although there most likely are few formal restrictions on communication in your small group discussions, you have probably noticed the tendency for talk to center periodically on one individual or another. Sometimes, for example, communication flows to and from unusually aggressive or dominant group members. Other group members may find themselves in focal positions while sharing extensive knowledge of the problem. Whenever the communication originates from or is directed toward one member of the group, the group is exhibiting the characteristics of the wheel network. The chain network may be apparent at other times if group members pass information from one to another, such as in business organizations or in the military. When all group members participate and communication tends to be distributed relatively equally, however, the group is using the all-channel network. Group structure is important for the individual group member as well as for the group, as you will see in the next section.

Effects of Structure

In addition to studying communication networks and discovering reasons that groups become structured, researchers have studied the effects of group structure. Noted researchers Dorwin Cartwright and Alvin Zander (1968) indicate that group structure has several potential effects. Two of these effects are (1) the consequences of structure for the individual group member and (2) the effects of structure on group performance.

Consequences of Individual Location in Group Structure. The position occupied in a communication structure produces several consequences for the individual, including morale and leadership.

Some research studies in group behavior (e.g., Berkowitz, 1978) have found that members who occupy the more central positions in a group's structure tend to be more satisfied with the group and have higher morale. This is presumably true because the individuals in the more central positions have the opportunity to send a greater number of messages and can interact more freely with the other group members. Because each individual may send and receive messages and has a relatively equal chance of being chosen leader, individual morale is generally highest in the all-channel network (see Figure 4.1). This may be one reason that individual morale and satisfaction are generally higher in a social group than in a hierarchical structure with primarily a one-way channel of communication (e.g., the army).

Studies also have investigated the relationship between an individual's location in the group structure and leadership. The group member who occupies a central position usually emerges as the group leader, generally because the central member has more information and can coordinate group activities. Although member satisfaction is generally lower in centralized networks like the wheel (see Figure 4.1), some research (e.g., Snadowsky, 1974) indicates that democratic leadership can produce satisfied group members in spite of centralized communication. Chapter Eight provides more information about leadership so that you can investigate it in your systems analysis, along with group structure.

One possible consequence of dissatisfaction with the communication is *subgrouping*. In subgrouping, private conversations take place within the framework of the larger discussion. Occasional private remarks between members who do not wish to take the group's time cause little concern. However, when the occasional remark becomes a conversation, the noise factor alone creates a distraction. In addition, the conversing members are not directing their energy toward assisting the group. When the group's communication structure is so highly centralized (or the group so large) that members do not have the opportunity to share their views, forming buzz groups (see Chapter Ten) may alleviate the problem caused by subgrouping and may enhance the performance of the group.

Effects of Structure on Group Performance.   The experimental studies in the area of communication structure have also shown that the performance of a group is affected by the communication structure (Hirokawa et al., 1996). Many researchers agree that some structures solve problems faster, make fewer errors, and send fewer messages.

When a task is relatively simple, for example, and primarily requires the collection of information, a centralized structure like the wheel tends to be more efficient in terms of speed and lack of errors. However, when the task is complex and requires analysis of information, decentralized networks such as the all-channel network tend to be more efficient (Berkowitz, 1978; Snadowsky, 1974). Members in the all-channel network are usually effective at developing creative solutions to problems because individuals in that network can freely express their ideas and opinions directly to one another (see Chapter Six for a discussion of brainstorming). Thus the effect of a structure on a group's performance depends in large part on the nature of the task.

Small group discussions in which you participate will probably not be typical of any specific communication structure for the entire duration of the discussion. However, during the interaction that occurs while the discussion itself is in progress, you may recognize the group's tendency to conform to a particular structural pattern.

Principles

1. A communication network is the pattern of interaction "linkages," or who talks to whom.
2. Groups exhibit differing communication structures for several possible reasons, including group efficiency and individual abilities.
3. An individual's position in a communication structure may affect morale and the probability of being chosen leader.
4. One possible consequence of dissatisfaction with the communication structure is subgrouping.
5. Centralized structures (e.g., the wheel) tend to be more efficient when the task is relatively simple and primarily requires gathering information. Decentralized networks (e.g., all-channel) may be better at developing plans for performing complex tasks.

Suggestions for Communicating Effectively in the Small Group

If a problem-solving group is to be effective, the members must not only be able to obtain the information they need to solve the problem but must also be able to effectively communicate and process that information. The following suggestions may help to improve your communication effectiveness in small groups. Remember, however, that no list of suggestions can guarantee your communication effectiveness. Only your participation in group discussion will determine whether or not you are communicating effectively.

1. *Thoroughly prepare for your small group discussions.* Know the agenda and find the information you need. Few people are "walking computers" with all the necessary facts. Rather than having the ability to speak "off the cuff," most knowledgeable participants have spent hours of research time.

2. *Seek information and opinions by asking questions of other group members.* If a single group member has all the information, there is little reason to form a group (see Chapter One). Because group members are responsible for sharing information, however, questions that demonstrate openness and are designed to coordinate information and opinions are essential to group problem solving.

3. *Speak clearly and stick to the point.* Although this suggestion may seem obvious, many group members do not communicate clearly. Some group members "ramble." Others often incorrectly assume that members share a common understanding. Still others may fail to clarify their intentions. In order to avoid these pitfalls, make clear statements with all the necessary information that group members need to understand the message.

4. *Keep an open mind.* Make a conscious effort to assess personal bias and to be flexible. Openness probably is the foundation of supportive, rather than defensive, communication. Be open to all ideas and views and respect individual differences. If all group members looked the same and expressed the same opinions, the discussion probably would be boring.

5. *Encourage a cooperative group climate.* If other group members seem reticent, encourage them to contribute, as all ideas and views are important. Foster the sense of "we-ness" in the group, and remember to cooperate with the group to reach the group goals even if your proposal isn't selected.

6. *Listen attentively and provide clear feedback.* Try not to interrupt the member who is speaking, and withhold the temptation to "chit chat" while the group is goal oriented. (Specific suggestions for listening and for providing feedback are given in the next chapter.)

7. *Manage interpersonal conflict.* Although some conflict is healthy and desirable, it is important to keep the conflict manageable and nonthreatening. Chapter Nine examines conflict management.

8. *Stay within ethical boundaries.* Value honesty and fairness. Say "I don't know" rather than fabricate evidence. Check information for accuracy, and remember to acknowledge the source. Analyze ideas rather than criticizing personalities, and be aware of hidden agendas and ulterior motives. Sometimes ethical choices are obvious; sometimes they are not.

9. *Keep an appropriate sense of humor.* The fact that a group is having fun doesn't necessarily mean that it is wasting time. Used appropriately, humor can redirect tension and potentially reduce defensive communication. But resist the temptation to use humor to minimize the value of others' contributions and/or to lead the group astray.

Ideas for Discussion

1. How would you describe your communication behavior in a problem-solving group? What are your strengths? In what areas do you wish to gain skills? You may wish to verify these perceptions with your instructor.

2. What are some potential effects of stereotyping on defensive communication? On supportive communication? What attitudes support these stereotypes?

3. Do you think that the leader can help group participants achieve a desirable discussion attitude? Explain your answer.

4. Which communication structures are more likely to emerge in authoritarian groups? Democratic groups? Would the size of the group affect the communication structure?

5. What are the effects of disagreement on group cohesiveness? Is it possible for group members to use defensive communication without adversely affecting group cohesiveness? Under what conditions?

Suggested Projects and Activities

1. Make a checklist of manifestations of positive and negative attitudes that group members display. Then, select and observe a group for twenty minutes while you apply your checklist to the group. Revise, if necessary, on the basis of your original checklist.

2. Think about a communication problem or misunderstanding that you have had with one or more group members. In a paragraph, describe (1) your attitudes (toward the problem, yourself, other participants), (2) examples of defensive communication, and (3) examples of supportive communication. Did the misunderstanding affect your attraction to the group? Why or why not?

3. Attend meetings of three different small groups (e.g., classes, religious groups, fraternities, clubs), and diagram the type of communication network employed in each. Compare and contrast each network discovered in terms of group efficiency and effectiveness.

4. Observe a small group at least twice. Record the amount of time during which each member speaks, and note your subjective evaluation of whether the communication was defensive or supportive. Did the amount of speaking time and/or the type of communication relate to (1) contribution of the individual to the group, (2) credibility of the individual, or (3) attractiveness of the individual to the other group members?

References _____

Bavelas, A. A mathematical model for group structures. *Applied anthropology*, 1948, *7*, 16–30.

Berkowitz, L., ed. *Group processes*. New York: Academic Press, 1978.

Bettenhausen, K. L. Five years of groups research: what we have learned and what needs to be addressed. *Journal of management*, 1991, *17*, 345–381.

Cartwright, D., and A. Zander, eds. *Group dynamics: research and theory*, 3rd ed. New York: Harper & Row, 1968.

Elias, F. G., M. E. Johnson, and J. B. Fortman. Task-focused self-disclosure: effects on group cohesiveness, commitment to task, and productivity. *Small group behavior*, 1989, *20*, 87–96.

Gibb, J. R. Defensive communication. *Journal of communication*, 1961, *11*, 141–148.

Gilchrist, J. C., M. E. Shaw, and L. C. Walker. Some effects of unequal distribution of information in a wheel group structure. *Journal of abnormal and social psychology*, 1954, *49*, 554–556.

Goodman, P. S., E. Ravlin, and M. Schminke. Understanding groups in organizations. In L. L. Cummings and B. M. Staw, eds. *Research in organizational behavior: an annual series of analytical essays and critical reviews*. Vol. 9. Greenwich, Conn.: JAI Press, 1987, 121–173.

Gully, S. M., D. J. Devine, and D. J. Whitney. A meta-analysis of cohesion and performance: effects of level of analysis and task interdependence. *Small group research*, 1995, *26*, 497–520.

Hirokawa, R. Y., L. Erbert, and A. Hurst. Communication and group decision-making effectiveness. In R. Y. Hirokawa and M. S. Poole (eds.), *Communication and group decision making*. Thousand Oaks, CA: Sage, 1996, 269–300.

Langfred, C. W. Is group cohesiveness a double-edged sword? An investigation of the effects of cohesiveness on performance. *Small group research*, 1998, *29*, 124–143.

Littlepage, G. E., L. Cowart, and B. Kerr. Relationship between group environment scales and group performance and cohesion. *Small group behavior*, 1989, *20*, 50–61.

McGrath, J. E., and I. Altman. *Small group research: a synthesis and critique of the field*. New York: Holt, Rinehart & Winston, 1966.

Mudrack, P. E. Defining group cohesiveness: a legacy of confusion? *Small group behavior*, 1989, *20*, 37–49.

Prapavessis, H., and A. V. Carron. Cohesion and work output. *Small group research*, 1997, *28*, 294–301.

Shaw, M. E. Group structure and the behavior of individuals in small groups. *Journal of psychology*, 1954, *38*, 139–149.

———.*Group dynamics: the psychology of small group behavior*, 3rd ed. New York: McGraw-Hill, 1981.

Snadowsky, A. Member satisfaction in stable communication networks. *Sociometry,* 1974, *37,* 38–53.

Spink, K. S., and A. V. Carron. Group cohesion effects in exercise classes. *Small group research,* 1994, *25,* 26–42.

Tziner, A. Differential effects of group cohesiveness types: a clarifying overview. *Social behavior and personality,* 1982, *10,* 227–239.

Zaccaro, S. J., and M. C. McCoy. The effects of task and interpersonal cohesiveness of performance of a disjunctive group task. *Journal of applied social psychology,* 1988, *18,* 837–888.

Zajonc, R. B. Social facilitation, *Science,* 1965, *149,* 269–274.

Suggested Readings

Elgin, S. H. *The gentle art of verbal self-defense at work.* Paramus, NJ: Prentice Hall Press, 2000. One of several books in the author's "gentle art" series, this book applies communication strategies to the work environment. The author explains how to recognize and defend yourself from subtle put-downs to racist or sexist language.

Hogan, K. *Talk your way to the top: Communication secrets to change your life.* Gretna, GA: Pelican Publishing, 2000. Communication is what you say as well as how you say it. This self-help book outlines methods for effective communication, both verbal and nonverbal, at the intrapersonal, interpersonal, and public speaking levels. Chapter 2, "Talking Yourself into Success," discusses communication apprehension.

Peurifoy, R. Z. *Anger: Taming the beast.* New York: Kodansha International, 1999. Many individuals have difficulty knowing when anger is appropriate or communicating anger appropriately. Filled with exercises and practical examples, this book discusses why we get angry and provides tools for managing anger.

Seiler, W. J., and M. L. Beall. *Communication: Making connections,* 4th ed. Boston: Allyn & Bacon, 1999. Chapter 1, "What Is Communication," provides a good overview of communication. Chapter 4, "Connecting Language and Communication," discusses the importance of language and its relationship to meaning and provides suggestions for using language more effectively.

5

Listening and Feedback in Small Groups

Study Questions _____

After reading this chapter, you should be able to answer the following questions completely and accurately:

1. What is the definition of listening?
2. How does listening differ from hearing?
3. What are three differences that occur when participants listen in a small group rather than in other communication situations (i.e., dyad, public presentation, watching T.V.)?
4. What responsibilities do listeners have during communication?
5. How do group members listen intrapersonally?
6. What is the major difference between active listening and passive listening?
7. What is social listening?
8. What is serious listening?
9. What are five listening pitfalls to avoid in the small group?
10. What are five suggestions for effective listening in the small group?
11. What is the definition of feedback?
12. What is the distinction between intrapersonal and interpersonal feedback?
13. What are three different types of feedback that indicate levels of comprehension on the part of the listener?
14. What are five specific response patterns?
15. What are three ineffective feedback responses?
16. What three effective feedback response skills are critical for group communication?
17. What are three listening strategies for reducing group conflict?

How many times have you been told to "listen"? The first time probably occurred when your parents were talking to you as a child while you were busy playing with a favorite toy. Occasionally, you still may be reminded to listen to someone while you are occupied with your thoughts or another project. Yet although most people are aware of the need to listen, few have made concerted attempts to improve their listening behavior.

A study examining communication activities of college students found that 53 percent of their communication time was spent listening (Barker et al., 1980). This percentage increases in the small group setting. Because of the amount of time you spend listening, it is important for you to become aware of the role listening plays in the small group situation. This chapter is designed to help you understand the responsibilities of listeners, to identify some common listening pitfalls, to provide suggestions for improving listening behavior, and to discuss the importance and types of feedback necessary for effective small group communication.

Listening has been defined as "the selective process of attending to, hearing, understanding, and remembering aural (and at times visual) symbols" (Barker, 1971, p. 17). Note that hearing is a *part* of listening, but it is not the same as listening. Hearing implies only that sound waves have been received or are capable of being received. Before you hear a message, you first have to attend. If you are not mentally prepared to listen, sound waves may reach your eardrums (i.e., you may hear), but you will not attach meaning to them consciously. Total listening adds to hearing the dimension of "meaning" or understanding. Only if you understand the verbal and nonverbal messages will you be able to remember the messages accurately.

In addition to attending, hearing, understanding, and remembering, listening also involves evaluating and responding to what has been communicated. Listening is not complete until there is a response or feedback. (Chapters 3 and 6 discuss the importance of evaluator roles and of evaluating evidence.)

Most of the principles and ideas in the other chapters of this book refer to the speaking (verbal or nonverbal) dimensions of small group communication. In most instances, however, individual participants in groups will be listening more than they will be speaking. For example, in a three-person group in which each member participates (speaks) the same amount of time, each individual member will be listening approximately 65 percent of the time. In a ten-person group, each person will listen about 90 percent of the time, and so on. Thus, since as a group member you spend considerably more time listening than speaking, it is essential for you to understand the need to sharpen your listening skills.

Listening and the Small Group

Differences between Listening in Small Groups and Listening in Dyads

The small group places demands on the listener that differ from other levels of communication. In the dyad, participants switch from speaker to listener and back to speaker again. The social pressure to listen to the other person in a dyad is great, because the listener knows that he or she will have to respond. The pressure to listen is also great in a small group because listeners must shift to speaking roles periodically during a discussion.

Yet even in a small group, there is less social pressure to listen constantly, because others in the group are expected to respond if one particular individual fails to do so. Thus, some listeners in small groups may tend to become *passive* and let the other person listen. The small group requires all participants to be *active* listeners in order for group efficiency and effectiveness to be maintained. *Active listening* implies that the person listens with the total self—including attitudes, beliefs, feelings, and intuitions.

The opposite of active listening is *passive listening,* in which the listener simply absorbs messages without critically evaluating them or making the effort to understand or remember them. Although it is easy to fall into a pattern of passive listening, especially in small groups when the discussion gets dull or one-sided, group members should always attempt to stay alert and active.

In the *public speaking* setting, there is somewhat less social pressure to listen, especially if you are a member of a large audience. However, unless the speaker is boring or the topic is uninteresting, you will probably listen actively in order to comprehend the message. Motivation to participate in a small group should be sufficient to generate a desire for members to listen carefully. Unfortunately, after several hours of discussion, or if one or two people dominate the conversation, it is easy to slip into the role of a passive listener and, at best, simply fake attention. The fact that listeners do occasionally become speakers in groups is the primary difference between the small group and the public speaking event.

Listener Responsibilities

It may be difficult for you to believe that your personal listening habits cause major problems in the groups in which you participate. Yet, each time you daydream or pay attention to a side conversation, you are jeopardizing the final group outcome. Repeating instructions, policy issues, or solutions to a problem because of poor listening is a waste of time. In fact, in a five-member group, repeating a two-minute dialogue wastes at least twenty group-member minutes. Poor listening habits cause some organizations to issue follow-up memorandums after meetings and others to appoint phone reminder committees. In addition to wasting group member time and money, poor listening also increases tension among group members. Try to remember the frustration you have felt when other group members failed to pay attention, interrupted others while they were speaking, or showed up unprepared because they did not *hear* the instructions.

It is important for us to develop our listening skills. Effective listening helps to shorten meetings, creates less paperwork, increases group member morale, improves accuracy, and raises productivity.

In the small group setting, group members alternate between speaker and listener roles. At one moment as a speaker, you may give information, offer an opinion, or ask for clarification. At other times, you may evaluate what others contribute, think about what you need to do later, or internally summarize the group solutions as a listener. Both roles are important, and effective group communication is dependent on responsible listeners and speakers, no matter which role they assume. At times we believe that it will not matter if we take a break from concentrated listening, but this just is not the case. You never know when you might miss critical information. Remember: poor listening risks unsatisfactory final outcomes.

Listening Intrapersonally

Individuals are constantly involved in intrapersonal communication during group meetings. For example, when you catch yourself reviewing the day's agenda, controlling tempers, making decisions, evaluating alternatives, and noticing hunger pangs you are intrapersonally listening. Many people are relatively unaware of how their intrapersonal processes can be used to improve communication among members in the small group. By listening to the messages you are sending verbally and nonverbally, you will be in a better position to evaluate your communication effectiveness.

Think for a moment about communication behaviors in others that tend to bother you while you are working in a small group. Behaviors that often cause breakdowns and frustration in groups include incessant talking, giving lots of advice, asking loaded questions, interrupting others, talking in generalities, and fabricating, misquoting, or identifying incorrectly (Geeting and Geeting, 1982). Through intrapersonal listening, you can check your own communication to see if you are also guilty of these or similar behaviors. If you tend to want to express your ideas, make sure that you are giving others a chance to express their ideas, too. Other methods of listening intrapersonally will be discussed later, when we focus on giving and receiving feedback.

Types of Listening

Listening scholars have found it helpful to classify listening behaviors in several different ways. Many of these classifications refer to a specific listening purpose or occasion, such as in the classroom or at a cocktail party. The classifications that follow refer primarily to types of listening needed or used in the small group setting.

Some writers have differentiated between social and serious listening (Barker, 1990). The type of listening used during small group communication should be matched to the group's purposes and goals.

Social listening is the type of listening usually employed in informal small group settings. Social listening is often used during the preliminary stages of both social and task groups. It is often associated with interpersonal conversations or entertainment. One subtype of social listening is *conversational listening,* which demands that the participant switch from the role of speaker back to the role of listener and so on. The listening that occurs serves as a framework for a response to the speaker.

Courteous listening is another form of social listening used in many small group settings. This type of listening may occur in interpersonal conversations, but it generally occurs in settings in which you are primarily the listener, not the speaker. Courteous listening is difficult because you may not be deeply interested in the subject under discussion, but you tend to demonstrate concern in order to reinforce others in the group or to avoid offending them. Giving feedback (see the last section of this chapter) is an essential behavior of a successful courteous listener.

In addition to social listening, participants in small groups may also engage in serious listening. Some social groups use serious listening, but it is often observed most in task groups. Serious listening is subdivided into *critical* and *discriminative listening.*

Critical listening involves listening to analyze the evidence or ideas of others in the group and making critical judgments about the validity and/or quality of materials presented. *Discriminative listening* involves listening for the purpose of remembering or understanding. It indicates a serious intent on the part of the listener but does not imply that he or she is making a critical judgment of the material presented. Both subtypes of serious listening occur in small group settings. You should determine your purpose in listening before engaging in small group interactions and then listen in the manner dictated by the listening setting.

Listening Pitfalls

Most listening experts agree that the first step in improving your listening behavior is to identify your bad habits. This section lists five listening problems that you might recognize in your own listening behavior. For a more complete list of potential listening problems, see Wolvin and Coakley (1996).

The suggestions given following each pitfall are intended to provide a basis for listening improvement. They are not intended to be an exhaustive list, however; understanding concepts about listening without trying to improve your own listening behavior is of relatively little value. Therefore, try to apply the information in the preceding sections to your own behavior in small groups in order to become a better listener and a better small group communicator.

1. *Getting overstimulated or emotionally involved.* This listening problem is created when participants are ego-involved, particularly with regard to the subject that is under discussion. For example, a group of women in a dormitory floor meeting may be discussing the fact that women on other floors seem to be more successful in getting dates. The fact that the women doing the discussing are involved with the topic on a personal level may cause them to react emotionally to some points in the discussion. The emotional involvement may distort or interfere with their acquisition of important information that might be useful in modifying the situation. The main problem implied here is that one's emotional involvement may cause an emotional deaf spot that must be identified in order to be corrected.

Compensate for main ideas to which you react emotionally. This is similar to the suggestion for emotionally laden works. Some specific suggestions to help compensate for emotional reactions to ideas include deferring judgment, empathizing with the speaker, and placing your own personal feelings in the proper perspective.

2. *Preparing to answer questions before fully understanding them.* This problem is particularly common in small groups that have developed considerable maturity and in which members know one another fairly well. Some members may predict what the end of another's sentence will be on the basis of what they know about him or her and, consequently, may jump to a hasty (and sometimes wrong) conclusion about the point being made. This habit can, at times, make members of small groups appear rude or perhaps not very intelligent. Be careful that you do not think so far ahead of the speaker that you begin to answer questions prematurely. By being cautious, you may not only save possible embarrassment but also derive deeper meaning from the discussion.

Hold your fire. Listen to complete ideas and messages before answering questions, evaluating others' ideas, or jumping to conclusions. If you do not listen to complete thoughts, you may be similar to participants on "Jeopardy" who miss out on thousands of dollars because they jump the gun and answer the wrong questions.

3. *Tolerating or failing to adjust to distractions.* Environmental distractions can create good rationalizations for not listening carefully. Such things as noise in the hall, music on the radio playing outside the room, paintings within the room, or furniture can cause distractions that make it difficult to listen with total efficiency. Failure to adjust to or compensate for such distractions is a common listening problem. If you cannot modify the environment in which you are communicating, then you must modify your internal listening behavior in order to assimilate fully the message transmitted within the group. In other words, you have to work harder at listening when distractions are present.

Establish a listening environment that is conducive to listening. The following are some specific suggestions for establishing an ideal environment for listening:

   a. Establish a comfortable, quiet, relaxed atmosphere in the room.
   b. Make sure the audience senses a clear purpose for listening.
   c. Prepare listeners for what they are about to hear.
   d. Break up long periods of listening with other activities.

4. *Allowing emotionally laden words to interfere with listening.* This habit is similar in part to the first problem noted. In this particular instance, however, group members react to specific words rather than to the general idea expressed in the message. Such words as *pig, fascist, communist,* and the like tend to have emotional connotations associated with them. Regardless of their context, such words often trigger what are called signal reactions, in which people react to the words and not their intended meanings.

Compensate for emotion-arousing words. Many words evoke reactions that are a function of habit or conditioning as opposed to cognitive deliberation. We must become aware of the particular words that affect us emotionally and try to compensate at the cognitive level for them. The following are some specific suggestions to help compensate for emotion-arousing words:

    a. Identify, prior to listening, those words that affect you emotionally.

    b. Attempt to analyze why the words affect you as they do.

    c. Try to reduce their impact upon you by using a defense mechanism. Examples of defense mechanisms are rationalization (e.g., attempting to convince yourself that the word really is not such a bad word) and repression (e.g., trying to relegate to your subconscious those meanings of words that are offensive to you). In other words, try to eliminate a conditioned or signal reaction to words and determine objectively what meaning the words hold for the speaker.

    5. *Permitting personal prejudices or deep-seated convictions to impair comprehension and understanding.* This habit is related to the concept of close-mindedness. It tends to exist when listeners hold positions that are strong and other members of the group threaten them by questioning or challenging those positions. This is a difficult listening problem to overcome, as it is a deep-seated (fully conditioned) one, and it is often a function of one's personality structure. However, if you are aware that you have certain deeply rooted biases or compunctions, you can at least sensitize yourself to them and learn to moderate your reactions if such topics are discussed.

    Be flexible in your views. Try not to be close-minded. Examine the basis for your views, and try to ensure that any inflexible views you hold are held strongly for a good reason. Try to acknowledge that other views contradictory to your own may be possible and may even have some merit, even if you cannot give them total acceptance. If you approach situations with an open mind, you will not only be a better listener, but you may help move the group more efficiently as well.

    These listening problems are only a few of the variety that may affect your listening in a negative way. Remember that as an individual, you are an open system and can conduct a personal systems analysis of your own listening behavior. If you note problems similar to these in your own behavior, begin changing them by recognizing them every time that they occur. By doing so, you will be in a position to eliminate them systematically.

    The suggestions, in part, were derived from research in listening. However, many of them could be classified as pure common sense. They are ideas about which you probably said, "Everyone knows that!"—and you were right. The key to improving listening behavior is to be sensitive to what you are doing while listening. You will then begin to increase your comprehensive skills and your general listening ability. So, view the suggestions as common sense, but examine each carefully to ensure that they are things that you are doing to improve your listening behavior. An occasional review of the list may help remind you of things you need to do to increase your effectiveness as a listener, particularly in the small group.

Additional Suggestions for Effective Listening in the Small Group

Professionals in business, education, government, and industry have used the following principles effectively. By identifying specific listening weaknesses and implementing plans of action, you too can become a successful listener (Steil et al., 1983).

1. *Prepare and commit yourself to active listening.* Effective listening requires you to "psych yourself up" to listen during small group interactions.
2. *Think about the topic and situation in advance.* Find ways to make the information useful to you. Thinking about the topic in advance increases learning and retention.
3. *Concentrate.* If you take "mental trips" or let your thoughts wander while listening, you will probably miss valuable information.
4. *Plan to report.* Commit yourself to repeat what you have heard to someone else later. A decision to be responsible for a message will change your listening behavior.
5. *Exhibit behaviors that are characteristic of good listeners.* The following are some behaviors that you should try to exhibit at all times:
   a. Concentrate your mental and physical energy on listening for a long period of time.
   b. Avoid interrupting the speaker.
   c. Demonstrate to the speaker that you are both interested and alert.
   d. Seek areas of agreement with the speaker.
   e. Search for meanings, and avoid arguing about particular words.
   f. Demonstrate patience by understanding that you can listen faster than the speaker can speak.
   g. Provide clear and unambiguous feedback to the speaker.
   h. Repress the tendency to respond emotionally to what is said.
   i. Ask questions when you do not understand something.
   j. Withhold evaluation of the message until the speaker is finished and you are sure you understand it.

By trying to imitate these behaviors, which are characteristic of effective listeners, you can improve your listening significantly. In this particular instance, imitation may not only be a sincere form of flattery; it also may help you become a better listener.

Principles
1. Listening has been defined as "the selective process of attending to, hearing, understanding, and remembering aural symbols." Listening also includes evaluating and responding to messages.
2. Hearing implies only that sound waves have been received; listening includes understanding.

3. There are at least three differences between listening in small groups and listening in other arenas.
   a. The listener experiences social pressure to listen in the dyad, because the listener knows that he or she will have to respond.
   b. There is less social pressure to listen in the small group, because others can be expected to respond if one particular individual fails to do so.
   c. There is little social pressure to listen in the public speaking setting, because the listener usually does not have the opportunity to become a speaker (as he or she occasionally does in the small group).
4. Poor listening increases the strain among group members while wasting valuable time and money.
5. Effective listening helps to shorten meetings, create less paperwork, increase group member morale, improve accuracy, and raise productivity.
6. Group members must assume responsibility for effective communication in both speaking and listening roles.
7. Active listening is listening with your attitudes, beliefs, feelings, and intuitions. Passive listening is absorbing messages without critically evaluating them or making the effort to understand or remember them.
8. Social listening is often associated with interpersonal conversations or entertainment. Social listening may be divided into conversational and courteous listening.
   a. Conversational listening demands that the participants switch from the role of speaker back to the role of listener, and so on.
   b. Courteous listening generally occurs when you are primarily the listener rather than the speaker.
9. Serious listening may be divided into critical and discriminative listening.
   a. Critical listening involves making critical judgments about the validity and/or quality of the evidence or ideas of others in the group.
   b. Discriminative listening involves listening for the purpose of remembering or understanding, without critically judging the material presented.
10. Five listening pitfalls to avoid in the small group are as follows:
    a. Becoming overstimulated or emotionally involved.
    b. Preparing to answer questions before fully understanding them.
    c. Tolerating or failing to adjust to distractions.
    d. Allowing emotionally laden words to interfere with listening.
    e. Permitting personal prejudices or deep-seated convictions to impair comprehension or understanding.
11. Five suggestions for effective listening in the small group are as follows:
    a. Compensate for main ideas to which you react emotionally.
    b. Hold your fire.
    c. Establish an environment that is conducive to listening.
    d. Compensate for emotion-arousing words.
    e. Be flexible in your views.

12. Principles of effective listening must be incorporated into all types of listening situations.
    a. Prepare and commit yourself to active listening.
    b. Think about the topic and situation in advance.
    c. Concentrate.
    d. Plan to report.
    e. Exhibit behaviors that are characteristic of good listeners.

Feedback

During the discussion of listening, you were encouraged to listen intrapersonally to see whether you were guilty of communication behaviors that cause breakdowns and frustration in groups. Now that you know more about listening pitfalls and methods for improving listening in groups, it is time to listen to the feedback that you send yourself and others. You engage in two levels of feedback during group interactions: intrapersonal and interpersonal. Intrapersonal feedback, or self-feedback, takes place when you listen to your own messages. By listening to your own internal and external feedback processes, you get an idea about how you communicate. For example, after taking a course in creativity, a professor may realize that she has thwarted her student's innovative ideas by being overly critical. When she thinks about what she wants to accomplish during her next class, she decides to use a creative brainstorming activity to generate ideas for solving the undergraduate advising problem. Concentrating on watching her internal reactions, she is careful as she walks around the room not to respond verbally or nonverbally to any of the groups' ideas. It is not until after the creative process is complete that she provides suggestions and ideas of her own. You also use internal self-feedback to monitor and correct yourself during conversations. By listening, you catch and alter an inappropriate phrase, tone of voice, or mispronunciation.

Interpersonal feedback concerns the responses you send and the effects that others' responses have on you. Think of the many verbal and nonverbal messages that you send back and forth to others during your group meetings. You may exchange knowing looks with a friend who agrees with you, frown at a person who contradicts your point of view, laugh out loud after a humorous remark, or congratulate another member who has made a good point.

Verbal and Nonverbal Feedback Combined

As in most face-to-face interaction, the majority of group members respond to a speaker's message both verbally and nonverbally. You are usually unaware of sending verbal and nonverbal feedback simultaneously unless someone calls your attention to your gestures. However, you would probably experience difficulty in explaining the directions to the campus administration building with words alone. You most likely would use gestures to accompany each verbal "left" and "right."

Feedback and Response in the Small Group

Imagine that you are watching a television suspense thriller. The leading character is about to be murdered. Just as the villain raises his weapon, you scream, "Look out!" As if the hero doesn't hear you, he blunders into the villain's trap. It takes a full sixty minutes for him to escape, because he didn't respond to your warning. You remind yourself that this is not real life, and you continue to watch the program.

But what if in real life you were forced to observe group discussions in the same way that you watch television? What if you could observe other members but not respond to them? You would probably miss much of what others said, because you could not question messages you did not understand. You would undoubtedly feel frustrated and perhaps aggressive.

The previous example illustrates the principle of *feedback*—a perceived message transmitted to indicate some level of understanding of and/or agreement or disagreement with a stimulus or verbal message from another. As mentioned earlier, the listening process is not complete until there is a response. There are three classes of feedback: positive, negative, and ambiguous.

Positive feedback is feedback that demonstrates that a message has been received and understood. However, it does not necessarily mean that the responder (i.e., giver of feedback) agrees with the speaker's point of view. From a communication framework, the term positive feedback means that the process of communication has been completed and that a potential for continued interaction exists. In small groups, members often send positive feedback nonverbally through a nod of the head, a smile, a frown, a hand gesture, or other similar cues.

Negative feedback, conversely, suggests that the message has not been received or understood. It does not necessarily mean that the responder disagrees—merely that the message didn't get through, at least in the form intended by the speaker. In small groups, negative feedback often results when members do not listen carefully or when there are distractions in the group or environment. When a speaker notes via negative feedback that the message is not received or understood, he or she usually will send it again, either in different words or in a different way (such as by shouting the message instead of speaking it in a normal voice).

At times, listeners send feedback correctly, but speakers interpret it incorrectly. Misinterpretation of the feedback message may result from *prior experiences and distortion.* Messages (whether feedback messages or speaker-initiated messages) are interpreted in light of prior experiences. Misunderstanding of feedback will occur to the extent that experiences of the speaker and listener differ. For example, if one group member has been taught to show respect by lack of eye contact, and another group member has been taught that lack of eye contact shows inattention to the message, the feedback will not have the same meaning for both of the participants. The meaning of verbal language differs between people, just as the meaning of nonverbal language differs; word meanings differ from individual to individual and from group to group.

A third type of feedback is *ambiguous,* in that the speaker is not certain whether or not you correctly understood the message. Just looking at a person and not verbally responding to his or her request for a ride home is ambiguous feedback; the group member is not sure that you even heard the request.

On occasion, a speaker may interpret *silence* as ambiguous feedback. Suppose, for example, that a group member was asked if he or she would be willing to accept the task of researching the cost of newspaper advertising in surrounding localities. If the group member failed to respond either verbally (e.g., "yes" or "no") or nonverbally (e.g., nodding or shaking his or her head), the silence might be misunderstood. For example, the other group members might interpret silence as inattention, not hearing the question, indecisiveness concerning acceptance of the task, and/or not wanting to accept responsibility for the task.

This example illustrates the risk involved in responding to a speaker's message with silence. Verbal and nonverbal messages that are easily interpreted help to improve accuracy in communication. Ambiguous feedback may be transmitted if the speaker is not sure of the meaning of silence. In more extreme cases, a communication breakdown may result if the speaker misinterprets the silence (e.g., the group members believe that he or she does not want to accept responsibility for the task). Silence should be distinct in meaning because it places a greater interpretive burden on the speaker.

Specific Response Patterns

Suppose that a group member proposes that someone interview the president of the university to learn his or her views on exchange programs with foreign students. One group member responds, "That's a fantastic idea!" Another group member responds, "I'd like to hear more about this." By agreeing with the speaker, the first group member hopes that the group will accept the proposal. The response of the second group member (neither agreement nor disagreement) is designed to get the speaker to explain the proposal further. This example illustrates the specific response patterns of *rewarding or punishing feedback* and *directive or nondirective feedback.* The specific patterns may employ silence or verbal and/or nonverbal patterns of response.

Rewarding versus Punishing Feedback. Learning theorists generally agree that reward and punishment change behavior and feedback in groups. For example, you may recall a situation in which you were especially good and your parents gave you a treat in the hope that it would maintain your new behavior. On the other hand, you can probably recall a situation in which your parents punished you in the hope of changing your behavior. In this chapter, *punishment* will be used to denote words or actions suggesting either disagreement with the speaker or misunderstanding of the speaker's message.

Punishment such as disagreement may have a similar effect in group discussion. A group member who is continually disagreed with (or punished in other ways) will probably decrease the frequency of his or her contributions. (In the case of an overtalkative group member, this may be desirable.) Generally, disagreement should be worded tactfully so that group members still will contribute to the discussion.

Reward (agreement) appears to have the opposite effect; that is, reward tends to increase the frequency of contributions. Collectively, reward and punishment may be effective tools for stimulating involvement in the discussion and regulating the participation of overtalkative group members. A systems analysis will help you decide when to use rewarding or punishing feedback with specific members. You should also examine who should give the feedback. For example, John may accept punishing feedback from Mary but not from Steve, even though there is good communication among all of them.

Nondirective versus Directive Feedback. The terms *nondirective* and *directive* are borrowed from counseling theory.[1] *Nondirective feedback* essentially is an attempt by the listener to replicate the message. The purpose of nondirective feedback is to encourage the speaker to further explain the message (ideas and/or feelings). *Verbal nondirective feedback* includes a questioning repetition of the last few words spoken by the speaker and other feedback such as "Would you explain a little more?" "Really?" "Oh?" The tone in which verbal nondirective feedback is uttered is important; an unsympathetic tone may cause the speaker to withhold or distort information.

Similar to verbal nondirective feedback, *nonverbal nondirective feedback* expresses an interest in the speaker's message. This includes nodding the head, leaning toward the speaker, and maintaining eye contact. *Directive feedback* puts a value judgment on the message and usually hinders further interaction. A leader who says "I have decided how we should divide the list of names for the

---

[1]Both Carl Rogers's and B. F. Skinner's positions have been simplified in this section to the point that they represent only portions of their total contributions to counseling theory.

phonothon," cuts off further input and discourages further discussion. Unlike directive feedback, nondirective feedback encourages more discussion by keeping options open. Another leader might say, "Since we have decided to divide the list of names for the phonothon, what would you suggest?" This leader is asking for contributions and stimulating further discussion.

To be an effective listener, a group member should not rely solely on either directive or nondirective feedback. Suppose, for example, that the group members continued to send nondirective nonverbal feedback to a speaker for a considerable length of time. The speaker would probably feel that he or she should continue talking even after the message had been communicated. Distortion, repetition, and irrelevant responses would likely result. Alternating between nondirective and directive feedback is much like driving a car on slippery pavement; as the car skids, you adjust your steering to compensate for the skid. Similarly, you will need to alternate between directive and nondirective feedback as you determine which you need to keep the discussion flowing smoothly among all participants.

Immediate and Delayed Feedback.   Immediate feedback occurs directly after a group member makes a comment. As one member offers a suggestion, others might say "Good idea," "Are you kidding? That would never work," or "That's one way to look at it. Does anyone else have something to say?" Each of these comments provides immediate feedback to the speaker. Delayed feedback, on the other hand, takes time before a response is received. Groups may consider options and vote during another meeting, send a recommendation to another committee and wait for a decision, or hear that a group member disagreed with the rest of the group after the meeting had ended.

General and Specific Feedback.   General feedback gives a broad idea about how a message or comment was interpreted, while specific feedback gives clear-cut comments about how a message or comment was interpreted. Group members usually prefer specific rather than general comments when working together. Think about how you would feel if, after you presented the idea of starting a new masters program, you received the following response: "That's the most ridiculous idea we've heard yet!" Now consider this response: "Tell me more about your idea. I can't see why you'd make that suggestion when we've been turned down for two new faculty positions for next year, we have more students than we can handle in our classes as it is, and there are three masters programs in the state." General feedback, the first response, may be clear, but because it does not provide reasons for the response, it will probably create conflict among group members. The second response, by contrast, gives specific reasons for questioning the suggestion, maintains good relations, and does not create a defensive climate.

Restrictive and Nonrestrictive Feedback. When group members are concerned about the consequences of being open and honest during a meeting,
they may use restrictive feedback. For example, employees may be afraid to
give their frank opinions about management decisions when their supervisor
is present or is the group leader. In other work situations, employees may feel
free to be completely open and use nonrestrictive feedback. Responses are
based on whether or not the receiver is willing and/or able to accept feedback.

Ineffective Feedback Responses

Many of your feedback responses are habits that you use without thinking.
Some of you have developed good feedback habits, while others have developed poor ones. The most common ineffective, frustrating feedback
responses are ones that are irrelevant, interrupting, or tangential.

Irrelevant Feedback. *Irrelevant feedback* is a response that does not apply to
the situation that is being discussed at the time. Group members may hear
only part of a message and respond as though they have heard it all. Group
members who are late to meetings, for example, often miss valuable information or decisions that have already been made. Even so, some group members
make comments without knowing what has already been discussed.

Interrupting Feedback. *Interrupting feedback responses* break into the words
or thoughts of another person. Although the anecdotal evidence suggests that
man interrupt more than women, recent research suggests that the differences in interrupting patterns are small (Canary et al., 1997) and that men and
women interrupt for different reasons (Stewart et al., 1996). Men often interrupt to dominate the conversation while women interrupt more often to
express support or show enthusiasm for the speaker's point of view. Interruptions are especially irritating during meetings, since it is important to
encourage everyone's participation and input. Members who are interrupted
may lose their train of thought or may be reluctant to participate in the future.

Tangential Feedback. *Tangential feedback responses* tend to sidetrack a conversation. While the response may be related to the initial topic, tangential
responses divert the group from the purpose of the discussion. You can probably relate to the following situation. The officers of a campus environmental
club met to discuss their proposed budget. The president explained how proposed university budget cuts would affect their plans. As the president finished
his point, another officer said, "I can't believe the university plans budget cuts!
My tuition has gone up each year since I got here. There has got to be a way for
the administration to keep costs down." As the topic turned to tuition increases,
the discussion got completely off track. Groups waste time after becoming sidetracked and find it difficult to get back to the real purpose for the meeting.

Effective Feedback Responses

Effective feedback responses do not occur automatically; they require practice, thought, and effort. Competent communicators must learn to adapt their responses to the needs of each person and situation. Attending, following, and reflecting are critical skills for highly competent group communicators.

Attending Responses.   The most obvious indicator of feedback is degree of attentiveness. Attending responses demonstrate interest and involvement in what others are saying. How you attend to others can influence whether or not interaction will continue and signals others that the process of reception is taking place. At least nonverbally, attentiveness suggests that a person is being empathic, tolerant, caring, and interested. You show others that you are listening through your eye contact, a forward lean, physical closeness, questions, and comments. *Asking questions* and *requesting clarification*, responses that show that you are listening, probably should be used more often. When you ask questions and request clarification, you increase your chances of interpreting the speaker's message accurately.

Following Responses.   *Following responses* encourage speakers to continue talking. Following responses include door openers, minimal encouragers, infrequent questions, and attentive silence (Bolton, 1979). *Door openers* are noncoercive invitations that encourage speakers to begin talking. When you see a co-worker during a meeting look anxious or nervous, you might say, "It looks as though you have something to say. What's on your mind?" You are, thus, using a door opener and allowing the other's feelings to surface. *Minimal encouragers* help group members to continue talking. Nodding your head or saying "Go on . . . " or "Really?" signals the person that you are interested in what he or she is saying. *Infrequent questions* help the listener to better understand the speaker without directing the conversation. Although you often need to ask questions or request clarification, you should not ask so many questions that you control the conversation and compel others to respond to your agenda. *Attentive silence* is probably the most important and most difficult feedback response. Many people feel so uncomfortable with silence that they fill pauses with questions, advice, and compulsive chatter. They don't allow others time to express themselves completely. During periods of silence, we should attend to and observe the other and think about what the other is communicating. The effective listener learns to both speak and listen as appropriate and feels comfortable with either.

Reflective Responses.   Another response that can contribute to accurate interpretation is reflecting. *Reflecting* is a way of restating the speaker's message. When you reflect, you express the message in your own words; you paraphrase and check your paraphrase with the speaker to make sure you understand. Reflecting responses include not only paraphrasing content but also reflecting feelings—that is, attending to the speaker's nonverbal messages or emotions. Because of the tendency of listeners to rivet attention on content, the emotional dimensions of both interpersonal and group interactions are often overlooked. Then group members scratch their heads when they find themselves embroiled in a conflict they didn't anticipate.

Reflective responses restate the feelings and/or content of what a speaker is communicating and show understanding and acceptance. A reflective listener paraphrases, reflects feelings and meanings, and uses summary reflection. Paraphrasing puts the essence of what the other person is saying into your own words. When a listener reflects feelings, he or she attends to the person's nonverbal messages. The messages give an accurate indication about how the person is responding emotionally to the situation. A person who says "I can't believe he would criticize me in front of the whole group!" is expressing feelings of anger, embarrassment, and hurt. Reflecting on meanings requires an understanding of a person's feelings and causes of the feelings. Finally, during summary reflection, the listener tries to recap the key themes, main point, or major ideas that have been discussed. When a group leader provides a brief review of what has been accomplished, it is usually easier for the group to continue.

Attending, following, and reflecting are appropriate responses in conjunction with all the listening behaviors previously described if the emotional context is intense and obscures or distorts the message. As you practice these digging strategies, you will be rewarded with greater success in conflict management, because you will have acknowledged the importance of emotion in both interpersonal and group conflict.

Using Listening and Feedback to Reduce Group Conflict

In Chapter Nine, conflict is discussed. Conflict often develops among group members who interact regularly. When conflict occurs, members try to either ignore it or resolve it. Since ignoring conflict hinders openness and the flow of quality information, it is important to find ways to manage group conflict constructively (Borisoff and Victor, 1998; Wilmot and Hocker, 1998).

One of the best ways to manage conflict is to keep channels of communication open. When the lines of communication among group members are maintained from the beginning of the conflict interaction, there is more potential for cooperation in resolving the conflict (Littlejohn, 1999). Effective listening is the key to maintaining open communication and therefore, the key to conflict management.

Listening to a person in a one-to-one conversation is very different from listening in a small group as we said at the beginning of this chapter. In small groups, you usually spend far more time listening than speaking. In a three-person group in which members participate equally, for example, each person will listen approximately 65 percent of the time. In a ten-person group, each person will listen 90 percent of the time. When one person fails to respond, others usually will. Thus, group members may become passive in their listening behavior, relying on others to take responsibility for active listening.

Appropriate listening increases understanding of other group members' motivations and values. When you understand others, you begin to accept their opinions and decisions while at the same time holding on to your own, without frustration, hostility, or the urge to make a convert. By listening effectively, you can consider differing points of view and then apply appropriate problem-solving and decision-making strategies.

Three Listening Strategies

Think for a moment about group situations that have caused you to feel tense, angry, argumentative, or defensive. Just as any of these negative feelings may have the potential to develop into conflict, positive listening behaviors have the potential to manage it. Using constructive listening strategies such as *dampening, diverting,* and *digging* (Barker et al., 1997) helps to minimize the effects of conflict.

Dampening consists of those listening behaviors that rely on hearing out the speaker—listening with minimal response and maximum acceptance. When we practice dampening behaviors, we temporarily refrain from arguing our opinions and feelings and concentrate instead on listening to and accepting (i.e., dampening) the viewpoint of the group member. In some listening settings, the needs of one person to speak are so great that the appropriate response from others is to listen quietly. Insisting on voicing our opinion may be interpreted as rudeness and evoke more hostility. Listening to other group members and indicating acceptance can keep communication open and build team spirit.

Diverting includes those listening behaviors that manage conflict by focusing attention on the message content. We use diverting behaviors when we respond to a group member by asking questions, restating the message, and providing feedback. Diverting is helpful in group situations requiring feedback and message clarification. Used skillfully, diverting manages group conflict by clearly identifying the real areas of conflict. When you listen critically to a group member whose opinions on abortion differ from yours, you may discover that you agree about the importance of human life but disagree on when life begins. You may believe life begins at the moment of conception, while your friend thinks that life begins at a later point in fetal development. Or perhaps you both disapprove of abortion, but one of you thinks it should be allowed by law under some circumstances and the other does not. By using diverting behaviors to identify areas of agreement and disagreement, we are better able to receive the message content the speaker intends.

Digging is characterized by listening behaviors that rely on empathy and attention to nonverbal messages. While diverting helps to clarify message content, digging clarifies feeling. When we use digging behaviors, we maintain communication by reflecting emotion. Understanding emotion helps us to interpret the message in the proper context. It is useful in groups when the real issues are obscured by emotion. Digging is critical when the real agenda is obscured by feeling, self-interest, or lack of insight. Empathic responses enable us to communicate to the speaker that we understand. For example, one group member, John, had a difficult time suppressing disagreement with other members' points of view. Instead of asking questions or giving opposing opinions, he didn't say a word. Other members, who wanted John's input, began to look for signals of how he felt. After a few meetings, they discovered that John jiggled the change in his pocket whenever sensitive issues or difficult topics were addressed. Using his nonverbal message (change jiggling) as a signal, group members directed genuine expressions of empathy toward John to build a supportive environment, to reduce defensiveness in the group, and to encourage him to make comments.

Group members who demonstrate empathy learn to listen to others before judging what is expressed. You need to remind yourself that when you make judgments, your values, motivations, and experiences often influence what you have heard. If you are sincerely trying to empathize, you must attempt to understand the other person's point of view and suspend judgment until you have heard the entire message. By practicing behaviors in the digging category, group members display empathy.

During your next group meeting, identify behaviors that hinder group outcomes and encourage conflict. Instead of being caught off guard, remember to use dampening, diverting, and digging listening strategies. Each strategy has the potential to help manage and reduce group conflict.

Methods of Improving Feedback Effectiveness

Feedback given and received during small group interaction influences the effectiveness of group outcomes. The following guidelines should help small group participants (adapted from Johnson 2000; Watson and Barker, 1990).

Giving
1. Give feedback in a form that group members can understand.
2. Quality feedback is more important than quantity; try not to overload the system.
3. Give feedback to help the other members, not for your own satisfaction.
4. Ask questions and make statements that are important.

Getting
  1. Listen carefully to the feedback messages and understand the response before you defend your position.
  2. Remember that suppressing, avoiding, and denying are methods of not letting feedback get through to you.
  3. Use feedback to learn about your own communication behavior and its influences on others.
  4. Adjust your communication behavior based on the feedback you receive.

Principles
  1. Feedback can be defined as a perceived message transmitted to indicate some level of understanding of and/or agreement with a stimulus or verbal message from another.
  2. The three different classes of feedback include positive, negative, and ambiguous feedback.
     a. Positive feedback demonstrates that a stimulus or message has been received or understood. It does not imply agreement with the speaker.
     b. Negative feedback suggests that the message was not received or understood.
     c. Ambiguous feedback suggests that the speaker is not certain whether the message was correctly understood.
  3. Five specific response patterns are rewarding versus punishing feedback, directive versus nondirective feedback, immediate versus delayed feedback, general versus specific feedback, and restrictive versus nonrestrictive feedback.
     a. Punishment (e.g., disagreement) will probably decrease the frequency of a group member's contributions. Reward (agreement) tends to increase the frequency of a group member's contributions.
     b. Nondirective feedback (an attempt by the listener to replicate the message) tends to encourage a group member to further explain the message. Directive feedback (placing a value judgment on the speaker's message) has the same effect as rewarding and punishing feedback.
     c. Immediate feedback occurs directly after a person makes a comment. Delayed feedback is not received until after a meeting is adjourned.
     d. General feedback gives a broad idea about how to interpret a message. Specific feedback gives distinct comments about how to interpret a message.
     e. Restrictive feedback occurs when members are afraid of the consequences of their comments. Nonrestrictive feedback occurs when members feel completely free and open to express their comments.
  4. Irrelevant, interrupting, and tangential responses are three forms of feedback that discourage or frustrate other group members.
  5. Three feedback response skills that encourage group members to continue making contributions to the group are attending, following, and reflecting.

6. Three listening strategies that can help reduce intragroup conflict are dampening; diverting, and digging.

Summary

This chapter focused on the importance of listening and feedback in the small group. Listening was defined as the selective process of attending to, hearing, and understanding aural symbols. Several differences between listening in small groups and in other levels of communication were identified. In addition, several types of listening were discussed.

A large portion of the chapter was devoted to a discussion of five listening problems to avoid in the small group and five suggestions to improve listening in the small group.

The role of feedback and interpersonal response in the small group was discussed, and several types of feedback were identified. Specific response patterns of individuals in groups were noted, and some suggestions for interpreting the feedback messages were given.

Problems in providing undesirable feedback were identified from the point of view of the participant-listener. Conversely, the problems in interpreting feedback messages were discussed from the point of view of the observer-speaker. Finally, strategies were given for reducing intragroup conflict.

Ideas for Discussion _____

1. How can group members modify the listening setting in order to make listening during the meeting more efficient and effective?

2. What kinds of words and ideas do people tend to react to emotionally?

3. What unique demands does the classroom place on the listener?

4. In what ways does the listener manipulate the speaker's behavior in a group?

5. Is nondirective feedback ever rewarding or punishing? If so, when?

6. Which of the listening suggestions included in this chapter is the hardest to implement successfully? Why?

7. What are some ways group members may become more sensitive to (i.e., aware of) their own listening habits in order to improve their listening skills?

Suggested Projects and Activities _____

1. Have each member of your small group keep a log of the amount of time he or she spends listening during a given day. Ask members to bring the logs to class

and compare the relative amounts of time each member spent listening. What variables may have accounted for differences?

2. Tape record a fifteen- to thirty-minute small group discussion in which you participate. Two weeks later, ask all group members to recall the ideas that were presented in the discussion (record them on paper if possible). Next, play back the tape and see how much information was remembered accurately, how much information was remembered inaccurately, what ideas were identified as having been presented that were not presented at all, and how much information was not remembered at all. Discuss the possible reasons for the discrepancies.

3. During a fifteen-minute period of a small group discussion, blindfold all group members so that no visual feedback may be received. After the time is up, discuss the feelings of group members concerning their not being able to receive visual feedback and their perception of its importance.

4. In a group of from four to six members, conduct a five-minute brainstorming session (see Chapter Six) to find as many ways as possible to improve listening in a group. (Use the suggestions in this chapter to get started.)

5. Have each member of your class make a list of irritating listening habits during small group communication. Compile and number the habits and ask each member to evaluate one other small group member. Finally, ask class members to identify their own irritating listening habits.

References

Barker, L. *Listening behavior.* Englewood Cliffs, NJ: Prentice-Hall, 1971.

Barker, L. L. *Communication,* 5th ed. Englewood Cliffs, NJ: Prentice Hall, 1990.

Barker, L. L., P. Johnson, and K. W. Watson. The role of listening in managing interpersonal and group conflict. In Michael Purdy and Deborah Borisoff, eds. *Listening in everyday life,* 2nd ed. University Press of America, Ianham, MD, 1997.

Barker, L. L., R. Edwards, C. Gaines, K. Gladney, and F. Holley. An investigation of proportional time spent in various communication activities by college students. *Journal of applied communications research,* 1980, 101–110.

Bolton, R. *People skills.* Englewood Cliffs, NJ: Prentice-Hall, 1979.

Borisoff, D., and D. A. Victor. *Conflict management: a communication skills approach,* 2nd ed. Boston: Allyn & Bacon, 1998.

Canary, D., T. M. Emmers-Sommers, and S. Faulkner. *Sex and gender difference in personal relationships.* New York: Guilford Press, 1997.

Geeting, B., and C. Geeting. *How to listen assertively.* New York: International General Semantics, 1982.

Johnson, D. *Reaching out: interpersonal effectiveness and self-actualization,* 7th ed. Boston: Allyn & Bacon, 2000.

Littlejohn, S. W. *Theories of human communication,* 6th ed. Belmont, CA: Wadsworth, 1999.

Smeltzer, L. R., and K. W. Watson. Gender differences in verbal communication during negotiations. *Communication research reports,* 1986, 3, 74–79.

Steil, L. K., L. L. Barker, and K. W. Watson. *Effective listening: key to your success.* Reading, MA: Addison-Wesley, 1983.

Stewart. L., P. Cooper, A. Stewart, and S. A. Friedley. *Communication and gender.* Scottsdale, AZ: Gorsuch Scarisbrick, 1996.

Watson, K. W., and L. L. Barker. *Interpersonal and relational communication.* Scottsdale, AZ: GSP Publishers, 1990.

Wilmot, W. W., and J. L. Hocker. *Interpersonal conflict,* 5th ed. Dubuque, IA: Wm. C. Brown, 1998.

Wolvin, A., and C. G. Coakley. *Listening,* 5th ed. Dubuque, IA: Brown & Benchmark, 1996.

Suggested Readings

Barker, L. L. *Listening behavior.* Englewood Cliffs, NJ: Prentice-Hall, 1971. Reprinted (1988), New Orleans: SPECTRA Incorporated, Publishers. This book was designed to provide a foundation for effective listening. To provide methods to improve listening behaviors, the book discusses the importance of the listener, the listening process, variables influencing listening, listening problems, methods to improve listening, biased listening, and listener feedback and response.

Cloke, K., and J. Goldsmith. *Resolving conflicts at work: A complete guide for everyone on the job.* San Francisco: Jossey-Bass, 2000. Centering around listening, this book explores a number of techniques for communication and resolving conflict more effectively. The authors of this highly readable book are mediators and trainers in conflict resolution.

Stewart, J., ed. *Bridges not walls,* 7th ed. New York: McGraw-Hill 1999. Chapter 7, "Listening," includes three articles that discuss listening myths and feedback. Chapter 15, "Communicating Across Cultures," includes several articles on communicating interculturally.

Wolvin, A. D., and C. G. Coakley. *Listening,* 5th ed. Dubuque, IA: Brown & Benchmark, 1996. This text emphasizes the process nature of listening. It features sections on listening as a communication function and on discriminative, comprehensive, therapeutic, and critical listening.

Zimmerman, J., and Coyle, V. *The way of council.* Las Vegas, NV: Bramble Books, 1996. Inspired by Native American traditions, this book explores a group council. Effective listening is at the heart of the council process.

Problem Solving

Study Questions _____

After reading this chapter, you should be able to answer the following questions completely and accurately:

1. What are three general sources of problems?
2. What are the definitions of the following terms?
   a. Problem
   b. Topic
   c. Proposition
   d. Decision making
   e. Solution getting
3. What are three general types of problems?
4. What is evidence?
5. What are four rules that can help when opinions are used as evidence?
6. What are three tests to apply when support testimony is used as evidence?
7. What are three tests for all types of evidence?
8. What is the difference between inductive and deductive reasoning?
9. What are three types of reasoning in addition to inductive and deductive reasoning?
10. What are the eight major steps in systematic approach for problem solving in small group discussion?
11. What are four rules for engaging in the brainstorming process?

"Rain, rain go away! Come again some other day." Most problems, unlike the rain in the children's rhyme, generally cannot be solved simply by telling them to "go away." Problems have complex origins and require systematic thought, planning, and action to be solved or minimized. Problems that are purely personal in nature may be solvable by the individual who experiences them. However, many problems affect several people, large groups, or even society as a whole. These problems often can be resolved efficiently and effectively through group communication and problem solving. In a problem-solving group, the problem itself acts as an important variable that should be considered in a systems analysis. This chapter discusses many aspects of problem solving that should be examined in relation to other variables in your particular system or group.

Sources of Problems

Many small groups exist for the sole purpose of problem solving. The problems that these groups attempt to solve vary widely in scope and evolve from an infinite number of sources. However, most problems fall into three general categories: inherited problems, assigned problems, and self-discovered problems.

In many organizations and small groups, discussing old business brings many *inherited problems* to light. These problems are passed on from previous groups composed of different people with different needs. Some typical examples of such problems might be, "How can we get rid of 2,500 brooms left over from the spring fund raiser?" "Should we change our bylaws so that our group's treasurer can serve more than two terms?" "Does our insurance cover alternative care, such as chiropractic and soft tissue therapy?" In evaluating whether such inherited problems are worthy of group discussion, groups should assess the problem's current interest, appropriateness, and relevance to the present group or organization.

Perhaps the most common context in which a group is assigned a problem is in small group communication and discussion classes. Many other groups and organizations work on problems that are assigned or designated by chairpeople to subcommittees or subgroups. In addition, outside forces may create or delegate problems for organizations to solve. Assigned problems include such examples as developing a system to alleviate the parking problem on the main campus; raising $5,000 for flood relief victims; or finding an alternative to the high prices and limited menus at the campus cafeterias.

Although groups that are assigned problems may have no choice in deciding whether to attempt to solve them, they still may want to ensure that the problem is clearly presented, that possible solutions previously attempted are identified, and that they know to whom the group is directly responsible.

Many problems arise as a result of daily encounters, interactions, or pressures. Since these problems present what Dewey (1910) terms a "felt need" (i.e., an obvious or pressing need), they are generally more interesting to group members and are, thus, often afforded top priority for discussion. Small pharmacies discover their customers are buying less merchandise from them and more at large convenience stores and search for ways to keep their customers. A collegiate soccer club wants to become a varsity sport in order to receive increased university funding. These are only a few examples of typical *self-discovered problems.* When evaluating a self-discovered problem for potential discussion, group members should decide whether the problem is related to the needs of the entire group or to only a few individuals, whether it is of genuine interest and concern to the majority of the group, and whether it is really within the ability or scope of the group to effect a solution.

Problems may arise from many sources in addition to the three suggested here. These examples merely provide a foundation for further explanation of the problem-solving process via group communication and discussion.

Principles

1. Three general sources of problems are inherited problems, assigned problems, and self-discovered problems.
2. Problems involving a "felt need" are more interesting to group members.

Some Definitions

Before proceeding, several terms to be used later in the chapter that may be potentially confusing will be defined.

1. *Problem: A question proposed for solution or consideration implying that certain obstacles must be overcome.* A problem does not imply a difference of opinion, just an unbalanced state that creates tension, anxiety, danger, or discomfort for the group or others of concern to the group members.

2. *Topic: A description of an idea or concept to be discussed.* It is important to note that a topic is considerably broader than a problem. The topic of one discussion group was AIDS and the HIV virus on campus. The broad topic of AIDS and HIV included a variety of potential problems for discussion, such as, "What precautions does the student health clinic take regarding AIDS?" and "Should student health insurance pay for medications related to AIDS treatment?" Thus, topics may suggest problems for discussion, but they are not the problems themselves. This distinction is important to remember, for later in the chapter the importance of stating the problem in a manner suitable for effective group discussion is noted.

3. *Proposition: A statement advocating a particular plan or point of view.* Again, it is important to note differences between propositions and problems. Propositions such as, "Women should have to register for selective service" require participants to take sides on the issue. On the other hand, if the same proposition were stated in a problem form, such as, "Who should have to register for selective service?" participants could explore all dimensions of the topic without being forced to take an initial stand on the issues. Thus, propositions indicate advocacy, whereas problem statements attempt to stimulate groups to determine the best of several possible alternatives.

4. *Decision making: The process of selecting among several alternatives.* There is considerable overlap in the terms *decision making* and *problem solving*. All problem-solving discussions require that the group make a decision. However, all decisions made by groups do not necessarily reflect the presence of problems. *Decision making* refers to the process that a group follows in order to select among alternatives or to chart a course of action (Gouran, 1997). Problem solving involves the processes of problem identification, analysis, solution getting, and selection of the best solution from among those proposed. Thus, although decision making is a vital step in the problem-solving process, it may take place in group communication independent of problems or propositions.

5. *Solution getting: The process of discovering possible solutions relevant to a particular problem.* Solution getting is often confused with problem solving. However, like decision making, it is only one step in the problem-solving process. It is relatively easy to discover possible solutions. In fact, if you ask a friend how to solve a specific problem, he or she probably will gladly suggest a

ready solution. The only problem is that if you ask five different people for advice, and all five have different solutions for the same problem, it is possible that some suggestions might work well, some might work adequately, and some might not work at all. Thus, in order to solve a problem, you must not only obtain a possible solution, you must also implement it and later evaluate it to determine whether it can actually solve the problem.

Principles
1. A problem is a question proposed for solution or consideration implying certain obstacles that must be overcome.
2. A topic is a description of an idea or concept to be discussed.
3. A proposition is a statement advocating a particular plan or point of view.
4. Decision making is the process of selecting among several alternatives.
5. Solution getting is the process of discovering possible solutions relevant to a particular problem.

Types of Problems

Some types of problems *cannot* be solved through discussion, so it only wastes the group's time to talk about them. Other problems can be solved through discussion, but they require special sensitivity (or training) on the part of the group members in order to make the discussion meaningful. Still other types of problems are extremely relevant for discussion by small groups. This section will discuss three general types of problems and their appropriateness for discussion in small groups.

Problems of Fact or Perception

Facts generally may be verified through empirical or scientific methods and refer to events, happenings, or objects. In addition, facts are generally thought to be synonymous with the truth. If, in reality, the truth can be known or discovered, it makes little sense to waste time in discussing, for example, "What is the present position of the Republican party on abortion rights?" It would make more sense to go to the library for a copy of the Republican party's platform for the last (or next) election and read what the Republican leaders have said about the issue. Such factual information may be obtained through research not through discussion.[1]

On the other hand, much information considered factual may only be *perceived* to be the truth. In instances where the absolute truth can never be discovered, factual problems may be discussed to learn different people's perceptions of the problem in question. For example, if a group contained two members who

---

[1]This assumes that a knowledgeable Republican party officer is not present in the group to present "expert" testimony.

listened to a speech by a Republican leader concerning the issue of deforestation and reported different perceptions, it might be fruitful to probe deeper to determine which observer's perceptions were based on more objective and/or verifiable data. Problems of fact also may be discussed to help share information or to reinforce important points for group members to remember. However, when the purpose of a discussion is to inform, the facts discussed do not take the form of a problem but merely become a topic for discussion.

Problems of Attitude, Feeling, or Value

If problems involve attitudes and value judgments, objective facts may not be available. For example, the problem, "How can the election procedures in this town be made fair to all students who live here?" cannot be solved simply by accumulating some facts. In the final analysis, it rests on the class members' perceptions of the term *fair*. In a sense, it is somewhat dangerous to spend time discussing problems involving feelings or emotions. Unless all group members share the same emotions, or unless persuasion takes place within the group, no consensus can be reached through extended discussion. The primary value in considering this type of question for discussion is to help understand others' feelings and attitudes. However, groups must be sensitive to the dangers of discussing problems that have no real solution and must also attempt to avoid letting interpersonal disagreements lead to interpersonal dislike.

Problems of Policy or Behavior

Problems of policy or behavior are best suited for discussion in small groups. In policy problems, facts may be brought to bear on possible solutions, reasoning may be applied, and group consensus can be gained through interpersonal communication. Some problems—for example, "What role should the president of the university play in regulating Greek activities?" "What strategy should the coach take to win Saturday's football game against a team averaging more than 280 pounds per player?" "What changes can the campus cafeterias make to increase the student business?" —involve issues that may be objectively analyzed, studied, and finally solved. A major value of problem solving in groups is that by bringing more insights to bear on a problem, groups reap a greater variety of possible solutions. More drawbacks to the suggested solutions may also be discovered by groups than by single individuals. The "two heads are better than one" argument is relevant here.

Problems of policy take several different forms. One form asks the group to make a decision from several proposed alternatives (e.g., "Should we donate our funds to the United Way, UNICEF, or St. Jude's Hospital?"). Another type of problem of policy demands that the group bring together knowledge or facts from a variety of sources in order to solve the problem (e.g., "Why are we having a difficult time recruiting soccer coaches for our teams?"). Still another type of problem of policy involves an objective or implied action (e.g., "How can we raise enough money to send our band to Washington for the inauguration?"). Regardless of the form that this type of question takes, the problem-solving approach is relatively similar. Suggestions for specific procedures to be followed in group problem solving are provided later in this chapter.

Principles
1. Three general types of problems are problems of fact or perception; problems of attitude, feeling, or value; and problems of policy or behavior.
2. Not all types of problems can be solved through group discussion.

Evidence and Reasoning: Essentials for Problem Solving

In discussing problems in small groups, it is essential that group members possess (1) relevant facts or evidence and (2) the ability to reason logically. Evidence consists of facts and opinions used to prove some contention and provides a solid foundation for logical reasoning.

Evidence

Facts and perceptions (opinions) are often confused. Evidence consists of both facts and perceptions, but the two forms of evidence differ in their nature, persuasiveness, and potential value. In court cases, for example, the quality and quantity of evidence has been instrumental in swaying the jury (Pettus, 1990).

Remember that facts only "approach the truth." Some examples of facts that may be used as evidence include statistics, recording (books, records, tapes), objects, graphs and diagrams, and pictures. Although these examples of factual evidence are generally thought to be objective and unbiased, they still must be relevant to the issue being discussed if they are to be valuable. A common problem with factual evidence is people's tendency to twist a piece of evidence to prove a related point.

Because opinions are obviously more subjective than facts, they must be used with more caution. These rules can help when using opinions as evidence:

1. Use opinions of experts whenever possible.
2. Do not base an argument (or case) exclusively on opinion.
3. Make sure that experts are asked to offer opinions in their particular fields.
4. Be sure that you quote experts accurately and in the proper context.

Opinions of nonexperts may also be used as evidence, but their impact or credibility may be insufficient to be persuasive.

Testing Evidence.   Following are some tests you can apply to determine the validity of evidence (Grice & Skinner, 1998; McCroskey, 1997).

The first two tests are suggested when "support testimony" is used as evidence:

1. Is the authority biased? In other words, does the authority have a vested interest or a potential reason for taking a certain stand? If the authority is genuinely impartial, his or her opinion and testimony will have more credibility.

2. Is the authority qualified by training and/or experience? An entertainer who does a low-calorie soft drink commercial may have some positive appeal to the TV viewers, but his or her ability to make scientific judgments regarding the chemical additive used to replace sugar and the general healthfulness of the soft drink may be questionable.

The last four tests are appropriate for all types of evidence:

3. Is the evidence probable? Regardless of how objective a piece of evidence may appear it must still be viewed in light of prior experience and knowledge. A piece of evidence that does not coincide with logical expectations should be carefully examined.

4. Is the evidence consistent? Consistency may be gauged both internally and externally. *Internal consistency* primarily refers to consistency within a given, written or spoken message. If a witness is self-contradictory, the testimony will be questionable. Similarly, external evidence may be inconsistent if two experts in the same area have different perceptions of a particular concept or event. In the case of differing opinions among experts, either a third expert must be brought in, or the credibility of the two differing experts must be examined to determine which is the more qualified.

5. Is the evidence recent? Scientific research, for example, has changed considerably over the years.

6. Is there a sufficient quantity of evidence?

A single bit of testimony may be insufficient to persuade the others in the group. Generally, the more evidence of fact and opinion you can provide, the more persuasive your argument will be.

Reasoning

Although facts and opinions may provide a basis for a given argument, the reasoning process is generally used to demonstrate how the evidence proves a particular point. Reasoning involves cognitive appeals for the purpose of influencing belief. Most forms of reasoning may be classified as either inductive or deductive. *Inductive reasoning* proceeds from a number of specific statements to a general conclusion, whereas *deductive reasoning* begins with a general observation and leads to a specific conclusion.

Following are examples of inductive and deductive reasoning:

Induction
1. Mr. and Mrs. Terry Chapman both are musically talented.
2. Mr. and Mrs. Chapman's parents are musically talented.
3. Mr. and Mrs. Chapman's children, Jordan and Ariel, are musically talented. *(specific statements or premises)* Conclusion: Everyone in the Chapman family is musically talented. *(generalization)*

Deduction
1. Everyone in the Chapman family is musically talented.
2. Jordan and Ariel are part of the Chapman family. *(general statements)* Conclusion: Jordan and Ariel are musically talented. *(specific statements)*

It should be noted in these examples that conclusions from inductive reasoning often provide premises for deductive reasoning. Similarly, conclusions from deduction may provide premises for induction. Ideally, a combination of both types of reasoning will be used to help develop a case or argument.

Other ways you can reason include (1) from analogy, (2) from cause to effect, and (3) from effect to cause. Reasoning from *analogy* simply involves the assumption that if two concepts are shown to be similar in several respects, they will probably be alike in other unknown respects. Analogies may be either literal or figurative. Literal analogies are based on similarity of two objects or events in the same class. Figurative analogies compare objects or events in different classes. A literal analogy might be made between movie directors, one of whom is known to be successful at the box office. The analogy begins by demonstrating that the second director possesses the qualities that made the first director successful. It ends by concluding that the second director also must be successful. A figurative analogy is often presented in parable form. The parables of the many religions are among the most widely known figurative analogies. "Building a house on solid rock" is analogous to building one's life on a solid faith. Both analogies may be used in reasoning, but their effectiveness depends on (1) the relevance of the analogy, (2) the accuracy of the analogy, and (3) the degree of the relationship implicit in the analogy.

Reasoning from *cause to effect* involves the isolation of variables that are thought to cause a certain phenomenon and demonstrations of the logical relationship between the causes and their effects. Two questions must be answered in testing reasoning from cause to effect: (1) Is the cause strong enough to produce the effect? (2) Are there any restrictions that would prevent the cause from producing the effect? An example of cause-to-effect reasoning is: The electricity was off for twenty-four hours. Consequently, the food in the freezer thawed out and spoiled. The causal relationship between the lack of electricity and the food spoilage is the logical one that also satisfies the two test questions posed previously.

Reasoning from *effect to cause* involves observing a known effect and inferring its probable cause. For example, a college president who observed repeated protests and sit-ins on campus might attempt to isolate the causes, such as prominent national or international events (wars, assassination, etc.) or local campus events (restrictions on student rights of visitation, voting, etc.). In testing the validity of reasoning from effect to cause, it is necessary to ask: (1) Is the alleged cause of sufficient strength or importance to produce the observed effect? (2) Could other causes possibly have produced the known effect? In the case of the example of the college president, it would be very difficult to determine that a single cause produced this observed effect. Thus, reasoning from effect to cause can be misleading at times and should be used with caution.

Principles

1. Evidence consists of facts and perceptions (opinions).
2. The following four rules can help you in using opinions as evidence:
   a. Use opinions of experts whenever possible.
   b. Do not base an argument (or case) exclusively on opinions.
   c. Make sure that experts are asked to offer opinions in their particular fields of competence.
   d. Be sure that you quote experts accurately and in the proper context.
3. Two tests to apply when "support testimony" is used as evidence are as follows:
   a. Is the authority biased?
   b. Is the authority qualified by training and/or experience?
4. Four tests for all types of evidence are:
   a. Is the evidence probable?
   b. Is the evidence consistent?
   c. Is the evidence recent?
   d. Is there a sufficient quantity of evidence?
5. Inductive reasoning proceeds from a number of specific statements to a general conclusion.
6. Deductive reasoning begins with a general observation and leads to a specific conclusion.
7. In addition to inductive and deductive reasoning, it is possible to reason from analogy, from cause to effect, and from effect to cause.

A Systematic Approach to Problem Solving

Chapter Two discussed the concept of systems. In this section, the term *systematic* overlaps somewhat with the previously discussed concept of system, but it has a more limited meaning. This section will suggest a step-by-step plan for approaching problems in small group discussions. Some experts call a systematic plan an *agenda*. A specific plan or agenda is useful when the group members understand the steps, have time to use them completely, and see their usefulness in a particular instance. However, you should be aware that many problems do not lend themselves to the use of a complete agenda, so its use might be adapted to the particular problem, environment, and group.

The following steps are based in part on those proposed by Dewey (1910). The major additions are based on current thought concerning creative thinking and problem solving. This creative aspect of problem solving will be discussed later.

Define the Problem

Defining the problem involves delineating its exact nature and defining terms in the problem statement. Only the definition of terms will be discussed at this point, because delineation of the problem relates not only to specific terms in the problem statement, but also to problem limitation and analysis. In defining the key terms of the problem, you will want to remember the following:

1. Keep definitions short and to the point.
2. Avoid using the word to be defined in the definition.
3. Use clear and concise language.
4. Use examples when necessary to clarify meanings.

Attempt to phrase the problem statement in such a way that it cannot be answered simply yes or no. In other words, instead of stating the question as "Should the U.S. government continue the embargo against Cuba?" you should state the problem as "What should be the position of the U.S. government regarding trade embargoes against Cuba?" Whereas the first phrasing asks participants to take a position immediately (i.e., yes or no), the second phrasing helps keep the problem on an objective plane and allows all facts to be brought forth before solutions are suggested or positions taken.

After the problem is stated properly and key terms are defined, the next step is to limit the problem.

Limit the Problem

Most complex problems cannot be solved in a brief period of time. Therefore, it is important to make initial decisions concerning the most critical aspects of the problem that must be considered. Limitation of the problem area should be made in light of the following considerations:

1. Relevance to group interests and needs
2. Importance of the specific issue to group or others
3. Amount of time allowed for discussion and/or action

In classroom discussion, it is important to limit the scope of a problem so that it can be covered adequately during the class period. In real-life groups, time is also an important variable, so topic or problem limitations also must be made on a pragmatic basis.

A topic of national or international scope, such as "What should be the role of the United Nations in managing world crises?" obviously could generate discussion for days, months, or even years. Such a topic, if used in a discussion or small group class, should be limited substantially, perhaps by taking a specific subarea and limiting discussion to only that area. An example might be, "What should be the role of the United Nations in negotiations in Bosnia-Herzegovina?"

Once the problem is limited to a manageable size, it is necessary to begin problem analysis.

Analyze the Problem

Problem analysis is at the core of the problem-solving process. Unfortunately, many group members tend to slight or completely ignore this area and jump immediately into suggesting solutions. Unless members completely understand the problem, it is unlikely that the solutions they propose will serve to solve the problem adequately. The basic purposes of the analysis step are to collect evidence and information that will help describe and clarify the problem and to explore the scope and dimensions of the problem. In addition, if the topic relates to a specific group or audience that will receive help from your group, you should conduct an audience analysis.

Audience Analysis. Once your group determines the general purpose or problem that needs to be solved, it is important to look at the audience that will receive the information. Your intended audience or target group should determine how the topic is researched and how the information/report is presented. For example, suppose as a member of the student government you received complaints about library theft on campus. Since library theft will affect students, professors, and administrators differently, your group's report should use the examples and illustrations that relate most directly to the group you were to address. The administrators would probably be most interested in direct replacement costs; students and professors might be more interested in the effects of theft on their research.

Audience analysis, or the process of getting to know your audience, should be conducted after you have determined your group goals. Then as a group, you can conduct demographic, attitudinal, or purpose-oriented analysis. *Demographic analysis* considers how the age, educational level, socioeconomic status, occupation, sex, and group membership of a target audience will affect the reception of a message. For example, if your group were trying to improve the quality of care at the local humane society, demographic characteristics would help you know how to approach the audience. With a group of college students, you might ask them to volunteer to work twice a month. However, with a group of business professionals, you might make an appeal for tax-free donations.

Attitudinal analysis provides group members with information about the beliefs and values of their target audience. Since many of our beliefs and values are acquired in childhood, it is important to ask questions about what might influence your audience's thoughts and actions. *Purpose-oriented analysis* gives you an idea about how much information the audience members have and how they feel about the topic. If your target audience is favorable toward your position, all you have to do is to reinforce your ideas with a fresh approach. However, if the audience is initially opposed to your position, your challenge is to change their minds or to provide them with an alternative point of view.

Gather Information.   When your target audience is one about which you know relatively little, your goal is to gather information. The most obvious source of information is the person or persons who know the audience best. For example, if you are trying to get a neighborhood to join a neighborhood watch program, you will probably need to speak to the person who arranged the meeting. Then you would ask questions such as, "Have there been thefts in your neighborhood?" "What do your neighbors know about neighborhood watch?" "How long will we have to speak?" "How many people will attend?"

In other situations, you can gather audience information by reading books, newspapers, annual reports and newsletters. You also might gather information from the electronic media: the Internet, television, and radio. Being informed can help you in preparing examples and illustrations. Another source of information comes from public opinion polls and surveys. Generalizations from local pollsters and from sources such as *Gallup Opinion Index* and *Public Opinion Index* provide useful information about how people are likely to respond to a given topic.

When possible, it is desirable for group members to divide the labor of collecting information and evidence relevant to the problem. Once information is collected and ordered in a manageable form, it should be used to help isolate causes of the problems as well as to identify the major effects produced by the causes. The more thorough analysis a group performs, the more time it will save later in obtaining relevant solutions. In fact, in some rare instances, a complete analysis of the problem can almost serve to solve the problem.

After evidence and information have been collected, examined, and evaluated, and the cause-effect relationships relevant to the problem have been examined, specific criteria need to be suggested that will guide the selection of the final solution(s).

Establish Criteria

Some writers refer to the step of establishing criteria as the "problem reformulation phase." This step requires the group to set specific objectives that any or all solutions must meet. The specific objectives or criteria may be derived directly from the problem analysis step or may be generated independently. Establishing criteria or specific objectives in advance of establishing solutions is not only logical but also timesaving. If solutions are simply suggested without any basis for evaluation or completeness, it may take the group a long time to search out those solutions that will do the job.

Obviously, the first procedure involved in this step is to determine what is required of the proposed solution(s). Often it is more efficient to employ the brainstorming technique (discussed later in this chapter) in order to get a large number of criteria "on the floor" for later evaluation. Remember that if the brainstorming technique is to be successful, all group members must reserve judgment about the quality of the criteria until all have been proposed.

After the criteria have been suggested, the next step is for the group to decide on those criteria that are most important and relevant. Although criteria must be established specifically for each problem, two general ones that are often employed are: (1) the proposed solution should be workable and feasible (in terms of resources, time, and money), and (2) the solution should not protect the majority at the expense of the minority (or vice versa).

Specific criteria should normally be employed in addition to more general ones. Following are examples of specific criteria for solutions related to the problem of "What should be the role of the county in creating a new sewage treatment facility during the next five years?"

The solution should:

1. Ensure that taxes are not raised.
2. Ensure that the natural ecology will not be disturbed significantly (i.e., any disturbing of natural balance during construction phase will be rectified upon completion, and all outputs of the facility will be monitored and remain safe).
3. Not involve only lands owned or farmed by low-income groups and minority groups.

4. Not provide a basis for personal gain for large real estate corporations, particularly those with personal friends in state government.
5. Provide equivalent facilities for all surrounding communities.

Note that some criteria are stated in negative terms, implying what the solution should avoid. Others are stated in positive terms, suggesting what the solution should include. A good set of solution criteria will provide a balance of both negative and positive points.

Suggest Possible Solutions

The "solution-getting" phase of the problem-solving process should begin with an exploration of general classes of solutions that may be useful. Then, specific solutions appropriate to each general class should be examined. Once again, it is often desirable to employ the brainstorming technique to obtain a large quantity of potential solutions. Defer judgment until all solutions have been proposed. At this stage, seek quantity rather than quality, and don't be afraid to improve or build onto ideas suggested by others. When all possible solutions have been brought to light, then—and only then—initiate the evaluation process. The first step is to check each solution against the criteria previously established.

Evaluate the Solutions in Light of the Criteria

At this point, critical evaluations are called for. To keep the evaluation phase more efficient and effective, try to keep criticisms aimed at ideas rather than personalities. If possible, each specific solution should be compared with all of the established criteria. Solutions that do not satisfy the critical criteria should be discarded, and the remaining solutions should be ranked according to their satisfaction of the criteria.

Finally, those solutions that seem to meet the criteria must be evaluated on different bases to determine the one(s) most feasible and desirable. Considerations such as cost of implementation, ease of implementation, short-range versus long-range effects of the solution, and predicted adequacy of the solution should be considered. The final solution may be a combination of several different solutions. Once the group agrees to a plan of action or solution, the next step is to implement it.

Implement the Solution(s)

The implementation and evaluation phases of problem solving may not be executed in some classroom situations, but in real-life groups these phases are probably the most important. If an idealized solution cannot be implemented successfully, it cannot help to solve the problem.

The group must strive to discover the most efficient and effective plan for implementing the solution. If money is a factor, costs must be considered; if time is important, it must be taken into account. When all contingencies are accounted for, the group must finally agree on one or more plans of implementation. Plans may be adapted for individual group use. Once the plan has been implemented, it must be evaluated to determine whether the problem really has been successfully solved.

Evaluate the Success of the Solution

Before attempting to evaluate the success of a solution, you must wait a sufficient length of time after it has been implemented to give it a chance to work. Obviously, some proposals are long term, whereas others yield immediate results. Tests for the solutions must be devised, and the criteria agreed upon should be examined to see if the solution has met them adequately. Other questions that may be asked include: "Can improvements or alterations be made on the implemented solution to increase its effectiveness?" "Is the cost of the plan (in money, time, or energy) commensurate with the results obtained?" and "Has the plan created new problems that are equal to or more disturbing than the original problem?" In other words, the evaluation step requires that the group make a final decision concerning whether to keep the present plan of implementation in force or to alter, replace, or repair it in order to help it meet the needs.

The worth of a solution can be determined only after evaluation has taken place and effects of the plan are known. If the plan works, the problem has been solved. If it does not work, the group members must go back to their list of possible solutions and try another, and keep repeating the process until something is finally found to be effective.

Principles

1. The eight major steps in the systematic approach (i.e., agenda) to problem solving in small group discussions are as follows:
    a. Define the problem.
    b. Limit the problem.
    c. Analyze the problem.
    d. Establish criteria.
    e. Suggest possible solutions.
    f. Evaluate the solutions in light of the criteria.
    g. Implement the solution(s).
    h. Evaluate the success of the solution.
2. The intended audience or target group should determine how group members research a topic and present their information.
3. Audience analysis is the process of getting to know the characteristics of your audience.

4. There are three types of audience analysis:
   a. Demographic analysis considers the age, educational level, socio-economic status, occupation, sex, and group membership of the target audience.
   b. Attitudinal analysis provides information about the beliefs and values of a target audience.
   c. Purpose-oriented analysis gives the group members an idea about how much information an audience has and how they feel about a topic.
5. A group can gather audience information by a person or persons familiar with the audience or from print and electronic media sources.

Sources of Information for Problem-Solving Discussions

When gathering information for problem-solving sessions, it is important that your group maintain objectivity if at all possible. For example, it would be unfair for a city council committee considering a utility rate increase to use information only from the utility company or only from a consumer activist group. It is also a good idea to select from a wide variety of sources. Of course, the type and number of sources you use will depend on your group goals and objectives. Four sources of information are available to group members.

Personal Experience.   Whether you realize it or not, you are a valuable resource to your group. You and other group members have life experiences, observations, and knowledge that are unlike anyone else's. For this reason, as a group member you can often offer information unknown by others. As an illustration, consider the following example. The newly appointed chairperson of the "Shoe Leather Express" Board of Directors was discussing the mandate from her CEO to ensure that all franchises followed federal hiring practices. Because she was unfamiliar with the policies, she was going to do some research and schedule another meeting. Before she did, one of the other board members said, "There is no need to call another meeting. I served as a recruiter for several years, and I am familiar with the policies. If you want, I'll be happy to explain what steps need to be taken." As you can see, the experience of this board member saved the entire group research and meeting time.

Interviews.   At times the best sources of information are other people. In these situations, you will need to conduct either a survey or a personal interview.

A *survey* is a detailed gathering of information by means of a questionnaire, interview, or observation. Surveys allow a group to gather a cross-section of information or opinions. For example, recently a group of university planners surveyed its student body and faculty to determine whether either group would be interested in renting university apartments and townhouses, at what cost, and if the location would matter. After tabulating the results of the questionnaires, the administration decided to build housing only for students. The faculty did not seem to have sufficient interest because of the location. Because decisions are based on survey results, it is important to remember that the best surveys are ones that use standardized questions and get a representative sample of participants. The university in this example could have lost a lot of money if it had built housing for the faculty without asking about the importance of the location or by asking only a selected group of people.

In many situations, *personal interviews* may be more practical and cost efficient than conducting formal surveys. During a personal interview you meet with a person, one on one. The interviewee is selected because of his or her knowledge, experience, or accessibility to information related to your subject. For example, if you were participating in a panel discussion about AIDS, you might want to interview a doctor, a public clinic official, a person who is HIV positive, and the chairperson of the local AIDS outreach program.

Of course, when you are selecting a person to interview, your objective is to find the person or persons who will have the most credibility. It would usually be inappropriate to interview someone who is not knowledgeable about your topic. If you decide that a personal interview would help you gather the best information, there are several guidelines you should keep in mind.

1. *Make an appointment.* As a courtesy, you should call or write and ask for the interview. When scheduling the interview, be sure to allow enough time to cover the topic area adequately. You don't want either of you to feel rushed.
2. *Plan for the interview.* Before actually meeting with the interviewee, define your objectives and prepare an outline. Decide the types of questions you will need to ask to get the best information. You will want to avoid asking questions that elicit "yes" or "no" responses. Finally, consider the environment in which the interview will take place. If conducting a telephone interview, for example, be sure to control for interruptions.
3. *Be on time.* If someone has given you time out of his or her busy schedule, you must be punctual.
4. *Establish rapport.* Meeting new people can often be difficult. Your job is to make the interviewee feel as comfortable as possible. You might begin by discussing something of interest to the interviewee, such as a photograph on the wall or an outside interest.
5. *Listen attentively.* Pay close attention to the interviewee. Show that you are listening by leaning forward slightly, maintaining eye contact, showing appropriate facial expressions, and nodding appropriately. It is also important for you to pick up on things that the interviewee says.

Paraphrase at times to make sure that you have understood correctly, and feel free to ask questions other than the ones you have prepared in advance.

6. *Thank the interviewee.* After the interview, thank the interviewee for giving you the time and information. In addition, you may want to consider writing a note as another way of expressing appreciation.

Often before conducting an interview you will need to conduct preliminary research. In fact, after researching a topic, you may find that interviews and/or surveys are unnecessary.

Printed Materials.   Printed materials serve as some of the best sources of primary information. Books, magazines, journals, newspapers, pamphlets, diaries, encyclopedias, almanacs, and other reference works are examples of just a few printed materials that offer valuable information.

Of course, libraries are the most common places to find printed information. Therefore, it is important for you to know how to use a library efficiently. Inexperienced students save valuable time by taking a tour of a library, learning its reference system, and familiarizing themselves with the cataloguing system, databases and reference areas. Especially for group projects, it is a good idea to know how to find statistical information, government documents, current periodicals, reference works, indexes, and public opinion resources quickly.

Although the library is the most common source for printed materials, be sure not to overlook other sources. Special-interest groups often have newsletters and publications not offered in a university or public library. For example, in one major city, an advertising club houses a more complete library of printed resources than any of the area universities. In addition to historical and state-of-the-art documents, it also has both printed and video examples of award-winning print advertisements from around the world. If your group were asked to design an advertising campaign, it might be profitable to investigate sources other than the campus library for printed materials.

Electronic Media.   Technology provides us with another valuable source of information: the electronic media. Through the Internet, television, radio, and audio and video cassettes, we now have aural and visual documents that can be used as sources of information or to support a position. The visual images and on-site reports from South America and the Midwest, for example, made the floods of the late 1990s particularly real to those listening and watching. In fact, with the availability of television, computers and the Internet, most students have been exposed to more electronic media than print media.

Evaluating the credibility of electronic information is very important. Unlike books and newspapers that are reviewed many times prior to publication to verify information and check for accuracy of spelling, for example, Web documents can be created by anyone with a computer. Therefore, information on the Internet varies in quality and evaluating it becomes more important. Suggestions for evaluating Internet sources (e.g., Ballard, DiSanza and Legge, 2000; Harris, 1997) include the following:

1. Look for the author of the site (including her/his qualifications for writing on the topic) and a way to contact her/him.
2. Evaluate the sponsor of the site. Is the site sponsored by a national institution, the government, a university or company? Is the sponsor relatively free of bias?
3. Consider the date the Web page was built or last updated.
4. Try to verify the information through other sources.

There are many problems that can make Internet searches unproductive or unreliable. However, with critical thinking, practice, and patience, the Internet is a valuable supplement to other sources of information.

Principles
1. When gathering information for problem-solving sessions, the group should remember to maintain objectivity, select from a wide variety of sources, and select sources based on group goals and objectives.
2. A valuable source of information is personal experience.
3. Surveys or personal interviews are beneficial sources of information.
   a. A survey allows a group to gather a cross-section of information or opinions.
   b. A personal interview is conducted on a one-to-one basis.
   c. An interviewee is selected for his or her knowledge, experience, or accessibility to information.
   d. When conducting a personal interview, follow these guidelines:
      1. Make an appointment.
      2. Plan for the interview.
      3. Be on time.
      4. Establish rapport.
      5. Listen attentively.
      6. Thank the interviewee.
4. Printed materials serve as primary sources of information and are most easily found in libraries.
5. Electronic media sources such as television, the Internet, and audio and video cassettes serve as sources of information and evidence.
6. Suggestions for evaluating Internet sources include:
   a. Look for the author of the site, the author's credibility, and a way to contact him/her.
   b. Evaluate the sponsor of the site.

  c. Consider the date the Web page was built or last updated.
  d. Try to verify the information through other sources.

Brainstorming: Creative Solution Getting

Most of the emphasis on creative thinking and the brainstorming process has been derived from Osborn's text *Applied Imagination* (1962). Osborn and his colleagues conducted considerable research using brainstorming techniques that, in most situations, were found to be up to 44 percent more effective than traditional problem-solving methods. The major premise behind the brainstorming method is that everyone should experience total freedom to express ideas without fear of personal embarrassment or criticism from others. Osborn suggests the following rules for engaging in the brainstorming process:

1. Defer judgment on all ideas presented until everyone has had a chance to contribute.
2. Seek to obtain the greatest possible quantity of ideas.
3. Use the "chain reaction" technique associated with "freewheeling" (i.e., let your mind flow freely without precensoring ideas).
4. Try to combine and improve on the ideas of others.

Generally a brainstorming session should last for no longer than five to seven minutes, but groups may want to set a specific time limit for this phase of the solution-getting process. During this intensive ideation period, one or two persons may be asked to record the ideas. If two people are recording ideas, they can take turns recording in order to more efficiently commit to paper the suggestions that have been made.

Remember that the brainstorming session is a true verbal free-for-all. Criticism is ruled out, and all ideas are permitted without condemnation or ridicule. It generally takes a few trials or practice sessions for the group to get used to the idea of free expression without criticism. If possible, groups should pick topics with simple solutions to practice in preparation for engaging in brainstorming concerning more complex problems.

Key questions members can ask themselves to stimulate further ideation include: "Can I adapt something? reverse it? substitute something? modify it? rearrange it? combine it with something? minimize it? magnify it?" By rearranging your habitual thoughts about a problem, you may be able to come up with a new technique or slightly different solution.

In general, brainstorming groups with more than five people are difficult to manage. In larger groups, several people often do not get a chance to express their ideas. The ideal size is probably four or five, with one or more participants serving as recorders as well as contributors.

Leadership in a brainstorming group generally is not necessary, although at times a facilitator may be necessary in groups just learning the brainstorming technique. A facilitator should try to help remind the members of the group of the rules that must be followed in order for the session to be productive, for example, not to stop and criticize ideas or the group may lose its momentum (Offner et al., 1996).

If your group tries brainstorming and it doesn't work for you, there is a variation that might help: Have all group members work independently, with each person generating as many ideas as possible. This method may produce more solutions than when group members work cooperatively. If your group uses this variation, you can regroup and try to build on one another's ideas and then move on to the next stage of problem solving.

After the brainstorming session, the solution(s) or criteria advanced can then be evaluated. The evaluation stage may follow immediately after the ideation or brainstorming stage. However, in some instances it is useful to allow for an incubation period before beginning evaluation.

Principles
1. The following are four rules for engaging in the brainstorming process:
   a. Defer judgment of all ideas presented until everyone has had a chance to contribute.
   b. Seek to obtain the greatest possible quantity of ideas.
   c. Use the chain reaction technique associated with freewheeling.
   d. Try to combine and improve on the ideas of others.
2. Brainstorming is a process used to get solutions; it does not always solve problems.

A Note of Caution

Problem solving, at best, is a difficult issue to approach on any level. This chapter suggested that a system may be devised to approach problems logically through group interaction and discussion. However, there is little data to suggest that the *only* valid method of approaching problems through group discussion is through a step-by-step plan similar to the one presented in this chapter. You should examine the composition of your group, the nature of the problem, the time and energy available to solve the problem, the resources available to implement the solution, and the battery of other issues that may be relevant to your group in a given context before deciding upon a specific approach or approaches to solving the problem. All of these factors can affect the productivity of your group and should be examined with a systems analysis approach. Although some of these factors have been discussed in other chapters of this book, it is important to note here that group members may have the critical thinking abilities but may not use those abilities unless motivated to do so (Perkins et al., 1994). Consequently, your group should be motivated to reach a quality solution and should not try to rush the problem-solving process if it is not absolutely necessary.

In general, it is desirable to follow a systematic step-by-step program in solving problems, but creativity in approaching problems through communication is encouraged. It is probable that a combination of creative and systematic approaches to problem solving will stimulate the best possible solutions. The key is not to be tied to any specific system so that it serves as a straitjacket for the group. Any approach employed should serve as an aid to, not a constraint upon, the problem-solving process.

Summary

This chapter focused on problem solving in small groups. It examined three general sources of problems for small group discussion. Next, definitions of and distinctions among such terms as *problem, topic, proposition, decision making,* and *solution getting* were provided.

It was emphasized that certain types of problems are more appropriate for discussion than others, and types of problems appropriate for discussion were examined.

Evidence and reasoning were discussed next, particularly as they relate to small group problem solving. Distinctions were made between facts and opinions. Several tests of evidence also were provided.

The reasoning process was described, and several examples of various types were provided. *Inductive reasoning* and *deductive reasoning* were defined, as were reasoning from analogy, cause to effect, and effect to cause.

A major portion of the chapter was devoted to the delineation and explanation of a systematic approach to problem solving. This eight-step approach, if followed, helps guide groups systematically in problem solving from definition of the problem through checking on the effectiveness of solutions. Suggestions concerning information gathering and possible sources of information also were included.

Brainstorming techniques were discussed, including rules for their use and some guidelines for effective brainstorming.

Ideas for Discussion _____

1. What is the relationship between facts and evidence?

2. What are some examples of the use of testimony in radio and television advertising?

3. What types of topics are most suitable for brainstorming sessions? Give some specific examples.

4. What is the difference between problem solving and solution getting?

5. Which steps in the agenda for discussion presented in this chapter are absolutely necessary to follow? Which may be skipped on occasion?

6. What are some examples of inductive reasoning? What are some specific examples of deductive reasoning?

Suggested Projects and Activities

1. Using other textbooks for resource materials, compile a list of as many techniques and/or rules for problem solving in groups as you can find. Then, prepare a chart that illustrates the similarities and differences among the different systems. Finally, compose your own technique for group problem solving based on your research.

2. Observe three different problem-solving discussion groups in action. Record the steps they followed (if any) in attempting to solve their problem. Prepare a brief paper comparing and contrasting the effectiveness of each method observed.

3. In a four- to six-person group, conduct a five-minute brainstorming session to find as many ways as possible to get evidence.

References

Ballard, Spahr, Andrews, and Ingersoll, LLP. *Evaluating the quality of information on the Internet: checklist.* The Virtual Chase, 2000. Retrieved July 15, 2000 from the World Wide Web: *http://www.virtualchase.com/quality/index.html*

Dewey, J. *How we think.* Lexington, MA: Heath, 1910.

DiSanza, J. R., and N. J. Legge. *Business and professional communication: plans, processes, and performance.* Boston: Allyn & Bacon, 2000.

Gouran, D. S. Effective versus ineffective group decision making. In L. R. Frey and J. K. Barge, eds. *Managing group life: communicating in decision-making groups.* Boston: Houghton Mifflin, 1997, 133–155.

Grice, G. L., and J. F. Skinner. *Mastering public speaking,* 3rd ed. Boston: Allyn & Bacon, 1998.

Harris, R. *Evaluating Internet research sources.* Costa Mesa, CA: Vanguard University of Southern California, 1997. Retrieved February 27, 2000 from the World Wide Web: *http://www.vanguard.edu/Rhurris/bobhome.htm*

McCroskey, J. C. *An introduction to rhetorical communication,* 7th ed. Boston: Allyn & Bacon, 1997.

Offner, A. K., T. J. Kramer, and J. P. Winter. The effects of facilitation, recording, and pauses on group brainstorming. *Small group research,* 1996, 27, 283–298.

Osborn, A. F. *Applied imagination.* New York: Scribner's, 1962.

Perkins, D., E. Jay, and S. Tishman. Assessing thinking: a framework for measuring critical thinking and problem-solving skills at the college level. In A. Greenwood, ed. *The national assessment of college learning: identification of the skills to be taught, learned and assessed.* Washington, DC: National Center for Educational Statistics, 1994, 65–112.

Pettus, A. B. the verdict is in: a study of jury decision-making factors, moment of personal decision, and jury deliberations—from the jurors' point of view. *Communication quarterly,* 1990, 38, 83–97.

Suggested Readings _____

Chaffee, J. *Thinking critically*, 6th ed. Boston: Houghton Mifflin, 2000. This text not only provides a good overview of critical thinking but also includes numerous thinking activities and exercises. Chapter 3, "Solving Problems," examines problems and solutions while Chapter 11, "Reasoning Critically," looks at types of reasoning and logical fallacies.

Schmidt, W., and R. Conaway. *Results-oriented interviewing: Principles, practices and procedures.* Boston: Allyn & Bacon, 1999. Chapter 2, "The Interview Process," discusses the structure of the interview and question techniques. Chapter 13, "The Computer-Assisted Interview" discusses the types of computer-assisted interviews and their advantages and disadvantages.

Stewart, C. J., and W. B. Cash, Jr. *Interviewing: Principles and practices*, 9th ed. New York: McGraw-Hill, 2000. Chapter 4, "Questions and Their Uses," discusses a variety of different questions and special techniques while Chapter 6, "The Survey Interview," explores the survey as an information gathering tool.

Zimmerman, J., and V. Coyle. *The way of council.* Las Vegas, NV: Bramble Books, 1996. Inspired by Native American traditions, this book explores an alternative to traditional forms of decision making. The authors present the steps for conducting a council and share many stories from the councils they have led.

Nonverbal Communication
in the Small Group

Study Questions

After reading this chapter, you should be able to answer the following questions completely and accurately:

1. What is nonverbal communication?
2. How does "masking" relate to small group communication?
3. What are Knapp's four functions of eye contact as related to group communication?
4. What is the "look and look away" technique of eye behavior in interpersonal communication?
5. What are two factors that appear to influence the meaning of a movement?
6. In what way do group members use touch?
7. What feelings may group members express through touch?
8. What are artifacts?
9. What are stereotypes?
10. When are stereotypes harmful?
11. What is one factor that tends to affect the impression you form of an individual based on his or her clothing?
12. How does your physical appearance relate to your participation in small groups?
13. What information may group members infer from another member's vocal qualities?
14. What emotions may group members infer from the voice?
15. What is the difference between territory and personal space?
16. What are four variables that appear to affect how comfortable you are with the distance at which another individual stands or sits?
17. What are two potential effects of increasing the size of the group?
18. What are two potential effects of seating arrangement on communicative interactions?
19. What are two variables that may affect the seating position you choose in relation to other persons?

Ray Birdwhistell (1970), a noted authority on nonverbal behavior, estimates that the average person actually speaks words for a total of only ten to eleven minutes daily. If we speak words for a relatively short period of time, how do we communicate the rest of the time? In general, we spend most of our time communicating nonverbally.

Although there have been various definitions for *nonverbal communication,* for the purpose of small group communication, we define it as follows: all communicative forms other than the written or spoken word that impart meaning to an individual or group.

In most small groups, only one person at a time communicates orally. However, while one person is communicating orally, you may tend to overlook the nonverbal communication of other group members. A group member's smile, frown, or deadpan expression communicates a loud nonverbal message.

Nonverbal communication is significant in the small group setting, not only because nonverbal behavior communicates meaning, but also because the eye contact and physical behavior of group members generally change as the group meets together over time (Mabry, 1989). Is it possible that these differences in nonverbal behavior result from changes in power, status, or the emotional changes that frequently accompany conflict? Or, could leadership, the formation of friendships, or a change in interpersonal relationships affect nonverbal behavior? Perhaps even environmental changes affect nonverbal communication.

Nonverbal communication plays an important role in small group communication. In this chapter, nonverbal communication in the small group will be discussed, including physical behavior, physical appearance, vocal behavior, territory and personal space, and environmental variables. When conducting a systems analysis, you should take these factors into account.

Physical Behavior

A member of a group can affect the group's deliberations without saying a word. For example, if a person has a bored expression, stares out the window, and sits apart from the group, and if that person is an influential member, the other members may attribute his or her boredom to any number of factors, among them that the group is only repeating what has already been said. Group members usually make inferences about other members' internal states through such physical behaviors as facial expression, eye contact, body movement, and touching.

Facial Expression

Facial expressions can have significant effects in interpersonal and small group settings. Perhaps because of physical closeness, group members depend on facial expressions to gain additional information about another member's verbal message or about the group member's internal emotional state. Knapp and Hall(1997) note that at least six categories of emotion can be accurately detected from facial expressions: happiness, anger, surprise, sadness, disgust, and fear. Research suggests that emotions are recognizable across cultures (Ekman and Friesen, 1986) and that females tend to be better than men in identifying facial display of emotion (Rotter and Rotter, 1988; Stannors et al., 1985).

The perceptions that group members hold of one another's facial expressions can affect group interaction. For example, a study by Purvis and colleagues (1984) found that attentive facial expressions encourage conversation. Other research (Forgas et al., 1983) indicates that groups are more lenient to "wrongdoers" who have positive facial expressions. You, too, may have noticed this effect when trying to be angry at an "innocent looking" friend who is smiling at you.

Sometimes group members display facial expressions that are inconsistent with their true feelings. There are a variety of reasons for controlling or "masking" facial expressions. One reason members mask is to avoid hurting someone's feelings. For example, a member may poke fun at a solution to the problem that you offered, and rather than show how angry you really feel, you smile. Another reason that group members mask is to conceal information. You may know, for example, that one group member's recount of an incident is exaggerated, but you nod your head in agreement in order to avoid embarrassing that member.

Lack of perceptiveness and sensitivity to masked facial expressions has several consequences for group members. For example, suppose that one person embarrasses another group member; that person is insensitive to the masking smile and continues to hurt the individual's feelings. The hurt individual may withdraw from group participation. Or, on the other hand, the hurt individual may become aggressive, begin blocking proposals, and be insensitive to the feelings of other group members in addition to the feelings of the group member who caused the hurt.

Another consequence of lack of perceptiveness and sensitivity to masked facial expression in this example may be merely spending needless time resolving interpersonal problems. Another consequence might be failing to resolve a problem in a satisfactory manner resulting in one or more members leaving a group. You should try to be attentive to masked facial expressions to avoid potential interpersonal problems.

Principles

1. Group members depend on facial expressions to gain additional information about a verbal message or about the source of the message.
2. Six categories of emotions that can be accurately detected from facial expressions are happiness, anger, surprise, sadness, disgust, and fear.
3. Group members frequently will "mask" their true feelings by displaying facial expressions that do not represent what they inwardly believe or feel.
4. Group members may mask to avoid hurting another group member's feelings or to conceal information.
5. You should try to be attentive to masked facial expressions in order to avoid potential interpersonal problems.

Eye Contact

Communication teachers and scholars have long recognized the significance of eye contact. For example, students in public-speaking courses are taught to maintain eye contact with their audience. They learn to shift their glance from one part of the audience to another without appearing mechanical. Lack of eye contact or artificial eye behavior can distract from the speaker's verbal message.

Eye contact, or the lack of it, also affects interpersonal communication. Early in life we learn that it is not polite to stare at persons with disabilities or to make eye contact with people in elevators. We are also taught that gaze aversion when we are expected to maintain eye contact (e.g., in sales or negotiations in general) can communicate nonreceptivity or lack of trust (Burgoon et al., 1986) and can lead to perceptions of lower credibility. Noted researcher Mark Knapp (1997) explains that eye gaze behavior can serve to (1) regulate the flow of communication; (2) monitor feedback; (3) express emotions; and (4) communicate the nature of the interpersonal relationships. We can readily apply these general functions of eye behavior to a small group setting.

Regulating the Flow of Communication between Group Members.   Picture the following scene. The chairperson of a large sorority has called the chapter meeting to order and requested that the secretary review the business of the last meeting. At the end of the review, the secretary turns to the chairperson and looks into her eyes. Almost immediately after eye contact is made, the leader says, "Thank you, Megan, for reading the minutes. And now for the business of today." Although Megan never said, "I'm finished," the leader knew that it was her turn to take the floor. When eye contact is used to indicate that the speaker no longer wishes to speak, the speaker has used gaze to function as a "turn-yielding" behavior (Wiemann and Knapp, 1999; Kalma, 1992). That is, simply by looking at the chairperson, Megan was able to regulate the flow of communication and yield the floor.

Monitoring Feedback.   Eye contact plays an important role in transmitting feedback. Because it is difficult for more than one member to speak at a time, it is difficult to have the entire group verbally express agreement with an idea. Consequently, the speaker often relies on "reading" the faces of the members. Perhaps the easiest way to tell if someone understands is to look him or her in the eye. The speaker might ask, "Am I making my point clear?" and look into the eyes of the group members to determine if the message is indeed getting through.

Expressing Group Members' Emotions.   Although it is often difficult to read an individual's emotional state by looking at the eyes in isolation from the rest of the face, research by Ekman and colleagues (e.g., Ekman, 1982; Scherer and Ekman, 1984) has helped to identify specific configurations of the eye area while emotions are being displayed. For example, even though you might not be able to explicitly detect a look of disgust from only the eyes of a group member (without the rest of the facial expression to serve as a cue), you probably would still suspect that the individual disagreed with the ideas being presented. Although you could not verbally describe the emotion in the eye behavior of the other person, you knew it when you saw it. Often group members send emotional feeling through their eye behavior without even realizing it.

Communicating the Nature of Interpersonal Relationships between Group Members.   Have you ever been in a group where two of the members were a dating couple? You were probably able to tell that they were a couple just by observing their eye behavior. Have you ever been in a group where two of the members disliked each other? Again, by observing their lack of eye contact, you were probably able to determine the nature of their interpersonal relationship. We generally look more at people we like or who agree with us and less at people we don't like or who disagree with us (Farabee et al., 1993). Consequently, in group settings we can be expected to turn to our friends for potential reinforcement and avoid our enemies for potential punishment.

You may be wondering what the optimum length of a gaze is in small group communication. Usually a "normal" gaze lasts no more than ten seconds, although women typically gaze more than men, both while talking and while silent (Hall, 1984).

Most often a group member will look at the listener or listeners when beginning to speak and then will look away. This technique may be termed the "look and look away" technique of eye behavior in interpersonal communication. The speaker probably looks away so that he or she won't be distracted or lose the train of thought. Then the group member will briefly gaze at the listener at the ends of phrases to see if the listener understands and/or agrees. After once again looking away, the speaker will signal the end of the speech with a rather long look. In other words, a speaker looks at the listener, looks away to lessen distraction, looks back at the listener to seek feedback, looks away, and then looks back at the listener to signal the end of the speech.

Differences in the "look and look away" technique may occur in your small groups as a result of both individual and cultural variations. Some cultures such as the South Americans, Greeks, and Arabs, for example, have longer or more intense eye contact as evidence of sincerity and interest (Grumet, 1999) while some Native Americans tend to avoid direct eye contact during conversation (Martin and Nakayama, 2000). Even within the American culture there are individuals who do not follow the "look and look away" technique. Until group members recognize that this is the style of the particular individual, they may display signs of nervous tension. When the new members become accustomed to this individual's steady gaze, they often suggest that he or she simply seems to be more interested in them than most other people. The important thing to remember is that these differences are individual and cultural and may have little direct relationship to invitation for interaction, liking or disliking, believability, or the task.

Principles
1. As related to one's participation in small group interaction, Knapp explains that eye contact can
   a. Regulate the flow of communication between group members.
   b. Aid in monitoring the feedback of group members to the speaker.

     c. Serve as a method of displaying and expressing one's emotions.

     d. Indicate the nature of the interpersonal relationships that exist within the group.

2. When a group member employs the "look and look away" technique of eye behavior in interpersonal communication, he or she looks back at the listener to seek feedback, looks away, and then looks back at the listener to signal the end of the speech.

3. Violation of the "look and look away" technique occurs in small groups as a result of both individual and cultural differences.

Body Movements

Our society seems to depend a great deal on body movements as a form of communication. A student's raised hand, the traffic officer's wave, and a teacher's nod, for example, communicate as clearly as words. In addition, the performance of ordinary activities such as walking into a room, shaking hands with someone, and sitting in a chair communicates messages. Whenever one person visually observes another, there is a continuous flow of information about that person.

Body movements are important for regulating the flow of conversation in small groups. The term *requesting* refers to a nonverbal behavior that serves to tell other members of the group that you want to speak (Wiemann and Knapp, 1999). Suppose, for example, that you are involved in a heated discussion concerning the building of a new basketball complex. You have some statistics indicating that a strong basketball program would increase all the programs at the university. But no one will recognize you and give you the opportunity to speak. You're sitting on the edge of your chair, visually following the verbal interactions of the other members and waving your hand in order to attract attention. This behavior eventually attracts the attention of the other members, and you are given the opportunity to speak. Without ever saying a word, you nonverbally requested the floor.

Body movements also communicate affective states (e.g., moods or emotions). Suppose you are discussing a topic that makes you feel nervous or uptight because of relevance to your personal life. Body movements such as swinging your leg, tapping your fingers, or playing with your hair might indicate to the other group members that you are uncomfortable with the discussion. If a group member's movements suggest nervousness or tension, you may decide to back off until that person is more comfortable. Body movements serve as cues that help you respond in interpersonal communication settings.

Both researchers (e.g., Birdwhistell, 1970) and popular writers (e.g., Fast, 1970) have emphasized the variability in meaning of body movement. Factors that appear to influence the meaning of a movement include (1) the context in which the movement occurs and (2) individual learning.

The meaning of a movement primarily seems to depend on the context in which the movement occurs. Best known for his research in the area of body movement, Birdwhistell (1970) notes that a body movement may mean nothing at all in one context and yet may be extremely significant in another context. For example, parents who observe their son sticking out his tongue at himself in the mirror will probably smile and attach little significance to the event. However, if the child sticks out his tongue at a sibling after a quarrel, the movement probably communicates a significant message!

The meaning of a particular movement also may vary according to the differing contexts of discussions. For example, a group member who leans backward and away from the group in an informal group discussion held outdoors may be perceived to be relaxed. However, a similar movement in the formal context of a conference room may indicate lack of involvement, boredom, or even a sense of superiority. Therefore, you should exercise caution in applying broad generalizations of meaning to all group members in all situations.

The meaning of a movement also seems to depend on learning or the meaning that we have come to associate with a particular movement. The thumbs-up gesture (similar to the hitchhiker's gesture) usually means "good" or "O.K." in the United States but in the Middle East it is an obscene gesture. Similarly, when former President Nixon visited a Latin American country, he signaled "A-OK" with his hand to symbolize good faith. Unfortunately, he failed to realize that in that particular country, the "A-OK" gesture stands for an obscene act. Although learning differences are most prevalent in intercultural communication, they also exist in small group discussion. Group members should be aware of different meanings for movements in order to avoid potential misunderstandings.

Principles
1. Through their body movements, group members can send feedback, communicate affective states (e.g., moods or emotions), and request permission to speak.
2. Individual learning and the context in which a movement occurs appear to influence the meaning of a movement. Therefore, you should exercise caution in applying generalizations of meaning to all people in all situations.

Touching

Children learn through touching and through being touched. In fact, touch is one of the child's primary means of communicating with the environment. When children cry, they receive consolation by stroking and patting. When they explore the world, they touch and perhaps taste whatever is within their grasp.

As children grow, touching is reduced. The mother may substitute a verbal "You're all right" for a comforting pat. The response "Don't touch that," instead of a hand slap as a child reaches for an object, increases in frequency. In general, verbal language replaces much of tactile communication.

Group members also rely more on verbal language than on touch to communicate in small groups. You can imagine the confusion that would result if group members expressed agreement or disagreement through touch instead of through verbal language. Although touch is not a primary means of communication in small groups, group members may use touch as a means of communicating feelings such as consolation, encouragement, or emotional support. For example, a group member may place her hand on the shoulder of another group member while expressing consolation for a failed test. In addition, group members may use touch to convey liking or power (Heslin and Alper, 1983) as well as to gain compliance with a request (Nannberg and Hansen, 1994).

Because touch plays an extremely important role in interpersonal relationships, the potential effects of touch on group members should be examined. Have you ever sat next to a "chronic toucher"? Although this individual may have intended nothing more than casual friendship, you may have misinterpreted the friendly pat as an aggressive come-on. Noise may be created in the communication system when a group member misinterprets the intention of the touch. Although touch may be more effective than words in many ways, touching a group member at the wrong time may be as detrimental as any negative verbal comment.

Principles
1. Group members rely more on verbal language than touch to communicate in small groups.
2. Group members may communicate feelings such as consolation, encouragement, emotional support, or happiness through touch.
3. Group members may use touch to convey liking or power as well as to gain compliance with a request.
4. Touching a group member at the wrong time may be as detrimental as any negative verbal comment.

Physical Appearance

It is Saturday night, and a young man is getting ready for his first date with the recent Miss Homecoming. He chooses a blue, lightly starched oxford shirt to go with his khaki slacks, fresh from the cleaners. He carefully polishes his loafers and places a paisley handkerchief in the pocket of his navy blue blazer. After a long shower and a lathered shave, he dresses and finishes with a careful splash of aftershave. The next Monday, the young man is joining his intramural rugby team for practice. He throws cut-off sweats over his boxers and grabs a ragged t-shirt. He ties a bandanna around his hair and foregoes a shower or shave. He wears his oldest running shoes and socks that are not quite matches.

Our fictitious young man illustrates the idea that most individuals manipulate their physical appearance in an attempt to communicate messages to other individuals. For example, the young man may be trying to send a message such as, "I am worthy of escorting Miss Homecoming" to his date to "Time for serious rugby playing" to his teammates. However, has communication occurred? In other words, do people look at an individual's physical appearance and make inferences or judgments about that individual?

Clothing and Stereotypes

Suppose you are attending a committee meeting to discuss the university's policy on serving alcohol at university functions. You are the first to arrive, and you observe the other group members walk into the room. The first person to enter is a long-haired man in a tie-dyed shirt wearing a peace medallion. The second person to arrive is a female wearing faded blue jeans with a halter top and a rose tattoo on her shoulder. The third person is a blond haired female in casual clothes. The fourth person is an ensign in his Navy ROTC uniform, wearing aviator sunglasses. As each person enters the room, you size them up and make inferences about them as individuals and as members of the group. You probably inferred that the first two individuals were more "liberal" and the second two individuals were more "conservative." But did you also wonder which individuals would have more status or greater credibility or persuasiveness?

Research has attempted to answer questions like these about the effect of clothing on interpersonal communication. Some investigators have found a relationship between conventionality of dress style and conservatism of political beliefs (Bryant, 1975; Daley and Cooper, 1972). Other authorities have noted that attractive, well-dressed people have more credibility than individuals who are perceived to be less attractive (Napier and Gershenfeld, 1999). Clothing may even have a persuasive value that influences the behavior of others. Because we rely less on the appearance of group members as we gain information about them, however, you may wish to read the following paragraphs before investing in a new wardrobe!

Just as clothing may affect interpersonal perceptions, so also do artifacts. *Artifacts* are objects with which people adorn themselves and include, for example, wedding rings, perfume, tattoos, sunglasses, and earrings. All of these objects can provide information about group members.

Impressions quickly formed from physical appearance or from artifacts are frequently termed *stereotypes*. You have probably been taught that stereotypes are harmful, and this is true when the stereotypes are inaccurate. For example, suppose you are a member of a public relations club at your university. One of the new members comes to the first meeting dressed in a flannel shirt and faded jeans. Would you assume that you have little in common with this individual? Would you wonder why someone dressed like that had joined the club? As group members become acquainted, however, you learn that this individual is a volunteer firefighter and had just returned from a run. Under these circumstances, you might be inclined to reexamine your initial appraisal of the person. One potential negative consequence of inaccurate assessments of group members is that the group may waste much time in polite conversation before discovering that there was only a difference in style of dress and not a difference in opinion.

Research investigating the effect of clothing on interpersonal perception suggests that there is less reliance on clothing in forming impressions when people know each other (Knapp and Hall, 1997). For instance, suppose the individual in the previous example was a friend of yours. Although your friend usually dressed in casual slacks and sport shirts, he came to the meeting dressed in jeans and a flannel shirt. You probably would ask him where the fire had been. You would not assume that he had become a different person overnight. However, since we initially know nothing about strangers, we often use dress as a method of assigning accurate or inaccurate personality traits to them.

Personal Appearance and Projected Self-Concepts

While this discussion has focused primarily on physical appearance and its effect on the impressions you form of group members, you should not overlook the effect of your own personal appearance on your self-image. How you feel about the way you look can directly affect your behavior in communication situations (Dubler and Gurel, 1984). If you feel you look attractive, you are probably more confident and may participate more often in your group's discussion. If you spilled mustard on your shirt at lunch, you may feel self-conscious and be less motivated to interact with the group. This self-image (confidence versus insecurity) may affect communicative interactions with other group members. Thus, physical appearance may affect small group behavior in two ways: through reactions to impressions formed of group members, and through actions resulting from a group member's self-image.

Principles
1. Individuals manipulate their appearance to achieve an effect.
2. Group members make inferences about other members based on physical appearance.
3. Impressions quickly formed from physical appearance or details of clothing are termed *stereotypes.*
4. Stereotypes are harmful when they are inaccurate.

5. The amount of information you have from observation of a group member's behavior or from prior knowledge of the group member tends to affect the impression you form based on physical appearance.
6. Your physical appearance may affect your self-image, and your self-image may affect your interaction with group members.

Vocal Behavior

Imagine a small group discussion about an emotional topic. One female is particularly ego-involved with the topic. She responds to a challenge in a high, squeaky voice: "I am not upset." However, you realize that she *is* upset and suggest that the group take a short coffee break. Perhaps without realizing the contradiction between the verbal and vocal message, you relied on the vocal message as an indication of *true* feeling. In addition, you have probably noticed that your vocal messages sometimes contradict your verbal messages.

Vocal Contradictions

The contradiction between verbal and vocal messages may be intentional or unintentional. The previous example illustrates unintentional contradictions. Unintentional contradictions also may occur in the group situation when you are angry but the group context dictates that you speak cordially. You may be able to fake a polite verbal message, but you may slip and let your anger show through in your vocal qualities. One type of intentional contradiction between the verbal and vocal messages is sarcasm. For example, you may say "This group is really motivated" but mean that the group lacks motivation. If the other group members perceive that the meaning is in the way you say the words rather than in the words themselves, you have transmitted information about yourself (e.g., you are angry, or you may be a sarcastic individual) as well as about your observation.

Even when you do not consciously try to manipulate your voice, you transmit information about yourself. Group members estimate the occupations, sociability, intelligence, level of education, and many other qualities from the vocal characteristics of other group members. For example, you may recall someone making inferences about a man who had a high, effeminate voice or about a woman who had a deep, masculine voice. Perhaps unconsciously, group members form impressions of people based on their vocal qualities, and, right or wrong, we relate to these people as if the impressions were accurate.

Vocal Qualities

Voice qualities, or paralanguage, like other forms of nonverbal behavior, often transmit as much meaning as the words that are spoken. Research has indicated that through differences in rate and the use of pauses and pitch, the voice conveys emotions, such as contempt, anger, fear, grief, and indifference. For example, you may have recognized that a group member was angry or afraid by his or her faster rate of speech, shorter comments, and more frequent pauses or use of "uh" and "um." An increase in the number or length of pauses in a group member's speech may indicate indecision, tension, or resistance. If a person is indecisive, for example, you probably would not want to push him or her into making a decision on a critical issue. By perceiving and being sensitive to vocal qualities, you may be able to guide your responses constructively to avoid potential communication problems.

A word of caution is in order, however. When you make inferences about group members based on their vocal qualities, you should be aware that the vocal expressions vary from individual to individual in the group. For example, within the broad concept of "anxiety" there are wide individual differences. In your group discussions you have probably observed that some anxious members talk slower and have a lot of silent pauses and/or nonfluencies, whereas other anxious members do not. Thus, prior knowledge of the individual in situations other than the group context should affect your perception of the individual.

Silent Messages

You may think that avoiding verbal interactions is the answer to being misunderstood in your vocal messages. Not so, for silence can be as loud as words. Although silence generally is not valued in the United States, in other cultures, silence can be appropriate and highly meaningful (Martin and Nakayama, 2000). Since silence, as well as vocal behavior, can be misunderstood, the meaning of your silence should be made clear to other members of your group. Silence may communicate that you are listening attentively or that you are too angry to speak. Silence also can communicate that you are thinking or that you are not paying attention.

The vocal behavior you use in small groups probably will not be the only factor influencing your effectiveness in the discussion. However, it probably will influence the perceptions that the other members hold of you. Individuals respond to others in terms of perceptions rather than reality. For example, unless the members know that you talk loudly in all situations, they may think that you are upset or aggressive when they hear you speak loudly. Whether or not you are actually aggressive is less important than the fact that the other members perceive you as aggressive. Vocal behavior is only a part of the total behavior of an individual and, therefore, interacts with other behaviors to influence the responses of other individuals. Remember that individuals as well as groups are open systems with many interacting elements.

Principles
1. When your vocal message contradicts your verbal message, the contradiction may be intentional or unintentional.

2. Group members may infer occupation, sociability, intelligence, and other qualities from a group member's vocal qualities.
3. Group members may infer emotions such as contempt, anger, fear, grief, and indifference from differences in rate, pauses, and pitch.
4. Silence also communicates messages.
5. Individual differences in vocal expression vary widely.

Territory and Personal Space

Have you ever had someone take "your" parking place, sit in "your" seat in class, or put his or her books on "your" desk? What was your reaction? Obviously, you cannot physically move someone else's car (unless the keys are in it). However, you may ask an individual to change his or her seat, or you may move someone else's books.

This type of aggressive behavior is frequently used to respond to an invasion of one's "territory." The term *territory* may be thought of as a given area over which ownership is felt. Generally, an individual feels compelled to defend the area against those who may invade it. Ownership may be felt over a large area, such as a home, or over a small area, such as a favorite chair.

You should be aware that group members also may "claim" territory. For example, a group member may think that a certain chair or position at the conference table is his or hers. If you occupy that chair, the person might ask you to move. Or, initially repressing aggressive feelings, the group member may display aggression in the discussion although he or she ordinarily is not an aggressive individual. Group members who notice and try to cope with the aggressive behavior may be totally unaware of the precipitating cause.

Group members also may claim geographical locations such as offices, homes, and dorm rooms as territory. There is some evidence that the territorial meeting place for a group discussion may affect the group. Just as many athletic teams experience a "home court" advantage, so also may a group member who hosts the group meeting exert more influence over the group. Taylor and Lanni (1981) found this "resident advantage" to occur even if the hosting member is not predisposed to being a dominant or persuasive person and even if outnumbered by his or her guests. Thus, you should also include the influence of territory in your small group systems analysis.

The concept of personal space differs slightly from the concept of territory. Whereas territory may be thought of as a given area over which ownership is felt, personal space may be thought of as a "bubble of air" surrounding the individual that expands and contracts according to certain variables. (These variables will be discussed later in this section.) Although unwelcomed "invasion" of territory may result in aggression, an intrusion into personal space usually leads to withdrawal. For example, you may recall a group member who moved his or her chair too close to yours. You probably remember that your reaction was subtle rather than aggressive—

perhaps tapping a pencil, swinging a crossed leg, or in some cases moving your chair away from the "invader." You may have responded to the invasion of personal space by withdrawing from the discussion. You may have become preoccupied with an anxious feeling and lost interest in the discussion even if you could not perceive the cause of your anxiety. On the other hand, you can probably recall a similar instance in which a group member moved his or her chair too close to yours but you didn't feel threatened.

Several variables appear to affect how comfortable you are with the conversational distance at which another individual stands or sits. Four of these variables (Knapp and Hall, 1997) are *sex of the interactants, nature of the interpersonal relationship, topic or task,* and *setting for the interaction.*

Sex of the Interactants. You have probably noticed that in our society female group members sit closer to other females than to male group members (where group members know one another slightly). In a group discussion in which all group members are females, the members will tend to sit closer together than if there were both males and females in the group. Because males tend to interact at greater distance than females, an all-male discussion group will probably have greater physical distance between individual members.

Nature of the Interpersonal Relationship. You have probably noticed that there usually is greater physical distance between group members who do not know one another or who dislike one another. If unfriendly group members are forced to sit together, the individuals may lean further backward or face in the direction away from one another in an attempt to put as much space between them as possible. As group members become acquainted and friendlier, however, they tend to sit closer together.

Topic or Task. When group members are discussing impersonal topics, there is usually greater distance between group members. Individuals discussing intimate topics usually stand or sit closer together. Suppose that two groups who knew each other equally well were formed. One group was given an impersonal topic. It seems logical that you would be able to determine which group was discussing the intimate topic by observing how close together the chairs were in each group. However, remember that the sex of the interactants and whether or not they know or like one another interact with this variable. For example, a group composed of males who did not know one another probably would not sit as close together as a group of females who knew one another, regardless of the intimacy of the topic.

Setting for the Interaction. The comfortable distance between individuals also seems to vary from situation to situation. If you were to observe one individual in all the groups to which he or she belongs, you would probably notice that the individual allowed group members to stand or sit closer in some situations than in others. For example, a group member might allow group members to sit closer if an informal meeting were held outside under a large shade tree. On the other hand, a group member might keep other group members at a greater distance if the group meeting were held around a conference table in an average-size room. Thus, the distance between individuals also varies from situation to situation.

The next time you are in a group situation, observe the distance between group members. You may even observe variables other than the ones mentioned here affecting the distance of interaction. Age, race, culture, personality, crowding, and mood of the interactants can also affect the distance at which people interact. In addition, the setting for the interaction has a direct effect on the amount of personal space an individual requires. In the next section, we will examine more closely the importance of the environment in relation to the small group setting.

Principles
1. Territory may be thought of as a given area over which ownership is felt. Invasion of territory may result in aggressive behavior.
2. Personal space may be thought of as an expanding and contracting bubble of air that surrounds you. Invasion of personal space may result in withdrawal.
3. There are at least four variables that affect how comfortable you are with the distance at which another individual stands or sits.
   a. Sex of the interactants. In a group in which males and females know one another slightly, females tend to sit closer to females than to males.
   b. Nature of the interpersonal relationship. Group members generally sit closer to group members whom they like.
   c. Topic or task. Group members generally sit closer when they discuss intimate topics.
   d. Setting for the interaction. Group members generally allow group members to sit closer in certain situations.
4. The comfortable distance between group members varies from individual to individual.

Environmental Variables Affecting Group Discussion

It's obvious from systems analysis that we do not interact in a vacuum. Our environment affects how we think and behave. Some environments encourage us to interact, such as the recreation room in the student union building. Similarly, our small group interactions are affected by our environment. This section will discuss the effects of three environmental variables: group size, attractiveness of the surroundings, and physical arrangement of the group members.

Group Size

You probably have heard sayings like "two heads are better than one" and "the bigger, the better." Sayings like these might influence us to think that participating in large groups is better than participating in small groups. When resources for problem solving are considered, large groups do have the potential for giving a greater number of suggestions for solutions to the group problem. However, large groups often encounter problems because of less available interaction time per member and difficulty in reaching consensus.

Have you noticed that it is easier to become acquainted and to participate in smaller groups than in larger groups? It seems obvious that as group size increases, the time available for each member to participate decreases. In large groups, the forceful group members may monopolize the discussion, while the less confident members may feel intimidated and unable to speak. As a result, the morale of the less confident members often declines. Lack of motivation or involvement and even resignations from the group are potential problems that may result from the decline in morale.

In addition to noting less available interaction time per member in large groups, you also may have noted that it tends to be more difficult to reach consensus in large groups. Although large groups may have greater resources because they have more members, reaching consensus is often more difficult because there are more people expressing divergent opinions. Providing clear objective criteria for judgment (see Chapter Six) may lessen this difficulty in both large and small groups.

The terms *large group* and *small group* have been used throughout this discussion of group size. You may be wondering just what is the optimum size for a small group. Although there is no clear agreement on this issue, many authorities think that five (Napier and Gershenfeld, 1999) to seven members is the optimum size for small groups. A group of five, however, probably would not be the optimum size for a class in small group communication. It seems that the group task and goals affect the optimum size in a small group.

To select the appropriate size for a given problem, Thelen (1949) suggested "the principle of least group size." The group should be just large enough to include individuals with all the relevant skills necessary to solve the problem, yet small enough to provide opportunities for individual participation.

Principles
1. Small group communication can be affected by the environment in which the interaction occurs.
2. As group size increases, the time available for each member to participate orally decreases.
3. Large groups usually are an advantage in the information-giving phase of problem solving but a potential disadvantage when consensus must be reached.

4. The optimum size for a small group is a group that is just large enough to include individuals with all the relevant skills necessary to solve the problem and yet small enough to provide opportunities for individual participation. This is known as "the principle of least group size."

Attractiveness of the Surroundings

Another important environmental variable small groups should consider is the physical comfort and attractiveness of the surroundings. Two now classic research studies conducted by Maslow and Mintz (1956) and Mintz (1956) investigated the influence of interior decoration on human responses. The researchers selected three rooms for study—an "ugly" room (designed to give the impression of a janitor's storeroom), a "beautiful" room (with carpet, drapes, etc.), and an "average" room (a professor's office). Both experimenters and subjects attempted to avoid the ugly room. The ugly room was variously described as producing fatigue, headache, irritability, and hostility. The beautiful room, however, produced feelings of pleasure, comfort, enjoyment, importance, and desire to continue the activity. Similarly, the room in which small group discussions are held may affect the comfort and motivation of the group members.

Most frequently the leader or someone assigned by the leader assumes responsibility for the environmental conditions surrounding the discussion. If you are the leader, you should choose a room with pleasant surroundings whenever possible. Comfortable chairs and pleasant interior decoration may lessen the fatigue that frequently accompanies long tasks and may increase the desire to continue the discussion.

You may even choose to promote a more "at ease" state by substituting an arrangement of arm chairs for the conference table. Seating arrangements for small groups are discussed in the next session.

Principles
1. The attractiveness of a group's surroundings may affect the comfort and motivation of the group members.
2. The leader, or someone assigned by the leader, usually assumes responsibility for the environmental conditions surrounding the group.

Physical Arrangement

Suppose you have enrolled in a seminar in small group theory and research. As you enter the room you see a long rectangular conference table with twelve chairs. Where would you sit? At the head position? At a corner opposite the head position?

According to researchers, seating position affects the flow of communication. Classic experimental studies have suggested, for example, that individuals tend to interact more frequently with individuals seated on either side of them

(Steinzor, 1950). Additional research appears to indicate that individuals who sit at the corners of a rectangular table tend to contribute the least to the discussion, while the central and head positions generally are dominant (Reiss and Rosenfield, 1980). It is not clear whether the position determines the amount of participation or whether members who normally contribute a certain amount select the position that seems to suit them best. At any rate, the seating position you occupy may affect your communication with other group members.

There is some evidence to suggest that where you choose to sit is not accidental. Several variables may affect your choice of seating position, including leadership and introversion–extroversion.

Leadership.   Have you wondered why a leader will generally select a seat at the head of a rectangular table? Is it adherence to a cultural norm of dominance through height (e.g., a king ruling from his throne or a minister preaching from the pulpit)? Or does the head of the table simply provide the leader with greater visibility of the group? Research suggests that the ability to both see and be seen predicts participation (Baker, 1984) and that the flow of communication often predicts leadership emergence (Howells and Becker, 1962). Other research (Strodtbeck and Hook, 1961) indicates that those group members who just happen to sit at the head position are more often chosen as the leader. This information may be useful to you if you are a participant in a group that has not yet selected a leader.

Introversion–Extroversion.   Some evidence suggests that seating position relates to the personality variable of introversion–extroversion (Reiss and Rosenfeld, 1980; Patterson et al., 1979). Extroverts, for example, tend to sit opposite each other, while introverts generally choose positions that keep them more at a distance from others. Because individuals who withdraw from small group communication do not make a full contribution to the group, the group may not realize its potential.[1]

Knowledge of the effects of seating arrangement on interaction can be beneficial to the group member participating in a small group discussion. For example, if the leader knows two group members are talking, he or she may choose to minimize interruptions of the discussion by having them occupy seats at some distance from each other. Similarly, the leader may want to encourage group members who are shy by placing them toward the center instead of at the corners of a rectangular table. Or, for example, if the leader knows of potentially hostile group members, then he or she may choose to minimize this hostility by physically separating the unfriendly group members. As you can see, careful consideration of environmental variables is very important in a systems analysis of your small group.

---

[1]Systematic desensitization has been found to help reduce withdrawal behaviors. McCroskey (1972) proposed a program for implementation of systematic desensitization for communication anxiety.

Principles
1. Seating arrangement and interaction are related; individuals tend to interact more frequently with people seated opposite them; individuals who sit at the corners of a rectangular table tend to contribute the least to the discussion.
2. Leadership and introversion–extroversion are two variables that tend to affect the seating position you choose.

Summary

This chapter focused on nonverbal communication as it relates to your participation in small groups. The first section discussed various physical behaviors as they relate to small groups. Group members rely on facial expression, eye contact, body movement, and touch to communicate messages about their own internal states and to make inferences about the internal states of other group members. Sensitivity to these physical behaviors may help you to avoid potential communication problems in small groups.

The second section discussed the idea that individuals manipulate their physical appearance in an attempt to communicate messages to other individuals. Group members observe an individual's physical appearance and form an impression. Inaccurate impressions present problems for group members.

The third section discussed vocal behavior. Group members make inferences about other members based on vocal qualities. Sometimes there is a contradiction between verbal and vocal messages. Group members also rely on these contradictions to form impressions.

The fourth section examined the role of space in the small group context. When a group member invades your territory, you may react aggressively. However, if a group member were to invade your personal space, you would probably retreat. Variables were identified that appear to affect comfortable interaction distance.

The final section of the chapter provided you with information about the importance of the environment. Size of the group, attractiveness of the surroundings, and the physical arrangement of the group members affect interaction. Generally the leader or someone assigned by the leader assumes responsibility for environmental conditions surrounding the discussion.

The purpose of this chapter has been to increase your awareness of nonverbal communication, especially in small groups, rather than to present an overview of the field.[2] It seems obvious that the total nonverbal behavior

---

[2]Several books that take different approaches to the study of nonverbal communication are available for further study. Birdwhistell (1970) takes a more systematic approach, whereas Fast (1970) is a popular bestseller. One of the most recent books that contains a summarization and explanation of research findings is Knapp and Hall (1997).

of the group member (in part culturally learned) affects other members' responses to any one behavior. Thus, this chapter is only an appetizer for the study of the field of nonverbal communication.

Ideas for Discussion

1. What is the role and significance of nonverbal communication in small group communication?

2. What are possible explanations for the behavior of
   a. an overtalkative group member?
   b. a silent group member?
   c. an aggressive group member?
   d. a group member who laughs even when something funny has not been said?

3. What are several ways that you express your boredom with a group discussion through physical and vocal behaviors?

4. How do you know when someone is interested in talking with you if he or she does not verbalize an interest?

5. What nonverbal factors have you noticed in people of different cultures that might cause problems in group discussions with people of your culture?

6. What personality factors would you assign to
   a. an obese group member?
   b. an athletic and muscular group member?
   c. a thin group member?

   How might each of these persons react during a tense moment in a group discussion?

7. What nonverbal cues do you rely on to tell whether a group member is lying?

8. What are other environmental variables that might affect the group discussion?

9. Would total darkness be beneficial or detrimental to group discussions? Under what conditions, if any, might it be beneficial?

Suggested Projects and Activities

1. Without talking, conduct a five-minute small group meeting about the group's social climate. After the time is up, conduct a follow-up discussion to determine the accuracy of messages received during the no-talking period. Did the group understand more or less than they would have predicted in such a restricted communication setting? What kinds of messages were most easily transmitted and received during the no-talk period? What kinds of messages were hardest to communicate?

2. In a group of from five to seven members, prepare a discussion to be presented in front of the rest of the class in which the members of the group deliberately

attempt nonverbally to mask their true feelings and role-play different ones. After the discussion, ask the class members who were observing if they could detect any masking behavior in the group. Discuss the relative success of the group's attempt at masking and role playing.

3. In groups of three to four, conduct a study in a local restaurant. Order something to eat and watch for the effect of clothing on the service that customers receive (e.g., liberals—jeans, sandals, T-shirts—versus conservatives—coats, ties, dresses, etc.). Observe carefully the facial expression of the waiter or waitress, the verbal behavior, and the apparent attitude toward the customers. On the basis of this study, what conclusions can you draw about the effect of clothing on attitudes of waiters and waitresses and the consequent service you obtain?

4. Have one member sit on the floor in the middle of the group while the rest of the group sits on regular chairs and has a group discussion. Then have the group sit on the floor around a group member who is sitting on a chair and continue the discussion. What effects, if any, did the different heights of members in relation to the rest of the group have on the interactions and content of the discussion?

References

Baker, P. M. Seeing is behaving: visibility and participation in small groups. *Environment and behavior,* 1984, *16,* 159–184.

Birdwhistell, R. L. *Kinesics and context.* Philadelphia: University of Philadelphia Press, 1970.

Bryant, N. Petitioning: dress congruence versus belief congruence. *Journal of applied social psychology,* 1975, *5,* 149–155.

Burgoon, J. K., D. A. Coker, and R. A. Coker. Communicative effects of gaze aversion behavior: a test of two contrasting explanations. *Human communication research,* 1986, *12,* 495–524.

Daley, J. M., and J. Cooper. The "Clean for Gene" phenomenon: the effects of students' appearance on political campaigning. *Journal of applied social psychology,* 1972, *1,* 24–33.

Dubler, M. L. J., and L. M. Gurel. Depression: relationships to clothing and appearance self-concept. *Home economics research journal,* 1984, *13,* 21–26.

Ekman, P., ed. *Emotion in the human face,* 2nd ed. Cambridge, England: Cambridge University Press, 1982.

Ekman, P., and W. V. Friesen. A new pan-cultural facial expresssion of emotion. *Motivation and emotion,* 1986, *10,* 159–168.

Farabee, D. J., M. L. Holcom, S. L. Ramsey, and S. G. Cole. Social anxiety and speaker gaze in a persuasive atmosphere. *Journal of research in personality,* 1993, *27,* 365–376.

Fast, J. *Body language.* New York: M. Evans, 1970.

Forgas, J. P., K. V. O'Connor, and S. L. Morris. Smile and punishment: the effects of facial expression on responsibility attribution by groups and individuals. *Personality and social psychology bulletin,* 1983, *9,* 587–596.

Grumet, G. W. Eye contact: the core of interpersonal relatedness. In L. K. Guerrero, J. A. DeVito, and M. L. Hecht, eds. *The nonverbal communication reader,* 2nd ed. Prospect Heights, IL: Waveland Press, 1999.

Hall, J. A. *Nonverbal sex differences: communicator accuracy and expressive style.* Baltimore: Johns Hopkins University Press, 1984.

Heslin, R., and T. Alper. Touch: a bonding gesture. In J. M. Wiemann and R. P. Harrison, eds. *Nonverbal interaction.* Beverly Hills: Sage, 1983.

Howells, L. T., and S. W. Becker. Seating arrangement and leadership emergence. *Journal of abnormal and social psychology,* 1962, *64,* 148–150.

Kalma, A. Gazing in triads: a powerful signal in floor apportionment. *British journal of social psychology,* 1992, *31,* 21–39.

Knapp, M. L., and J. A. Hall. *Nonverbal communication in human interaction,* 4th ed. Fort Worth: Harcourt Brace Jovanovich, 1997.

Mabry, E. A. Development aspects of nonverbal behavior in small group settings. *Small group behavior,* 1989, *20,* 190–202.

Martin, J. N., and T. K. Nakayama. *Intercultural communication in contexts,* 2nd ed. Mountain View, CA: Mayfield, 2000.

Maslow, A. H., and N. L. Mintz. Effect of aesthetic surroundings: I. Initial effects of three aesthetic conditions upon perceiving "energy" and "well-being" in faces. *Journal of psychology,* 1956, *41,* 247–254.

McCroskey, J. C. The implementation of a large-scale program of systematic desensitization for communication apprehension. *The speech teacher,* 1972, *21,* 255–264.

Mintz, N. L. Effects of aesthetic surrounding: II. Prolonged and repeated experience in a "beautiful" and "ugly" room. *Journal of psychology,* 1956, *41,* 459–466.

Nannberg, J. C., and C. H. Hansen. Post-compliance touch: an incentive for task performance. *Journal of social psychology,* 1994, *134,* 301–307.

Napier, R. W., and M. K. Gershenfeld. *Groups: theory and experience,* 6th ed. Boston: Houghton Mifflin, 1999.

Patterson, M. L., C. E. Kelley, B. A. Kondracki, and L. J. Wulf. Effects of seating arrangements on small group behavior. *Social psychology quarterly,* 1979, *42,* 180–185.

Purvis, J. A., J. M. Dabbs, Jr., and C. H. Hopper. The "opener": skilled user of facial expression and speech pattern. *Personality and social psychology bulletin,* 1984, *10,* 61–66.

Reiss, M., and P. Rosenfeld. Seating preferences as nonverbal communication: a self-presentational analysis. *Journal of applied communication research,* 1980, *8,* 22–30.

Rotter, N. G., and G. S. Rotter. Sex differences in the encoding and decoding of negative facial emotions. *Journal of nonverbal behavior,* 1988, *12,* 139–148.

Scherer, K. R., and P. Ekman, eds. *Approaches to emotion.* Hillsdale, N. J.: Erlbaum, 1984.

Stannors, R. F., D. M. Byrd, and R. Brabriel. The time it takes to identify facial expressions: effects of age, gender of subject, sex of sender, and type of expression. *Journal of nonverbal behavior,* 1985, *9,* 201–213.

Steinzor, B. The spatial factor in face to face discussion groups. *Journal of abnormal and social psychology,* 1950, *45,* 552–555.

Strodtbeck, F. L., and L. H. Hook. The social dimensions of a twelve-man jury table. *Sociometry,* 1961, *24,* 297–415.

Taylor, R. B., and J. C. Lanni. Territorial dominance: the influence of the resident advantage in triadic decision making. *Journal of personality and social psychology,* 1981, *41,* 909–915.

Thelen, H. A. Group dynamics in instruction: principle of least group size. *School review,* 1949, *56,* 139–148.

Wiemann, J. M., and M. L. Knapp. Turn-taking in conversations. In L. K. Guerrero, J. A. DeVito, and M. L. Hecht, *The nonverbal communication reader,* 2nd ed. Prospect Heights, IL: Waveland, 1999, 406–414.

Suggested Readings

Birdwhistell, R. L. *Kinesics and context.* Philadelphia: Philadelphia Press, 1970. In this classic book, the father of kinesics presents essays on body motion communication. The book includes methods of isolating behavior, approaching behavior, collecting data, and research.

Guerrero, L. K., J. A. DeVito, and M. L. Hecht. *The nonverbal communication reader,* 2nd ed. Prospect Heights, IL: Waveland, 1999. This book is a collection of classic and contemporary research. Some of the articles include: "Social and Emotional Messages of Smiling," "The Power of Silence in Communication, " "Communicating with Touch," and "Turn-Taking in Conversations."

Knapp, M. L., and J. A. Hall. *Nonverbal communication in human interaction,* 4th ed. Fort Worth, TX: Harcourt Brace, 1997. This book is an excellent introduction to the study of nonverbal communication. In addition to coverage of the major areas of nonverbal communication, this book provides a good review of the literature.

Rogers, E. M., and T. M. Steinfatt. *Intercultural communication.* Prospect Heights, IL: Waveland Press, 1999. Chapter 6, "Nonverbal Communication," provides an overview of selected types of nonverbal communication and provides many examples of cultural differences and opportunities for cultural misunderstandings.

Samovar, L. A., and R. E. Porter, eds. *Intercultural communication: A reader,* 9th ed. Belmont, CA: Wadsworth, 2000. The readings in Chapter 5, "Nonverbal Interaction: Action, Sound, and Silence," explore a number of key areas in nonverbal communication. Chapter 6, "Cultural Contexts: The Influence of the Setting," focuses primarily on cultural differences in organizational settings.

8

Leadership in Small Groups

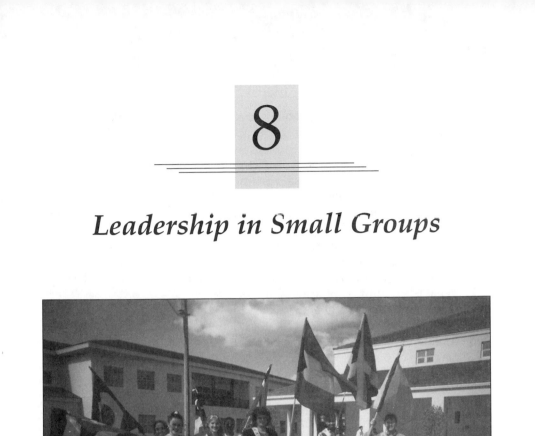

Study Questions _____

After reading this chapter, you should be able to answer the following questions completely and accurately:

1. What is the trait approach to defining leadership? What problems result from viewing leadership as traits?
2. What are three leadership styles?
3. What is the situational approach to defining leadership? What problems result from this approach?
4. What problems result from viewing leadership as an official position?
5. What is the leadership-functions approach to defining leadership?
6. What is the communication-competency approach to defining leadership?
7. What is a definition of leadership?
8. What is effective leadership?
9. What are task competencies?
10. Identify four task-related competencies and explain how differences across group situations relate to each one of the competencies.
11. What is procedural sensitivity?
12. What are relational competencies?
13. Identify three relational competencies and explain how differences across group situations relate to each one of the competencies.
14. What are nine suggestions for teambuilding?
15. What is self-monitoring?

Your favorite television program is interrupted one evening with an announcement. You hear the voice of the press secretary: "Ladies and gentlemen, the president of the United States." Most individuals would agree that the president is the recognized leader of our country. Consider the cabinet meetings, however. Does the president exert leadership, or does he merely preside over the cabinet meetings? Is he the only individual in the cabinet meeting to influence the group, or are there other individuals who also perform leadership functions? This chapter is intended to help you answer these questions. We will consider approaches to defining leadership, identify two types of communication competencies for effective leadership, and comment on the complexity of leadership in small groups and provide suggestions for teambuilding.

Approaches to Defining Leadership

When people read the term *leadership,* they tend to think of a single individual. The thought of a club president, a supervisor, or a professor may come to mind. An image may form of a person who has been elected or appointed to the task of assuming major responsibilities for the group's activities.

Before we propose our preferred definition of leadership, we would like to look at some previous approaches to the study of leadership.

Leadership Traits

The first serious attempt to understand leadership was the trait approach. The approach seems to be based on the notion that leaders are born and not made (the phrase "a natural, born leader" illustrates the point). Studies were conducted to identify traits or characteristics that leaders possess. The investigations have attempted to learn whether leaders are more popular, intelligent, aggressive, self-confident, enthusiastic, or physically attractive than those they lead. While such leadership qualities seem reasonable, the research studies have failed to achieve consistent results. Although many different physical and personality traits have been examined, few were found that could be used for *consistent* identification of leaders.

Leadership Styles

The styles approach to the study of leadership, like the traits approach, assumes that there is one person in the leadership position. This approach seeks to determine which of three styles of leadership is most effective: the democratic, the autocratic, or the laissez-faire.

Generally conceived to be a "guide" not a "controller," the democratic leader encourages group discussion, usually through the use of questions (e.g., "Are we ready to suggest criteria for solutions to the problem?"). Tasks tend to be determined by the group and divided according to individual abilities and preferences. Autocratic or authoritarian leaders, on the other hand, generally make decisions themselves and often give orders (e.g., "We will now begin listing our criteria."). Laissez-faire leaders tend to be the most difficult to analyze, because this style implies that the leader leads by not leading at all. Essentially, a laissez-faire leader performs leadership functions only when asked to do so by the group. In many cases, the group does not request the assistance, and it therefore becomes a "leaderless group."

Although most research shows a preference for the democratic style, studies have also indicated that no one leadership style is effective in all situations. Each of these three styles varies in effectiveness according to the type of group and the task. It seems obvious that in crisis situations (e.g., a hospital emergency room), a group might need a directive, authoritarian leader. It's probably just as obvious that people in community groups don't like to be given orders (e.g., "We're having a yard sale on Saturday. I want your things priced and at my house by 8:30 A.M. You have the noon-to-2:00 P.M. shift."). You probably can see that an analysis of leadership styles might be useful in identifying relationships (and problems) between group leaders and group members.

Situational Approach

The situational approach suggests that leadership is a function of the situation in which leaders find themselves. Different situations would require different types of leaders. Closely related to traits and styles, effective leadership would result from matching the situation with the "proper" person and personality style to lead the group. Because of the many different situations (e.g., task complexity, group size, power and status differences) as well as personality variables, it is impossible to account for every possible combination (Fisher, 1986). Even if all the potential situational variables could be identified, personal characteristics do seem to affect leadership as well.

Leadership Functions

The traits, styles, and situational approaches to the study of leadership assume that the person occupying the official position of power (i.e., the leader's office) is the leader and is, therefore, the person exerting leadership. Sometimes the occupant of the leader's office does in fact provide leadership for the group. At other times, however, someone other than the "official" leader provides leadership. As you know, the ability to lead is not necessarily magically granted to a person who assumes the role of leader (not all managers, for example, are effective supervisors). Rather than focusing on the abilities of a single individual, the functions approach examines leadership as a set of behaviors that may be performed by *any* group member.

The functions approach to the study of leadership emphasizes two types of behaviors that influence the group. The first set of behaviors helps groups accomplish their achievement goals (see Chapter Three). Examples include seeking and obtaining information from other members, summarizing key points, and reporting on progress toward the group goal. The second set of behaviors helps groups accomplish their maintenance goals. These behaviors include encouraging participation and relieving tension by arbitrating disputes. While both types of leadership functions are important for the success of a group, they may be performed by different group members. Fisher (1986, p. 202) notes that "leadership functions are not necessarily performed by a single person, not even a leader, throughout the history of a group interaction."

Communication-Competency Approach

One of the most recent approaches to the study of leadership is the communication-competency approach. The communication-competency approach is based on the assumption that leadership depends on communication skills (or competencies) that aid groups in adapting to situations (Barge, 1997). That is, leadership implies that in any given situation a group member is able to use communication skills to help the group reach a mutual understanding in order to overcome the barriers to goal achievement. Two types of communication competencies are required: task and relational.

Task competencies, the first type of communication competency, refer to the communication skills necessary to perform tasks and to manage group goals. For example, group members need to be able to analyze problems, generate criteria and solutions, and analyze the solutions in light of the criteria (see Chapter Six). Barge and Hirokawa (1989, p. 173) observe that "failure to be behaviorally skilled or competent in these areas will frustrate groups in fulfilling their tasks." The second type of communication competency is relational. *Relational competencies* refer to communication skills necessary for managing interpersonal relationships and group climate. Examples of relational competencies include balancing participation among group members and managing conflict.

The communication-competency approach further suggests that the situation or context affects which skills or competencies will be most effective in overcoming a problem. Because group situations evolve and change over the course of the discussion, an appropriate skill at one time in a group's development may be inappropriate at another time. This "adaptability" perspective is one of the important contributions of the communication-competency approach. Groups are dynamic, changing systems, and leadership skills that are effective in one situation may not be equally effective in another. Effective leadership involves the ability to respond to the everchanging nature of groups.

Definition of Leadership

Throughout this book, the importance of learning to communicate effectively in small groups has been emphasized. Because effective communication is central to successful groups, the following definition of leadership is proposed. *Leadership refers to those communication skills that move a group toward its recognized goal and/or maintain the group in any given situation.*

This definition of leadership does not assume that only the person occupying the leader's office exerts leadership. Neither is the definition based on the premise that there are natural leaders (persons with specific traits that enable them to influence others) or specific styles of leadership that are effective across all group situations. In fact, viewing leadership as communication skills does not assume that only one person influences the members of a group. To the contrary, *all* members have the potential to contribute to the process by which groups seek and achieve goals as well as manage interpersonal relationships.

The previous definition of leadership also supports our view that groups are complex systems. Because group contexts and situations are ever changing, skills that are useful in one situation may not be the same as skills useful in another situation. *Effective leadership is that which best meets the needs of a group at a particular point in time.* Like other variables discussed in this book, leadership is a dynamic process and should be studied in terms of a systems approach to small group communication.

Principles
1. The trait approach to the study of leadership attempted to identify traits or characteristics that leaders possess. Few traits were found that could be used for consistent identification of leaders.
2. The styles approach to the study of leadership attempted to determine whether the democratic, the autocratic, or the laissez-faire leader was the most effective. The styles of leadership vary in effectiveness according to the type of group and the task.
3. The situational approach to the study of leadership suggests that leadership results from matching the person with the situation. Because of the many different situational and personality variables, it is impossible to account for every possible combination.
4. The functional approach to the study of leadership suggests that leadership is a set of behaviors that can be performed by any member of the group.
5. The communication-competency approach to the study of leadership is based on the assumption that leadership depends on communication skills that aid groups in adapting to situations. Two types of communication competencies are required: task and relational.
6. Leadership refers to those communication skills that move a group toward its recognized goal and/or maintain the group in any given situation. This definition assumes that any member of the group, not just the designated leader, has the potential to exert leadership. The definition also supports the view that leadership is a dynamic process.
7. Effective leadership is that which best meets the needs of a group at a particular point in time.

Leadership Competencies

Effective leadership depends on two types of communication skills: task competencies and relational competencies. *Task competencies* refer to the communication skills necessary to perform tasks and to manage group achievement goals (see Chapter Three). *Relational competencies* refer to communication skills necessary for managing interpersonal relationships and group climate (i.e., group maintenance goals). In this section of the chapter we will look at each of these areas.

Task Competencies

Although groups vary considerably in the way they reach decisions, most groups will be concerned with the following task-related activities (Hirokawa and Scheerhorn, 1986): (1) *analyzing the problem,* including an investigation of the causes and effects of the problem; (2) *establishing criteria or meeting objectives* that need to be satisfied by the solution; and (3) *evaluating* the positive and negative consequences associated with *the various solutions* that have been posed by the group members. Barge and Hirokawa (1989) add (4) *establishing operating procedures.* Most of these task competencies involve the ability to think critically.

Analyzing the Problem. As groups explore problems and examine the causes and effects of those problems, they establish an information base. Sometimes this information is based on first-hand experience, while at other times group members report information from outside sources (see Chapter Six for sources of information). Gouran (1982, p. 92) observes, "Whether deliberately or accidentally distorted, inaccurate information increases the probability that a group will make a poor or ineffective decision." Therefore, the ability to explore the problem by analyzing that information is an important communication competency.

How is information analyzed? Because group situations vary, there is no one answer to this question. However, determining whether there is sufficient relevant information and analyzing the validity of the information is a good place to begin. First, is there enough relevant information? Suppose your group is analyzing problems encountered by students who commute daily at least fifty miles to campus. One group member has reported the results of a survey taken in a history class. Another member shares the results of an interview with the dean of Arts and Sciences. Has sufficient information been presented? Probably not. How will you know when sufficient information has been shared? Because of problem complexity, availability of sources, and many other situational variables, that question is difficult to answer. Nevertheless, the potential for faulty group decisions is greater if groups do not analyze sufficient information. The more relevant and valid the information, the greater the probability that effective decisions will be made.

Second, when analyzing information, it is also important to consider the validity of the information. Is the source potentially biased or unreliable? Evaluating the information in light of what the source "has going" with the issue, or stands to gain from the position taken, is important. While few people are free of vested interests, it is important to evaluate that information in light of those vested interests. Considering potential bias in a source is important to effective problem solving, but such an analysis is often difficult for group members. The difficulty may rest in part with human nature. Most individuals tend to accept information, regardless of its validity, if it supports a preferred idea or a favored position or decision. However, be careful of hastily rejecting information.

As group members analyze the problem, presenting and testing the validity of information, relationships are often established between "pieces" of information and/or the issues being discussed by the group. It is important to correctly identify the cause(s) of the problem. If the cause is not correctly identified, the solution may not solve the problem. Let's return to the hypothetical group that is exploring the problems of nontraditional female students. While discussing the causes of the problem, one group member observes that enrollment of nontraditional students at the university increased since a leading discount retailer opened its doors in the community. A causal relationship has been established: The opening of a discount store caused an increase in student enrollment. It seems illogical, doesn't it? Before you summarily dismiss the point, however, you need more information. Suppose the store's personnel department will hire employees with a high school diploma but requires those employees to be making reasonable progress toward an associate's degree. Remember, important communication skills include thinking through causal relationships in addition to seeking sufficient, relevant, and valid information.[1]

Establishing Criteria and Meeting Objectives.   Another communication competency involves setting objectives that the group wants to meet with its solution (see p. 105). The group can rely on information made from outside sources as well as on their own opinions and first-hand observations. Group members frequently rely on this information to stimulate their thinking and to get ideas for criteria. What criteria or objectives should the group establish? Again, because of situational differences, it is impossible to identify objectives or criteria appropriate for all groups and all problems. Objectives depend to a large degree on values—possibilities that group members want to see realized or want to avoid.

Suppose a group is formed to study crisis care in the emergency room of a large teaching hospital in a major metropolitan area. The area has a large homeless population, and the rate of violent crime is high. Although the hospital has been subsidized by the county, it is currently operating "in the red." Many complaints have been received about poor care, and the death rate is higher than the national average. The group was formed in an attempt to represent the divergent viewpoints of the community as well as the hospital. Group members include the physician in charge of the emergency room, the charge nurse, the director of fire and rescue services, a county commissioner, and a local police officer. The group has agreed on only two objectives: (1) the solution should improve the quality of care, and (2) the solution should be one that the group has the power to implement. Other objectives that the group discussed include the following: (3) the solution should reduce the staff-patient ratio, (4) the solution should not require more money from the county, (5) the solution should not be a "quick fix" for a complex problem, and (6) the solution should quickly respond to the needs of the patients. Group members are having difficulty agreeing on other criteria because their

[1]See Chapter Six for additional information on evidence and reasoning.

values differ. The emergency room staff sees patient numbers as a primary issue. The county commissioner sees money as a major issue but doesn't want the county to have to provide the additional revenue.

What communication skills are appropriate in this situation? First, as in the previous example, a group member will be able to help the group set objectives that logically follow from an exploration of the problem. Second, a skilled group member will also be able to distinguish between these objectives or criteria and the solutions which will be proposed in the next step. Remember, all group members can potentially exert leadership if they are skilled in establishing criteria.

Evaluating the Solutions.   Another important communication competency involves the ability to evaluate alternative solutions in light of the positive and negative consequences associated with each one. Essentially, groups are looking for an alternative or solution that appears to have the most acceptable combination of criteria or objectives that were set forth in the previous step. Sometimes when groups evaluate solutions, members prematurely accept a solution. Critical thinking skills can help your group avoid this trap.

Suppose one member of our hypothetical group suggests that a solution to this problem is to direct the rescue squad to transport 20 percent of their patients to other hospitals. At first glance this solution might appear to meet most of the objectives in the previous step. Looking further, however, we see that some assumptions are being made. The group has assumed that (1) reducing the number of patients brought to the emergency room will improve the overall quality of care for those who are treated, (2) the group has the power to direct the rescue squad to transport to other hospitals, and (3) other hospitals will accept the patients. Some commonly held beliefs don't affect groups. Other beliefs, however, do potentially affect the group outcome and, therefore, should be considered.

What if invalid assumptions are made by group members? You have several choices, including questioning the assumption, explaining how the assumption is flawed, and persuading the group to dismiss it, or suggesting other reasonable assumptions. Because some members become defensive when their assumptions are questioned, the most effective choice will depend on the personalities and status of the group members as well as on other situational variables. However, thoroughly evaluating each solution in light of its positive and negative consequences does tend to have the long-term advantage of reducing power plays and polarization around preferred solutions. So, as you can see, the ability to evaluate solutions is another important task-related competency.

Establishing Operating Procedures.   A plan for conducting a group meeting is often referred to as an *agenda* (Seibold, 1992; Seibold and Krikorian, 1997.) Although the degree to which groups follow their agendas often varies from group to group, failure to follow any overall plan can increase the probability of faulty decision making. Therefore, having a procedural plan is important.[2]

Another task competency for leadership in this area is procedural sensitivity. Procedural sensitivity is the ability to know when and how to minimize the group's digressions from the agenda. The question "Where are we now?" often reminds the group of the procedures it agreed to follow. Sometimes, however, it is necessary to point out the procedural violation and the potential problem (Gouran, 1997). If the group skips criteria, for example, the group might be reminded that selecting a solution will be more difficult in the absence of objectives that the solution should satisfy.

Because some groups have a need to be flexible and "free-wheeling" among agenda items, situational analysis is important. An agenda should be planned for each meeting. However, knowing when to be adaptable and deviate from the agenda and knowing when to be firm are part of procedural sensitivity. A leader may have prepared an agenda yet still need to develop procedural sensitivity. Even if you are not the designated leader, you have the opportunity to exert leadership with this important communication skill.

Central to all task-related competencies is the ability to ask good questions. Because of differences among groups and contexts, pre-planned questions which anticipate relationships among the issues are of little value. An important communication skill is the ability to specify information wanted and/or request potential relationships among the issues *at the moment.*

Stewart and Cash (2000) have summarized some of the basic principles of effective questioning. First, use language that you and the other group members understand. Avoid ambiguity and vagueness. Second, avoid complex questions. Keep questions simple and easy to understand. Third, be on guard against words that may bias responses. Be sure that your questions do not lead other group members to perceive that you are looking for a particular answer. Fourth, be sure that respondents see the relevance of each question to the group's purpose. If there is a possibility that a question may appear irrelevant, explain your reason for asking it. Fifth, ask questions that relate to the information that group members might have. Stewart and Cash note that "Questions beyond the respondent's information may cause embarrassment or resentment." (p. 94) Resentments that might be created as a result of a put-down could have long-term effects for the group and should be avoided. Maintaining a positive, open, communication climate (see p. 56) while asking questions is important.

Principles
1. Task competencies refer to the communication skills necessary to perform tasks and to manage group goals.

---

[2]Procedural plans, or agendas, are discussed in Chapter Six and Eleven.

2. Most groups are concerned with the following task-related activities:
   a. Analyzing the problem, including an investigation of the causes and effects of the problem
   b. Establishing criteria or meeting objectives that need to be satisfied by the solution
   c. Evaluating the positive and negative consequences associated with the various solutions
   d. Establishing operating procedures
3. A group member who is skilled in these task-related competencies can provide leadership for the group. Any group member, not just the designated leader, may provide task-related leadership.
4. The ability to ask good questions is central to all task-related competencies.

Relational Competencies

Communication skills that help to manage interpersonal relationships and group climate are as important to leadership as task competencies. Relational competencies are necessary for the maintenance and continued existence of the group. Although there are many relational competencies, we will discuss the following three competencies in this section: (1) balancing participation, (2) other orientation, and (3) conflict management.

Balancing Participation. One fairly consistent finding in the research on social interaction is that some people talk more than others. A general tendency may exist to perceive the most talkative group member as contributing the most to the solution of the problem. This is not always true! One problem is that group members who dominate the discussion limit the opportunities for hesitant members to enter the discussion. High contributors may also be so aggressive that they alienate members who contribute less frequently.

It would be nice if all group members were sufficiently self-disciplined that actions to balance participation were not necessary. Unfortunately, not all group members are self-disciplined. There are many alternative ways to assist in balancing participation, but a preferred technique is to visually ignore the talkative member. Most socially perceptive individuals will be quiet if they see that no one is listening to them. Another, and more direct, technique is to say, "Some members have not had the opportunity to participate. Why don't we give the others a chance?" Sometimes talking in private with an individual in an honest and supportive fashion about the effects of monopolizing a discussion is necessary.

Just as some group members talk too much, some group members are not involved enough. Involvement has to do with the degree to which an individual is willing to participate in the discussion of the problem and in the performance of group tasks. Some members are willing to share in the workload but, perhaps because of shyness or communication apprehension, they do not verbally participate. Other individuals may not have the opportunity to participate, perhaps because another member is talking too much.

Stimulating the involvement of quiet group members is also part of balancing participation. This may be as easy as placing the hesitant member in a more central seating position (see pp. 134–135). Or, if the member is uninvolved because the group is large and more aggressive members are doing the talking, breaking into "buzz groups" (see Chapter Ten) may give each member a more equal chance to participate.

Generally, you should not directly call on a quiet group member unless that person appears to want to contribute. Zander (1982) notes, "Addressing a question directly to a shy person to pull him into the interaction can be more frightening than reassuring for him unless he already is on the verge of talking" (p. 40). If the hesitant member is attempting to contribute but other members are not paying attention, recognizing the person by name may remind the other members that an attempt is being made to enter the discussion. Because the effectiveness of a group is reduced if even one of the members does not participate, it may be necessary to remind the group that the success of a discussion is dependent on the participation of all group members.

An individual who is skilled at balancing participation will consider the situational variables before using one of the foregoing techniques. The choice of the techniques to use will probably depend on the personality and status of the talkative or hesitant member, the hesitant member's nonverbal involvement, the overall progress of the group, and numerous other situational variables. If you are skilled in balancing participation among group members, you will be demonstrating an important relational competency and providing leadership for your group.

Other Orientation.   Think for a moment about the groups to which you've belonged recently. Can you remember being disappointed, frustrated, or "stressed out" during a group meeting? Probably. Groups are composed of real people. Real people are affected not only by what happens to them at meetings but also by their lives outside of the group context. A group member who demonstrates competency in other orientation is sensitive to other members and demonstrates support and cooperation.

A group member generally supports another through acceptance and positive regard. Suppose a disagreement between two group members has turned into a confrontation, with one of the group members being verbally attacked by the other. A person skilled in other orientation knows when and how to come to the aid of the person being attacked. Helping someone "save face" when an idea is rejected, listening to and supporting a shy or less confident group member, "stroking" people for important contributions—all of these techniques serve to support others.

A member skilled in other orientation is also cooperative. Cooperation involves working together for group benefit rather than for personal gain.

Behaviors that indicate willingness to cooperate include offering to divide the workload and assist others, helping to implement another solution after yours has been rejected, and offering your own resources (such as the use of your fax machine). Both cooperation and support are part of other orientation, a relational competency necessary for the maintenance and continued existence of the group.

Conflict Management. Most discussion groups with a history of working together experience some degree of conflict.[3] To the extent that conflict encourages a reexamination of the issues and expands alternatives, conflict can be a positive. When group members rely on destructive tactics such as issue avoidance, "buck-passing," or personalized attacks, however, conflict has become destructive. Thus, the ability to help a group manage conflict may be essential to its continued existence.

The first critical skill in managing conflict is to have a sense of timing and to know when conflict is becoming destructive (Folger et al., 2000). If viewpoints are becoming polarized and individuals are becoming either defensive or withdrawn, the conflict could potentially diminish group productivity and damage interpersonal relationships. There is a fine line between a healthy exchange of ideas and an ugly scene that can damage egos and hinder group members' ability to work together.

There are many other necessary skills in addition to the ability to recognize potentially destructive conflict. These skills (Putnam, 1986) include knowing (1) when to use information and expert testimony to resolve disagreements, (2) when to postpone a confrontation, and (3) when to discuss proposals one at a time.

An additional skill is the ability to prioritize disagreements: "Some conflicts are fundamental to a group's decisions and to its survival, while others are tangential to its goal and maintenance" (p. 193). A situational analysis will help determine which conflicts to consider and which to ignore. Remember, actions that are effective in one situation may not be effective in another. Competency in conflict management means making the effective choice for the situation at hand.

Many people believe that leadership means only opening and closing meetings and perhaps calling on a few group members for information. But you can now see that leadership is extremely complex. This complexity of leadership will be discussed in the next section.

Principles
1. Relational competencies refer to communication skills necessary for managing interpersonal relationships and group climate. Relational

---

[3]Chapter Nine explores conflict mangement in greater detail.

competencies are necessary for the maintenance and continued existence of the group.
2. Three relational competencies include:
   a. Balancing participation
   b. Other orientation
   c. Conflict management
3. A member who is skilled in these relational competencies can provide
   leadership for the group. Any group member, not just the designated
   leader, may provide relational leadership for the group.

Complexity of Leadership

Several of the approaches to leadership discussed at the beginning of this
chapter assume that only the person occupying the leader's office exerts
leadership over a group. Now that you have examined some task and relational communication competencies for effective leadership, it probably is
easier to see how all members of the group, not just the designated leader,
have the potential to affect group process. Barge (1997, p. 209) observes
"When a task is more complex, shared leadership makes good sense."

Shared leadership also allows for situational differences—differences
from one group to another as well as differences during the life of a single
group. Groups evolve and change, they are not static, and communication
skills that are useful in one situation may not be useful in another situation.
As you can see, leadership is indeed complex and if your group will be meeting together over time (as contrasted to a group that meets only one time),
you probably are interested in promoting group unity (cohesiveness) or
team spirit. This process often is called "teambuilding" and is the topic of the
next section.

Teambuilding

A review of employment advertisements will indicate that many companies
want to hire teamplayers. What about teambuilders? A teambuilder is a
group member who goes beyond the communication competencies discussed in this chapter. A teambuilder recognizes that teams are on-going
groups that meet together over time and therefore, seeks to create a sense of
"we-ness" or team spirit in the group. Because many of the following guidelines extend and integrate material from other chapters, you might want to
review the suggestions for effective communication (Chapter Four), for
effective listening (Chapter Five), for effective problem solving (Chapter
Six), for effective conflict management (Chapter Nine) and some of the suggestions for effective leadership identified earlier in this chapter. Together

with material from other chapters, the following suggestions can help you create an atmosphere in which team spirit can grow.

1. Develop group identity. A teambuilder might encourage group members to create a group logo and wear t-shirts (with the logo) on the days of group meetings or on a designated day of the week. Celebrating the birthdays of group members and using "we" rather than "you and I" also reinforce the sense of group (team) identity.
2. Promote a common purpose and model appropriate behaviors. Place group concerns above personal self-interests, care for others by not laughing at jokes that belittle individuals or groups (particularly ethnic groups), and praise others.
3. Respect others. A teambuilder listens openmindedly, avoids interrupting others, analyzes ideas rather than people and if necessary, disagrees tactfully.
4. Share rewards with the group when goals are achieved. Rewards may be as inexpensive as purchasing coffee cups for the group or as expensive as treating members to lunch. The rewards build team pride.
5. Promote face-saving. If a group member is creating a problem for the group, a teambuilder first talks to the individual in private and helps the member to see the situation from the group perspective.
6. Express expectations clearly and treat members accordingly. Teambuilders foster a sense of responsibility in team members, they are not caretakers.
7. Support other members when they act according to group policies. A teambuilder does not leave other team members hanging to take responsibility for a group decision.
8. Encourage differences of opinion to avoid groupthink. Rather than advocating positions, however, ask members to treat conflict in a spirit of inquiry with openness to alternative positions.
9. Keep within ethical boundaries. A teambuilder communicates accurately, without exaggeration, and does not manipulate or coerce others.

If teambuilding and leadership are so complex, how does a group member become more effective? A necessary step in the process is "self-monitoring" (Ellis and Cronshaw, 1992). By watching yourself (and later reflecting on your behavior), you can learn to make choices depending on what is happening in the group at the moment. No matter how well you plan for a meeting, however, it is impossible to anticipate every possible situation that might arise. Yes, prepare thoroughly for the meeting and then, during the discussion, be self-disciplined and alert to the continuously changing group situation. You can learn to be a teambuilder and you can improve your skills by reflecting on your experiences in groups.

Principles
1. All group members have the potential to affect group process.
2. Because groups evolve and change over the course of a discussion, skills that are useful in one situation may not be useful in another situation.
3. Nine suggestions for teambuilding (creating team spirit) include:
   a. Develop group identity.
   b. Promote a common purpose and model appropriate behaviors.
   c. Respect others.
   d. Share rewards with the group when goals are achieved.
   e. Promote face-saving.
   f. Express expectations clearly and treat members accordingly.
   g. Support other members when they act according to group policies.
   h. Encourage differences of opinion to avoid groupthink.
   i. Keep within ethical boundaries.
4. Self-monitoring can lead to more effective leadership and teambuilding.

Summary

The beginning of this chapter examined five approaches to defining leadership: leadership as personality traits, leadership according to style, leadership as a function of the situation, leadership as functional behaviors, and leadership as communication skills or competencies. The chapter indicated that most of these theories either view leadership as a role position or fail to provide for situational differences in groups. It suggested that you view leadership as communication skills that move a group toward its recognized goal and/or maintain the group in any given situation. The chapter also emphasized that effective leadership is that which best meets the needs of a group at a particular point in time.

Two types of leadership competencies were identified: task and relational. Task competencies refer to the communication skills necessary to perform tasks and to manage group achievement goals. There are four important task-related competencies: analyzing the problem, establishing criteria or objectives that need to be satisfied by the solution, evaluating the positive and negative consequences associated with the various solutions, and establishing group operating procedures. All group members can potentially exert leadership if they are skilled in adapting their communication to the group and the group situation at that point in time. The ability to ask good questions is central to all task-related competencies.

Relational competencies refer to communication skills necessary for managing interpersonal relationships and group climate. Three relational competencies—balancing participation, other orientation, and conflict management—were discussed. Finally, the complexity of leadership was noted. This chapter emphasized that groups are dynamic, and communication skills that are useful in one situation may not be useful in another situation.

The chapter also discussed teambuilding, or creating an atmosphere that fosters a sense of we-ness or team spirit. Nine suggestions were given for teambuilding. Lastly, the chapter emphasized that all group members can learn teambuilding and leadership competencies and improve their skills through self-monitoring.

Ideas for Discussion

1. Is it possible for small groups to achieve goals without a leader?

2. Do you have a stereotyped image of leaders? What physical characteristics do you expect leaders to have? How do you expect a leader's voice to sound?

3. What are some ways of coping with overly talkative and silent group members that will not embarrass them?

4. When you are a member of a group that is in trouble because no one is skilled at leadership, how do you react? Are you skilled at leadership, or do you feel more comfortable waiting for someone else to lead? Why?

5. In groups to which you belong, are there designated leaders? Under what conditions might it be desirable not to have a designated or official leader?

6. What cues would indicate to you that the leadership needs of a group were not being met?

7. In those groups to which you belong, are you usually most interested in getting the job done or in maintaining warm interpersonal relationships among the members? Why?

Suggested Projects and Activities

1. In a group of five to seven persons, role-play the situations listed here, with one person playing the role of leader and other group members playing the role(s) called for by the situation. Change roles so that all group members get a chance to participate actively.
   a. The leader wants to get a silent group member to participate in the discussion.
   b. The leader wishes to discourage a group member from being overly talkative without hurting his or her feelings.
   c. The leader wants to resolve conflict between two members over an issue.
   d. The leader wants to resolve a conflict of personalities between two group members.

2. Considering all the small groups in which you have participated, who was the best leader? Make a list in which you describe what this person did that made him or her an effective leader. How does your behavior as a group member differ from that of the best leader you have known?

3. With two or more classmates, attend and observe a meeting of a small group. Take notes on the task and relational competencies that you observed. Compare your observations with those of your fellow students. Do they differ? If you had been a member of the group, what actions would you have taken to satisfy group needs?

References

Barge, J. K. Leadership as communication. In L. R. Frey and J. K. Barge, eds. *Managing group life: communicating in decision-making groups.* Boston: Houghton Mifflin, 1997, 202–233.

Barge, J. K., and R. Y. Hirokawa. Toward a communication competency model of group leadership. *Small group behavior,* 1989, 20, 167–189.

Ellis, R. J., and S. F. Cronshaw. Self-monitoring and leader emergence: a test of moderator effects. *Small group research,* 1992, 23, 114–115.

Fisher, B. A. Leadership: when does the difference make a difference? In R. Y. Hirokawa and M. Poole, eds. *Communication and group decision-making,* Beverly Hills: Sage, 1986.

Folger, J. P., M. S. Poole, and R. K. Stutman. *Working through conflict,* 4th ed. New York: Longman, 2000.

Goodall, H. L., Jr. The skills of leading small groups in American business and industry. In R. S. Cathcart and L. A. Samovar, eds. *Small group communication: a reader,* 5th ed. Dubuque, IA: Wm. C. Brown, 1988.

Gouran, D. S. Effective versus ineffective group decision making. In L. R. Frey and J. K. Barge, eds. *Managing group life: communicating in decision-making groups.* Boston: Houghton Mifflin, 1997, 133–155.

Gouran, D. S. *Making decisions in groups: choices and consequences.* Glenview, Il: Scott, Foresman, 1982.

Hirokawa, R. Y., and D. R. Scheerhorn. Communication in faulty group decision-making. In R. Y. Hirokawa and M. S. Poole, eds. *Communication and group decision-making.* Beverly Hills: Sage, 1986.

Nanus, B. *Visionary leadership: creating a compelling sense of direction for your organization.* San Francisco: Jossey-Bass, 1992.

Putman, L. L. Conflict in group decision-making. In R. Y. Hirokawa and M. S. Poole, eds. *Communication and group decision-making.* Beverly Hills: Sage, 1986.

Seibold, D. R. Making meetings more successful: plans, formats, and procedures for group problem solving. In R. S. Cathcart and L. A. Samovar, eds. *Small group communication: a reader,* 6th ed. Dubuque, IA: Wm. C. Brown, 1992, 178–191.

Seibold, D. R., and D. H. Krikorian. Planning and facilitating group meetings. In L. R. Frey and J. K. Barge, eds. *Managing group life: communicating in decision-making groups.* Boston: Houghton Mifflin, 1997, 270–304.

Stewart, C. J., and W. B. Cash, Jr. *Interviewing: principles and practices,* 9th ed. Dubuque, Iowa: Wm. C. Brown, 2000.

Zander, A. *Making groups effective.* San Francisco: Jossey-Bass, 1982.

Suggested Readings

Blanchard, K., B. Hybels, and P. Hodges. *Leadership by the book: Tools to transform your workplace.* New York: William Morrow, 1999. Like Ken Blanchard's bestselling *The One Minute Manager,* this book is written in parable format. The authors link spiritually to organizations and develop the concept of servant leadership.

Cashman, K. *Leadership from the inside out: Becoming a leader for life.* Provo, UT: Executive Excellence Publishing, 1999. Based on extensive interviews with more than fifty chief executive officers as well as the author's personal experience, the book relates leadership to personal growth.

Hackman, M. Z., and C. E. Johnson. *Leadership: A communication perspective,* 3rd ed. Prospect Heights, IL: Waveland, 2000. Chapter 2, "Leadership Communication Styles," explores in greater detail the differences between the authoritarian, democratic, and laissez-faire leadership communication styles. The authors also discuss four significant research attempts to identify the communication patterns of leaders: the Michigan leadership studies, the Ohio State leadership studies, McGregor's Theory X and Theory Y, and Blake and McCanse's Leadership Grid.

Shockley-Zalabak, P. *Fundamentals of organizational communication: Knowledge, sensitivity, skills, values,* 4th ed. New York: Longman, 1999. Chapter 8, "Leadership and Management Communication," distinguishes between leadership and management and identifies characteristics of transformational leadership and principled leadership. The chapter includes communication competencies that contribute to leadership effectiveness.

Williams, P. *The magic of teamwork: Proven principles for building a winning team.* Nashville, TN: Thomas Nelson Publishers, 1997. Written by the senior executive vice president of the Orlando Magic (and former general manager of the Philadelphia 76ers), the easy-to-read book explores universal lessons that can be learned from the world of sports. The message centers on turning a collection of individuals into a team.

Conflict Management and Resolution in Small Groups

Study Questions

After reading this chapter, you should be able to answer the following questions completely and accurately:

1. What is task conflict?
2. What is interpersonal conflict?
3. What is procedural conflict?
4. To what extent are issues in conflict situations not clearly defined?
5. What is intercultural conflict?
6. What are three positive effects of conflict?
7. To what extent can conflict in groups be potentially negative?
8. What is groupthink?
9. What are eight symptoms of groupthink?
10. What are four suggestions for assisting groups in avoiding the groupthink condition?
11. What are five decision-making strategies in groups?
12. What is the difference between conflict resolution and conflict management?
13. What are nine suggestions for conflict management in small groups?

Radio and television news thrives on conflict between people and between nations. However, only the most serious conflicts make the headlines. It's no wonder that the term *conflict* has negative connotations for most of us.

Obviously, all conflicts are not the same. We face minor conflicts each day in our personal relationships. We may have disagreements with our families, friends, or employers. An employee who requests a 20 percent raise, for example, will probably experience conflict with his or her employer. If the employer agrees to the raise, the conflict has been resolved. As you know, however, conflicts are rarely resolved this easily. Most conflicts are "managed" as individuals work out differences and reach agreements that are acceptable to both parties.

Conflict resolution in groups is often difficult. Through the decision-making process, group members work together to find a solution that is acceptable to the group. This process often involves managing conflicts. This chapter will discuss various types of conflict and examine some of the advantages of conflict. Next it will examine groupthink, a condition that sometimes occurs when groups deliberately suppress conflict. Then this chapter will look at some of the procedures used by groups for making decisions. Finally it will present some suggestions for conflict management.

Types and Values of Conflict

Think for a moment about the small groups to which you belong. Are most of those groups ongoing groups, or are they "one-time meeting" groups?

You probably belong to groups that meet together over time, perhaps even on a regular basis. Have these groups been free of even brief periods of tension, anger, or anxiety? Probably not, for periods of conflict are inevitable as individuals interact with one another on a continuing basis. In this section, we will identify the types of conflict that groups may experience, and we will examine the positive values of conflict.

Types of Conflict

In previous chapters, we identified three basic group needs: task needs, procedural or guidance needs, and relational or maintenance needs. *Task needs* refers to the movement of the group toward its goal or objective. This is the first area for potential conflict among group members. Group members may disagree about facts or opinions from authorities. The interpretation of evidence may be questioned. In other words, disagreement about the substance of the discussion is called *task conflict*. Task conflict can be productive and can improve the quality of decisions through idea testing. This value of task conflict will be discussed in the next section.

The second need that groups experience is in the area of guidance. The term *guidance needs* refers to the orderly movement of the group toward its goal or objective. *Procedural conflict* exists when group members disagree about the procedures to be followed in accomplishing the group goal. New procedures may be formulated and a new agenda suggested. Even the group goal may be modified. Procedural conflict, like task conflict, may be productive.

Groups also experience maintenance needs. *Relational or maintenance needs* refer to the interpersonal strengthening of the group as members develop and preserve harmonious relations. This is another potential area for conflict, and the term *interpersonal conflict* is used to indicate the disagreement that most people call a "personality clash." Sometimes interpersonal conflict results when group members "rub each other the wrong way." At other times the conflict may result from interpersonal rivalry and the attempt of one person to dominate one or more other group members. While personality clashes may take the form of antagonistic personal remarks, the conflict is more often expressed through subtle nonverbal behaviors. There may be icy stares or, at the other extreme, an avoidance of eye contact. Interpersonal conflict may be inevitable, but it is not as useful to the group as task conflict and tends to be more difficult to manage.

Issues in conflict situations are not always well defined. In some situations, for example, what appears to be task or procedural conflict may be a result of hidden agendas (unrevealed personal goals). Individuals may appear to be challenging the merit of ideas, but a closer look may reveal that personal motives are the cause of the conflict. In other situations conflict may be illusionary, and members may falsely believe that they disagree. Reducing defensive communication (see Chapter Four) and improving listening and feedback skills (see Chapter Five) will help alleviate this false conflict.

Some groups may experience an additional type of conflict. Conflict that results from cultural differences among group members is called intercultural conflict. Little is known about how to deal with intercultural conflict (Martin and Nakayama, 2000) but we do know not all cultures view conflict in the same way. As do individuals from many Western cultures, the authors of this text see conflict as useful. On the other hand, individuals from many Asian cultures share a tendency toward avoidance of confrontation and absence of direct expression of feelings (Toupin, 1980). Imagine a multicultural group, for example. A group member from a typical city in the Midwest asks a member from an Asian culture about his/her opinion. Several comments are made, none of which seem to clearly support or disagree with the majority opinion. Responding "Do you agree or not?" might do more harm than good to the group process. Once again, there might be a perception of conflict when conflict does not actually exist.

Because the small group is a continuously changing system, group members may experience more than one type of conflict simultaneously. How do group members know whether the conflict they are experiencing is productive? In the next section we will examine some of the positive aspects of conflict.

Some Advantages of Conflict

Three types of conflict have just been identified, and it was noted that conflict can have positive effects on groups. Three of these positive effects are (1) improving the quality of decisions, (2) stimulating involvement in the discussion, and (3) building group cohesion.

Improving the Quality of Decisions.   Suppose your group is discussing the merger of city and county governments. You and another member disagree about the population of the city. What would you do? Would you continue affirming your position or would you walk to the telephone and call the city manager's office to request the population information contained in its records? Most group members will look for more information to resolve task conflict. This often means that the group must adjourn while more thorough investigation into the problem is conducted. When the group meets again and does reach a decision, that decision will be based on the additional information that probably would not have been obtained without the expression of the conflicting views. The result generally is a better decision.

Stimulating Involvement.   One of the greatest threats to goal achievement in small groups is member apathy and one of the most obvious "side effects" of task and procedural conflict is excitement. Although some of the feelings generated by conflict may be negative, they are evidence of involvement. Group members may be angry, but at least they are involved in the group discussion. Thus, a good argument may be an effective antidote to apathy. Individual involvement helps groups become more cohesive.

Building Cohesion.   You probably have a friend, or perhaps a mate, who has a difficult time handling conflict. Conscious efforts on your part to avoid disagreement may produce feelings of tension and anxiety as you try to watch what you say. When repeated often, these tense interactions become increasingly unpleasant. Similar situations can occur in groups. Carefully wording statements to avoid conflict restrains participation and results in tension and frustration. As group members tend to edit their thoughts before communication with others, the feeling of group unity is adversely affected.

Obviously, building group unity through interpersonal conflict is difficult at times. Suppose, for example, that you become extremely angry during an already heated discussion and call another group member a "turkey." If individual and group trust exists and members do not take remarks as personal rejection, the group can grow through the confrontation. Group members learn that together they can confront even personality clashes and as a group work to solve them. In the words of Ellis and Fisher (1994), "The group that fights together stays together" (p. 224). The conflict should be managed, however, before it degenerates to verbal assault and irreparable damage to individual egos occurs.

As we have seen, conflict has several positive aspects and working through conflict constructively can result in more satisfying relationships (Canary et al., 1995; Nicotera, 1997). Understanding these advantages may be sufficient help for those groups operating under the myth that conflict in any form is bad. Remember, however, that conflict is also potentially destructive in groups when it consumes individual members' energies. Conflict can interfere with group process and create so much interpersonal hostility that group members may become unwilling or unable to work with one another. This chapter should increase your understanding of conflict and help you use conflict constructively. The next section will discuss groupthink, a condition that can occur when groups deliberately suppress conflict.

Principles

1. Periods of conflict are inevitable as individuals interact with one another on a continuing basis.
2. *Task conflict* refers to the disagreement about the substance of the discussion.
3. *Procedural conflict* refers to disagreement about the procedures to be followed in accomplishing the group goal.
4. *Interpersonal conflict* refers to the disagreement that most people call a "personality clash."
5. *Intercultural conflict* refers to conflict that results from cultural differences.

6. Three advantages of conflict are that it improves the quality of decisions, stimulates involvement in the discussion, and builds group cohesiveness.
7. If conflict is not managed, it can interfere with group process and create interpersonal hostility.

Groupthink

Imagine a board meeting at a large pharmaceutical company. Seven well-educated individuals have come together to decide whether or not to market a highly controversial new drug. The chairperson and chief executive officer is a highly respected man in his mid-50s. A large picture of his father, the founder and president of the company, hangs on the wall behind him. Although today's meeting seems like any other, at least one group member recognizes that it is different. This member presents the results of experimental studies revealing that the new drug has the potential to cause serious side effects, and she cautions against premature marketing of the drug. Avoiding eye contact with her, the group members direct their attention to the CEO. Another member responds by stating, "This company has built its reputation on the tradition of quickly providing the newest drugs to alleviate the pain and distress of ill people. We would never market a dangerous drug." The CEO calls for a vote. Even the member who noted the serious side effects votes for approval. Quickly leaving the room following adjournment, she still wonders why she didn't maintain her position.[1]

The previous example illustrates a condition that Irving Janis (1972; 1982) termed *groupthink*. Groupthink occurs in some groups when pressure to both reach the group goal and conform to group opinion are so great that individual members surrender their own beliefs, avoid conflict, and view the issues from the group's perspective. Believing that they have a unanimous decision, group members often stop their deliberations (Cline, 1994).

We would like to believe that groupthink is a rare occurrence and without serious consequence, but that is not the case. There is some evidence, for example, to indicate that groupthink was operating in the group decision to advise President Kennedy to support the attack on Cuba (the Bay of Pigs invasion), in the Committee to Re-elect the President when it authorized the burglary at Democratic headquarters in 1972 (Watergate), in Iran-Contra, and in the Challenger disaster (Jaksa and Pritchard, 1994).

At this point you may be wondering whether there are some warning signs indicating that a group is experiencing groupthink. With groupthink, a group norm usually develops that encourages members to remain loyal to the

---

[1]While this situation is hypothetical, similar circumstances may have occurred at the Food and Drug Administration when the decision was made to approve thalidomide, an anti-nausea drug for pregnant women. After the birth of severely deformed babies, the drug was taken off the market.

group and to follow the policies to which the group has already committed itself. A sense of group loyalty causes members to accept proposals without carefully examining the advantages and disadvantages of those proposals; furthermore, the group may tacitly discourage the expression of opposing views by group members who may have misgivings about the proposals. Janis (1982; 1989a; 1989b) identifies the following eight main symptoms of groupthink:

1. *Illusion of invulnerability.* Group members may feel that they can do no wrong. This provides them with some degree of reassurance, and they tend to become overly optimistic and take extreme risks.
2. *Illusion of morality.* Group members ignore the ethical or moral consequences of their decisions.
3. *Collective rationalization.* Group members may rationalize criticism and/or reduce credibility of those who disagree with the group in order to reduce the impact of the criticism. The group members can then recommit themselves to their past policy decisions without being concerned about the quality of those decisions.
4. *Shared stereotypes.* Group members generally share common stereotypes of opposing groups. These stereotypes tend to derogate opposing groups and implicitly reaffirm the inherent "goodness" of their own group.
5. *Self-censorship.* Group members tend to avoid expressing views that are inconsistent with group opinion. Not only may they be silent, but they may even mentally convince themselves that their misgivings are not justified.
6. *Illusion of unanimity.* Group members may falsely perceive they have reached consensus. The illusion of unanimity may result from silence on the part of some group members being perceived as agreement.
7. *Direct pressure.* Group members are pressured into going along with the group so as not to threaten the esprit de corps of the group. The pressure for loyalty to the group need not be verbal; it may be as subtle as a facial expression.
8. *Emergence of self-appointed mind guards.* Some of the group members in effect become "gatekeepers." They protect the group from adverse information that might interrupt the complacency about the effectiveness of the group's decision.

Is there a way to lessen the possibility that your groups might succumb to groupthink? Before responding to that question, it must be emphasized that the lack of disagreement among group members does not necessarily mean that the group is experiencing groupthink. Sometimes people concede their viewpoints because they have been persuaded that another idea is better. Because it is the subtle pressure to *conform at all costs* that is dangerous, the following suggestions based on Janis's work are offered. These suggestions can help your group reduce the possibility of, but cannot ensure that your group will avoid, the groupthink condition.

1. *Encourage critical, independent thinking.* Groups most prone to groupthink are those that have high-status leaders. Individuals in high-status positions tend to be most influential. The influence, however, is based on authority rather than persuasion, because their ideas are not critically evaluated. Group members may "rally 'round the leader" without evaluating his or her ideas on their own merits. The person occupying the leader-role position should assume responsibility for encouraging open, unbiased inquiry into available alternatives. Group members should try to critically evaluate all ideas without being influenced by the status of the members who present those ideas.

2. *Assign the "devil's advocate" role to a group member.* Because members of highly cohesive groups tend to share similar viewpoints, you may find it necessary to assign someone the role of "disagreer." Supporting rejected alternatives, raising objections to preferred solutions, and critically analyzing ideas encourage the group to explore a wider range of alternatives. The group will find it more difficult to ignore facts and opinions that do not support the policy preferred by the group if those critical ideas are presented by someone chosen to fulfill the role of critic. Conflict of this nature, therefore, is desirable in that it will help improve the quality of the group's decision.

3. *Suggest alternative decision-making strategies.* Consensus is generally a preferred decision-making strategy. However, there is evidence that when used in highly cohesive groups, consensus can interfere with open-minded vigilant problem solving (Janis, 1982; 1989a). On occasion, your group might choose majority vote to reach decisions. Group members may be willing to voice disagreement anonymously because they don't have to make their opinions public.

4. *Invite an "outsider" to group meetings.* After his analysis of decision-making groups, Janis (1972) observed that a group insulated from "outsiders" makes it easy for the symptoms of groupthink to become dominant. Your group, for example, might invite a topic expert and/or a process observer to attend one or more group meetings. The topic expert could share his or her expertise on the topic area the group is discussing. Or, the group could invite someone who could act as an observer to summarize and evaluate the group's decision-making process. Sometimes an outside viewpoint, whether from a topic expert or a process observer, can help the group avoid groupthink.

Principles

1. The term *groupthink* refers to a situation in which group morale and uniformity of opinion become more important than the critical analysis of ideas.
2. The main symptoms of groupthink are as follows:
   a. Illusion of invulnerability
   b. Illusion of morality
   c. Collective rationalization

    d. Shared stereotypes

    e. Self-censorship

    f. Illusion of unanimity

    g. Direct pressure

    h. Emergence of self-appointed mindguards

3. You can help your group avoid the groupthink condition by

    a. Encouraging critical, independent thinking

    b. Assigning a "devils advocate" role

    c. Suggesting alternative decision-making strategies

    d. Inviting someone from outside the group to attend group meetings

Decision Making and Conflict Management

Suppose you are a member of the advisory group of a food cooperative in a city that is primarily a "university town." The cooperative has grown in size from a few families buying food in quantity and distributing out of a home to a moderately sized cooperative with a small run-down storefront in the downtown area, approximately two miles from campus. Although the majority of the members are students, some nonstudent families are joining the cooperative to take advantage of the savings on cheese, juice, and other food items. All members are required to work at the store a given number of hours each month. With increasing numbers of customers, workers have experienced difficulty keeping the small food bins adequately stocked, and the customers are finding the aisles a "tight squeeze." The storeroom is no longer large enough to store food from one delivery until the following delivery. All board members agree that the cooperative needs more space.

    Various solutions to the problem have been suggested, and all but two of them have been rejected. One potential solution involves renting a warehouse some distance from the store for food storage and expanding the back wall several feet in the alley behind the store. The other solution involves moving the store to a location in a small shopping center. The second proposal would cost considerably more than the first proposal but would provide space for a juice and sandwich bar. There are several ways of resolving the disagreement on the two proposals. In the following section, we will discuss some of the ways groups make decisions, and then we will present some suggestions for conflict management.

Methods of Decision Making

There are many differences between the individual decision-making process and the group decision-making process. A group, for example, usually has a variety of viewpoints to consider.[2] The decision-making method selected by

[2]See Chapter One for a discussion of the differences between individuals and groups.

the group will generally be determined by the complexity of the problem or task, the personalities of the group members, and the amount of time that the group has for making a decision. Five decision-making strategies that will be examined in more detail include force, majority vote, compromise, arbitration, and consensus.

Force.   Suppose the president of the board of directors in the previous example said, "The board has been discussing expansion versus moving to a new location for the past three meetings and obviously cannot reach a decision. Since this group elected me president, I am going to make the decision." As a member of this group, how would you feel? Angry—because someone was making a decision that you should participate in? Depressed— because this is one more group that's been "spinning its wheels?" Anxious to hear the president's decision—what if he or she disagrees with your point of view? Anger, depression, and anxiety are not positive feelings and tend to adversely affect group morale. When group members don't feel good about a decision, they generally don't want to work to implement it. The decision may have been made, but it's generally not worth much.

This illustration concerns, in part, the effect of *status* on conflict and decision making. If you perceived yourself as equal in status with the president of the cooperative, your dissatisfaction with the decision would be increased. Conversely, were the president of obviously higher status (with "deserved" power), you might be more willing to accept without discontent the authoritarian decisions that he or she might make.

Majority Vote.   As you read of the disagreement among the board members concerning the proposed move to a larger location, you might have thought: *Take a vote.* The democratic ethic seems to center on voting. Certainly when time is at a premium, majority vote allows a group to make a decision quickly. There are dangers to majority vote, however. One danger is that the rush to achieve closure on the issue may be more important than concerns for group harmony or equal representation of the differing points of view. Another danger results in dividing group membership. It also seems reasonable to assume that as members of ongoing groups, sometimes individuals will be on the side of the "winning" majority and sometimes on the side of the "losing"minority. Sometimes, however, a member loses more than wins. When the losses are taken as personal defeats (i.e., a rejection of my ideas is a rejection of me as a person), then majority rule can be destructive.

Compromise.   The members of the board of directors could compromise and agree to rent a warehouse and look for a suitable location for a juice and sandwich shop. Compromise involves mutual concessions. No one completely wins—but no one completely loses, either. Half of a falafel sandwich is better than none, right? The compromise solution *is* better than doing nothing at all, but compromise does not solve the additional storefront problems of inadequate space for food bins and crowed aisles. Realizing that the "solution" is not going to completely solve the problem and feeling as though they gave more than they gained, both sides of the controversy may have low motivation to implement the solution. Although group members often can work together to find much better solutions, compromise may be the best possible solution in some conflicts. Compromise, for example, can be useful as a temporary solution. The board may use the time to investigate other rental possibilities.

Arbitration.   If the board members see no way to resolve their differences and are becoming bitter about the continuing conflict, the group may have to resort to arbitration. During arbitration, the group brings in a disinterested third party to make the decision.[3] Labor-management disputes are often handled in this manner. Arbitrators generally resolve disagreements at some middle-ground position, and often the decision seems like compromise in that no one completely wins and no one completely loses. Potential low group motivation toward implementing the decision may result here as well.

Consensus.   There are occasions when group members agree on a decision—not a false sense of agreement as in groupthink, but a genuine, honest consensus. In contrast to the previous decision-making strategies, consensus initially centers on goals rather than on alternatives. Conflicts involving "my way" versus "your way" often result in discussion of the superiority of personal solutions. When members shift their attention from solutions per se to the goals, solutions can be developed that permit both sides to obtain goals. (See Chapter Three for a discussion of goals.)

Suppose that the board of directors for the food cooperative is meeting. The members seem to have become divided into the expansion-versus-new-location viewpoints. At this point, a group member asks each other member to state his or her goals. The members favoring expansion generally indicate their concern over finances; their goal is to keep the monthly rent within reasonable limits (feelings are that rent is too high in a shopping mall). The members favoring a new location generally want a nicer-looking storefront and an increase in membership; their goal is an attractive store in a location with good customer traffic. After some discussion, the meeting adjourns, with group members feeling positive about group progress and agreeing to investigate other rental possibilities before the next meeting.

At the next meeting, other alternatives are discussed. One alternative is a storefront two blocks from campus. Customer traffic is good and the store

---

[3]If using arbitration in multicultural groups, consider that individuals in some cultures may fear the loss of face in mediation (Rogers and Steinfatt, 1999). Participants in arbitration may have similar concerns.

is large. The rent is reasonable because the inside of the building is in need of repair. Because of the member work requirement, labor to repair and paint the inside of the building is available. Several cooperative members are experienced construction workers and could provide the necessary labor. After perceiving that many members favor the proposal, the president asks if the group consensus is to move to the near-campus location or if anyone wants to "block" the move. Although one group member doesn't like one of the businesses adjoining the prospective store, he doesn't block, agrees to give his assistance to the group effort and consensus has been reached. Both the group goal (more space) and individual goals (reasonable rent and attractive location with good customer traffic) are achieved. Group morale is high, and group members leave the meeting with eager anticipation to accomplish the many necessary tasks before the cooperative opens its doors for business in its new location.

Consensus can be a highly desirable decision-making method, but obviously not all consensus results in better-quality decisions. It is entirely possible that groups can unanimously agree on a completely incorrect solution to the problem. When groups approach the task systematically and rationally, however, the consensus decisions do tend to be better ones (Hirokawa, 1982).

Although consensus can be a desirable decision-making method, it can also be more difficult for groups than the other methods of making decisions. Doubts and reservations need to be openly expressed. All members must be responsible both for expressing their own needs openly and honestly and for listening openly to the needs of other members. All group members should also understand themselves well enough to know when they can agree to work for group effort (although they may not totally agree with the proposal) and when their personal viewpoints differ to the point that blocking is necessary. Consensus seems to work best in mature, ongoing groups in which honest expression (at the risk of interpersonal conflict) is valued and commitment to the group is strong.

There is no single strategy for decision making that should be used by all groups. Nor is there a strategy for decision making that should be used by any one group to make all of its decisions. This book suggests that consensus has certain benefits that may make it most desirable. It enhances creativity, promotes understanding, and provides an atmosphere that promotes trust and cooperation. However, it also seems to work best in mature groups and is time consuming. In situations where the group is under a time pressure, majority vote may be the preferred decision-making strategy. Decision-making strategies are tools. It is important to select the right tool to get the job done and then use it as skillfully as possible.

Principles
1. Five decision-making strategies are force, majority vote, compromise, arbitration, and consensus.

2. Force generally is an ineffective decision-making strategy, because group members often do not support decisions that they do not make.
3. Majority vote can save time when a quick decision is necessary, but the strategy can be destructive when group members take losses as personal defeats.
4. Compromise solutions involve mutual concessions; no one completely wins and no one completely loses. If group members feel as though they gave more than they gained and/or that the problem is not completely solved, motivation to implement the decision may be low for both sides of the controversy.
5. During arbitration, the group brings in a disinterested third party to make the decision. Sometimes arbitration has the same effects as compromise in that no one completely wins and no one completely loses.
6. Consensus initially centers on goals rather than alternatives, and the group attempts to formulate a new solution that will meet the goals of both sides of the controversy.

Conflict Management

The perspective on conflict in small groups has changed in recent years. Sociologists initially viewed conflict as a disruptive force in society (Coser, 1956). Conflict in groups was once seen as an undesirable (although sometimes necessary) temporary occurrence. The objective was to resolve the conflict. More recently, conflict has been viewed as an inevitable and integral part of group process (Nicotera, 1997). Many conflicts (e.g., the struggle for civil rights in this country) cannot be brought to a speedy conclusion. Sometimes, finding ways in which the parties to the controversy can communicate is more important than immediate resolution of the conflict with a single solution. Whether the issue is civil rights, labor-management relations, or campus concerns, people do sit down and talk. In this way, the conflict becomes "managed." Conflict management does not exclude attempts to resolve conflict, but the emphasis is on communication rather than on termination of the disagreement.

Conflict cannot be managed unless communication channels are kept open. To walk out of a group meeting or to refuse to confront the issues creates more problems than it solves. Because of the importance of communication to conflict management, we offer the following suggestions to increase your effectiveness with this important variable in group process.

Identify Your Problem and Desires.   Stop and think before you speak. Is the problem that is creating the conflict in you? Are *you* the person who doesn't agree with the group? Why? Perhaps, for example, you don't agree with the group because you feel that you will have to do most of the work; you feel that the group is taking advantage of you. After you are clear about your desires, you may be more ready to state those desires or needs in a descriptive way.

Describe Your Problem and State Your Desires. If you disagree with the group, the group cannot work through the conflict unless you communicate what you want. It is up to you to describe the situation as specifically as possible. You might say, for example, "I have a problem. It really upsets me that the rest of the group wants to do another mailing to the cooperative membership. Last time we did a mailing no one helped, and I'm concerned that I will have to do the mailing by myself again. I would like to help, but I'm carrying eighteen hours at school this term and can't do the mailing by myself." This clear statement lets the other members know what you are experiencing. It's amazing how many group members argue without ever sharing what is really bothering them.

Express Disagreement Tactfully. Avoid defensive communication (see Chapter Four). Filley (1975, p. 14) states: "The most important consideration in determining the outcome of the conflict is whether the situation is personalized or depersonalized." *Personalized* situations are situations in which the whole being of the group member is threatened (i.e., the individual rather than the idea is what is being judged). In *depersonalized* situations, the group member's behavior is described as creating a problem. "You are careless" is a personalized statement. "It's difficult for me to keep up with you. When you stuff these envelopes so fast, some of the ZIP codes get out of order" is a depersonalized statement. Some authorities refer to a depersonalized statement as "sticking to the facts, not criticizing the personalities." Personalized statements (criticizing personalities) often result in interpersonal conflict. Depersonalized situations (discussing behaviors) lend themselves to conflict management.

Listen Actively. Active listening was discussed in Chapter Five. It requires that you attend to the feelings and emotional tone of the message as well as to the content of what the other group member is saying. Contradictions are sometimes apparent between what group members say verbally and what they say nonverbally (see p. 128). Perhaps a group member is unwilling to disagree due to fear of personal rejection. Some group members would rather not express disagreement than have a friend no longer like them. Be supportive, encourage the individual, and listen. Understanding the desires and needs of another member is necessary if you are to offer solutions that can potentially meet those desires and needs.

Persuade Others of the Value of Conflict. How group members view conflict determines to a large extent how they deal with it and how successful they are in managing it. If a member views conflict as something to be avoided, he or she may respond defensively. The group member may even pretend that everything is fine and that the group is "sailing along a smooth ocean." However, "choppy waters" and cohesiveness are not necessarily opposites. Avoiding conflict may appear effective in the short run, but it generally is not satisfactory in the long run with ongoing groups.

Develop Intragroup Trust.   Conflict is neither a fight that should be avoided nor a fight to be won at another's expense. Group meetings are not the place for personal vendettas. Conflict should be viewed as cooperative problem solving. The degree of trust within your group will be directly related to the group's ability to handle conflict constructively.

Don't Take Disagreement as Personal Rejection.   If group members disagree with what you say, you may think that they don't like you or are "out to get you." The perceptions we hold of ourselves are a result of years of conditioning, and they cannot be changed immediately (see p. 53). Be careful not to let your ego interfere with the goals of the group.

Demonstrate Cooperativeness if Your Plan Is Rejected.   Cooperativeness is your responsibility to group effort, even though your personal opinions may not be in agreement with the group opinion. In essence, the group goal becomes more important than personal opinions.

Structure the Group Carefully.   If possible, you should choose group members who get along. This is not to say that members must hold the same viewpoints. Remember that with a variety of opinions and information, there is a better chance of improving the quality of the decision. This is also not to say that group members must have such high personal regard for one another that they fall into the group-think condition. What *is* necessary is that members be able to get along interpersonally. If, however, it is impossible to select participants who get along, and you are aware that potentially hostile individuals are group members, you may wish to spend additional time on group maintenance needs and select a seating arrangement that will separate the potentially hostile individuals.

     One solution to conflict that usually is not desirable but that ends the conflict is to dissolve the group. Individuals may choose to leave the group rather than to conform to group opinion. Research (Hare, 1976) indicates that there are at least three cases in which an individual is more likely to conform to group opinion: if the member must make his or her opinion public, if the majority holding a contrary opinion is large, and if the group is especially friendly or cohesive.[4] If the deviant member does not conform to group opinion, he or she will probably either remain a deviant or leave the group.

     The decision of whether or not to leave the group is not totally the choice of the deviant member. Groups are systems with interdependent ele-

---

[4]Extensive work in the area of conformity has been conducted by Solomon Asch.

ments. The deviant member may be rejected by the group and forced to leave if the group decides that it can operate more effectively without him or her. Obviously, rejection of a group member is not an optimal technique for conflict resolution. Gaining the conformity of the member through the use of persuasive techniques is preferred.

Principles

1. Conflict management emphasizes communication rather than termination of the disagreement.
2. Nine suggestions for conflict management in small groups are as follows:
   a. Identify your problem and desires.
   b. Describe your problem and state your desires.
   c. Express disagreement tactfully.
   d. Listen actively.
   e. Persuade others of the value of conflict.
   f. Develop intragroup trust.
   g. Don't take disagreement as personal rejection.
   h. Demonstrate cooperativeness if your plan is rejected.
   i. Structure the group carefully.
3. One solution to conflict that usually is not desirable but that ends the conflict is to dissolve the group.

Summary

This chapter began with a discussion of the types and values of conflict. *Task conflict, interpersonal conflict,* and *procedural conflict* were defined. The three advantages of conflict that were discussed were: (1) improving the quality of decisions, (2) stimulating involvement in the discussion, and (3) building group cohesion.

The next section discussed groupthink, a condition experienced in some groups when pressures to reach the group goal and to conform to group opinion are so great that the group members conform to group opinion in order to avoid conflict. Eight main symptoms of groupthink were identified, and four suggestions to assist groups in avoiding the groupthink condition were noted.

The last section of this chapter concerned decision making and conflict management. Force, majority vote, compromise, arbitration, and consensus were discussed as decision-making strategies. In addition, nine suggestions for increasing your effectiveness with conflict management were presented.

Reading a chapter on conflict resolution will not solve all of the problems you might encounter with group conflict. The adage "practice makes perfect" should be amended to include the restriction "except when conflict occurs." In other words, there are many variables in the system, and conflict is probable as individuals work together. Practicing the suggestions we have discussed will not instantly resolve group conflict, but the techniques will assist you in conflict management.

Ideas for Discussion

1. Do you agree with this chapter's approach regarding conflict? Has it overemphasized its value or slighted its limitations? Explain your answer.

2. Which of the decision-making strategies are used in the groups to which you belong? Which strategy works best? Which strategy is least effective? Why?

3. How do you communicate when in a conflict situation? Do you have any emotional reactions? Which of the suggestions for conflict management do you already practice? Which of the suggestions do you need to acquire?

4. Do you think the leader has an effect on attitudes toward conflict resolution? Explain your answer.

5. What types of problems lend themselves to increased potential for group conflict?

6. How would you arrange a room for a meeting during which there is likely to be conflict? What arrangement might minimize status differences? What arrangement might reduce the possibility of confrontation?

7. Is a group ever justified in asking a member to leave the group? Under what conditions?

Suggested Projects and Activities

1. In a four- to six-person group, have a five-minute brainstorming session to find additional suggestions for managing conflict.

2. Observe a group and write down any personalized statements that you hear. Edit the ideas on your paper so that they are expressed more tactfully (in a depersonalized manner).

3. Attend a meeting at the level of city or county government (e.g., city council). What styles of decision making are used? Is conflict apparent? What type? Was the conflict managed? How?

4. In class, design a role-playing situation that involves proponents of different views. Include the three types of conflict. Have the actors demonstrate as many of the suggestions for conflict management as possible. Ask the class to analyze the group's effectiveness in handling the conflict.

References

Canary, D. J., W. R. Cupach, and S. J. Messman. *Relationship conflict*. Thousand Oaks, CA: Sage, 1995.

Cline, R. J. W. Groupthink and the Watergate cover-up: the illusion of unanimity. In L. R. Frey, ed. *Group communication in context: studies of natural groups.* Hillsdale, NJ: Lawrence Erlbaum, 1994.

Coser, L. *The functions of social conflict.* New York: Free Press, 1956.

Ellis, D. G., and B. A. Fisher. *Small group decision making: communication and the group process,* 4th ed. New York: McGraw-Hill, 1994.

Filley, A. C. *Interpersonal conflict resolution,* Glenview, IL: Scott, Foresman, 1975.

Hare, A. P. *Handbook of small group research,* 2nd ed. New York: Free Press, 1976.

Hirokawa, R. Y. Consensus group decision-making, quality of decision, and group satisfaction: An attempt to sort "fact" from "fiction." *Central states speech journal,* 1982, *33,* 407–415.

Jaksa, J. A., and M. S. Pritchard. *Communication ethics: methods of analysis,* 2nd ed. Belmont, CA: Wadsworth, 1994.

Janis, I. L. *Victims of groupthink: a psychological study of policy decisions and fiascoes.* Boston: Houghton Mifflin, 1972.

———. *Groupthink: psychological studies of policy, decisions, and fiascos.* Boston: Houghton Mifflin, 1982.

———. *Crucial decisions: leadership in policymaking and crisis management.* New York: Free Press, 1989(a).

———. Groupthink: the desperate drive for consensus at any cost. In J. S. Ott, ed. *Classic readings in organizational behavior.* Belmont, CA: Wadsworth, 1989(b), 223–232.

Nicotera, A. M. Managing conflict communication in groups. In L. R. Frey and J. K. Barge, eds. *Managing group life: communicating in decision-making groups.* Boston: Houghton Mifflin, 1997, pp. 104–130.

Martin, J. N. and T. K. Nakayama. *Intercultural Communication in Contexts.* Mountain View, CA: Mayfield, 2000.

Rogers, E. M., and T. M. Steinfatt. *Intercultural communication.* Prospect Heights, IL: Waveland Press, 1999.

Toupin, A. Counseling Asians: psychotherapy in the context of racism and Asian-American history. *American journal of orthopsychiatry,* 1980, *50,* 76–86.

Suggested Readings

Folger, J. P., M. S. Poole, and R. K. Stutman. *Working through conflict: Strategies for relationships, groups, and organizations,* 4th ed. New York: Harper Collins, 2000. Featuring real life conflict situations, this book focuses on conflict and communication interactions. Chapter 6, "Climate and Conflict Interaction," discusses the effects of climate on interaction and decision making in organizations. Chapter 7, "Doing Conflict: Styles, Strategies, and Tactics," describes conflict styles and presents a model for style selection based on strategies in conflict and negotiation.

Johnson, D. W. *Reaching out: Interpersonal effectiveness and self-actualization,* 7th ed. Boston: Allyn & Bacon, 2000. Chapter 9, "Anger, Stress, and Managing Feelings," differentiates between constructive and destructive anger, discusses functions of anger, identifies anger arousers and guidelines for managing anger constructively, and provides suggestions for dealings with an angry person. The exercises are especially useful.

Pickering, P. *How to manage conflict,* 3rd ed. Franklin Lakes, NJ: Career Press, 2000. A practical guide for managing conflict, this easy to read book explores the relationship between communication and conflict and provides suggestions for dealing with the emotional aspects of conflict. Activities to improve conflict management skills are included.

Stewart, J. *Bridges not walls: A book about interpersonal communication,* 7th ed. New York: McGraw-Hill, 1999. Chapter 14, "Conflict," includes several articles on conflict management.

Ury, W. *Getting to peace: Transforming conflict at home, at work, and in the world.* New York: Viking Penguin, 1999. Written by the co-founder of Harvard's Program on Negotiation and co-author of the bestseller *Getting to Yes*, this book examines our culture of conflict and presents ten ways to prevent, resolve, and/or contain conflict. The author uses his profits from the sale of the book for peace education.

Weaver, G. R., ed. *Culture, communication and conflict: Readings in intercultural relations.* Needham Heights, MA: Simon & Schuster, 1998. Conflict management principles are not universal and this edited book includes a variety of readings that explore cultural differences primarily in international conflicts. The following readings are helpful for understanding cultural approaches to conflict: "Achieving Integrative Agreements in Negotiation," "Culture and Business: Interacting Effectively to Achieve Mutual Goals," and "Culture Clash."

Wilmot, W. W., and J. L. Hocker: *Interpersonal conflict,* 5th ed. Boston: McGraw-Hill, 1998. Chapter 4, "Power," provides a useful overview of the relationship between power and conflict management. Chapter 9, "Third-Party Intervention," discusses a variety of intervention modes and differences across cultures.

10

Special Forms and Techniques for Small Group Communication

Study Questions

After reading this chapter, you should be able to answer the following questions completely and accurately:

1. What is a definition of a forum? What is its purpose or function, and when would you be likely to use a forum alone?
2. What are the characteristics of a forum?
3. What is a definition of a panel? What are some purposes the panel might serve effectively?
4. What are the characteristics of the panel and its operations that make it unique?
5. What is a definition of a symposium? What purpose does it serve most effectively?
6. What are the distinguishing characteristics of the symposium and its operation?
7. What is a definition of a colloquium, and what special purposes does it serve?
8. What are the unique characteristics of the colloquium?
9. What are the characteristics of a forum, panel, symposium, and colloquium that differentiate each from the others? What are the similarities across two or more of these four forms of public discussions?
10. What is the distinction between a public discussion and a private discussion?
11. What are the distinguishing characteristics of quality circles?
12. Why is it important to involve middle managers in quality circle efforts?
13. What are self-directed or natural work teams?
14. How are they different from quality circles?
15. What is teleconferencing?
16. What are the distinctions among audio, video, and audiographic conferencing?
17. How can audio and video conferencing difficulties be overcome?
18. What advantages are there for using media-assisted groups?
19. What advantages are there for using computer-mediated communication?
20. What are the differences between self-help and therapy groups?
21. What are some of the benefits of belonging to such groups?
22. What is the purpose of a buzz session, and how is it structured?
23. Why is role playing an effective group involvement technique for human relations problems?
24. How does the structured six-step role-playing process work?
25. What is the purpose of using a listening team?
26. How can the nominal group technique be used during group meetings?

Earlier chapters examined the nature of small group communication and attempted to suggest principles to improve the effectiveness of its operation. Most of the attention has been centered on those factors that influence the effectiveness of small group deliberations. Because you are likely to engage frequently in both informative and problem-solving discussions, a chapter has been devoted to each of these formats and processes. However, there are still other forms of small group communication to which you can successfully apply the concepts and principles discussed earlier.

This chapter will describe some of the selected special forms of small group communication. Special forms of public discussions are examined first; these include consideration of the forum, panel, colloquium, and symposium. The second section deals with special forms of private discussions, including a description of quality circles, teleconferencing, role-playing groups, buzz sessions, listening teams, the nominal group technique, and brainstorming. For each of the special forms of small group communication, this chapter will define the form, specify its purpose or function, identify its characteristics, and provide an example of its use.

Selected Public Discussions

The primary focus throughout this book has been on the interpersonal level of communication as it is applicable to small groups. In addition, there has been a tendency to emphasize a setting or context that may be characterized as private. In other words, the book has stressed the operation of small groups in seclusion from the presence, sight, or intrusion of others. Obviously, small groups can and do function in public as well as in private settings. This section will examine four common forms of public discussions in which you will probably be asked to participate within the next few years. These forms are labeled "public," because the discussions take place in the presence of an audience. Some types of public discussions invite and depend upon audience participation. The forum, the panel, the colloquium, and the symposium will be considered.

The Forum

A *forum* is a general form of public discussion in which the full audience participates from the outset of the meeting under a chairperson's leadership. In its pure form you will find that there are no formal presentations by either individuals or a group. Rather, under the leadership of a chairperson or moderator, the members of the audience examine a subject, topic, or problem by giving impromptu speeches from the floor, taking issue with what has been said, asking and answering questions, and responding briefly to questions and comments (see Figure 10.1). Thus, the general purpose of a forum in its pure state is to provide the audience with an opportunity to share information on a

FIGURE 10.1   *The Forum*

topic or problem. Wagner and Arnold (1965, pp. 182–183) have provided an excellent summary of the purposes of the forum:

1. To enable an audience to gain supplementary information from experts or knowledgeable persons, since in no form of public discussion can those who participate in the stimulation stage express all their knowledge, views, and preferences.
2. To give final form and organization to the views and information which the listeners derive from pre-forum discussion.
3. To provide an opportunity for correcting intentional or inadvertent bias, distortion, or misunderstanding.
4. To give an opportunity for verbal expression by the audience, an important adjunct to silent thinking.

The forum is seldom implemented as a separate form of public discussion, although it may be so used in rare instances. Typically, you will observe the forum used in combination with other types of public discussion, as in a panel-forum or symposium-forum. When it is used in combination with other types of public discussion, a period of time is usually set aside for the forum. This period of time ranges widely, running from twenty minutes to forty-five minutes, depending on various conditions. The forum, whether employed as a separate form or in combination with other types of public discussion, may be conceived of as the audience's participation time.

Heavy responsibility falls on the shoulders of the chairperson or leader of the forum. The chairperson begins by gaining control of the audience. Next he or she provides a brief orientation to the topic or problem and the occasion. Then he or she instructs the audience concerning procedures for questioning, responding to questions, making remarks, and any other appropriate limitations placed on the forum's methods of operation. The chairperson also stimulates the members of the audience to get the forum under way and keep it moving along by asking leading or provocative questions and by identifying key issues. The chairperson is similarly responsible for controlling and guiding the discussion. In meeting these responsibilities, he or she will attempt to keep questions, responses, and remarks on target and framed in a clear and concise manner. Obviously, with many unknown audience members participating in a forum, a comprehensive systems analysis is virtually impossible. However, during the meeting, the leader should try to identify people with different viewpoints and give all factions access to communication.

The following guidelines are appropriate for any forum, whether it is employed separately or in combination with other forms of public discussion (Wagner and Arnold, 1965).

The chairperson or forum leader is responsible for the following:

1. Instructing the audience as to the mode of participation desired—whether informal discussion, questions and answers only, comments from the floor, or some combination thereof. The chairperson should also advise the audience of any limitations on questioning or speaking that will apply during the forum period.

2. Stimulating participation by asking leading questions, offering striking statements, and posing the issues brought out in the previous discussion.

3. Encouraging brevity, clarity, and integration of ideas through apt questions, suggestions, restatements, interpretations, and transitions.

4. Guiding the progress of questioning or discussion as in any group discussion. It is especially important that the chairperson keep questions and comments, and the length of the forum as a whole, within reasonable bounds. He or she must deal tactfully but firmly with irrelevant, obscure, emotional, and other difficult questions and comments. The objective should be to encourage free and frank participation without allowing a few tiresome persons to monopolize the time or defeat the majority's effort to explore the main questions.

5. Emphasizing the importance of selecting a preferred solution in order to increase the audience's reflective thinking and bring about organization and progress.

6. Rephrasing and restating questions and comments whenever there is any doubt that all have heard and understood what was asked or said.

7. Taking responsibility for referring questions and statements to the proper person if an answer or comment seems to be needed. (Naturally, those who ask questions or offer comments should be free to direct their remarks to persons of their own choice.)

8. Bringing the forum to a satisfying close by summarizing aptly and briefly while there is still a lively interest in the problem. Only in this way can the audience be sent away still thinking about the subject. Forums that drag on too long can diminish interest in the subject and thus defeat their main purpose.

According to Wagner and Arnold (1965, pp. 183–184), those who participate as members of the audience should do the following:

1. Ask questions useful to themselves *and others.* The interests of the *group* are paramount; personal, trivial, and irrelevant questions and comments are out of place.
2. Phrase their questions and comments clearly, simply, briefly, and interestingly.
3. Phrase questions and comments in such a way as to maintain a reflective attitude on the part of everyone. Good taste and good temper should be maintained no matter how controversial the problem.

Those who respond to audience questions and statements are duty bound, as in informal discussion, to be:

1. Free from contention and dogmatism in their comments.
2. Helpful in maintaining the climate of opinion conducive to group thinking. (See precautions enumerated in (4) under duties of the chairperson.)
3. Frank and cooperative in providing the data and advice needed for effective problem solving.

With some basic understanding of the forum, now consider an example of this form of public discussion. The forum can serve as a useful form of public discussion for providing both access and input to some individual or group charged with making recommendations or decisions concerning a problem or topic. Suppose you were appointed by the president of your university to a task force on student publications composed of faculty and students. During an early phase of the task force's work, the group decides to hold an open meeting on the campus to permit students, faculty, and staff to express their views relevant to the current operation of student publications.

The chairperson of the task force might very logically select the forum as the type of public discussion to be used in this instance. The forum would provide an opportunity for interested members of the campus community to express their views on matters relevant to student publications, thus providing access and input to the task force for later deliberation. The chairperson of the task force might serve as the moderator for the forum, performing all those duties described previously for the forum leader. Note that in this example the forum was used as a form separate from other types of public discussion. Later in this section, examples in which the forum is used in combination with other forms of public discussion will be considered.

The Panel

A *panel* is a form of public discussion in which a group of four to eight persons, including a leader, discusses a problem in front of an audience (see Figure 10.2). The presence of the audience can act as an important external variable on the

FIGURE 10.2 *The Panel*

panel and can significantly affect the discussion. Consequently, its potential effect on the group members should be considered in a systems analysis. On the basis of such an analysis, the leader may decide to exclude from the panel any members who tend to be nervous or excitable. The members of the group are usually experts or are at least reasonably knowledgeable about the problem under discussion, and their views on the problem may vary widely. They follow the problem-solving format described earlier, proceeding through the discussion in an orderly and logical manner. You will find no prepared speeches and no particular order designated for individuals in the group to speak. As in private discussion, the interaction among members is informal, characterized by frequent interruptions and substantial give and take under the leadership of a moderator or chairperson.

Panels are *public* discussions, and as such they are presented for the benefit of the audience. Accordingly, the primary purpose of a panel usually is to give the members of the audience information about a problem and its possible solutions. The members of the panel attempt to solve a problem (one level of purpose), but they do so for the purpose of informing the audience (another level of purpose). Thus, it is possible for you to conceive that the panel has two simultaneous levels of purpose or a kind of dual purpose, with the essential purpose being to inform the audience. Panels are used frequently on radio and television to publicly present various points of view.

Because a panel is presented before an audience, it is important that all of its members be seen and heard by those observing the event. For this reason, the panel is sometimes seated on a platform in the front of a room. Tables and chairs are arranged so that the panel members may see one another easily and so that all members of the panel may be seen by the audience.

These environmental conditions may affect the informal group process when the group is transplanted onto the platform in front of an audience. As you might expect, the informality that is characteristic of private group discussions is reduced in public panel discussions. For example, all members must speak loudly enough to be heard by the audience. The public nature of panel discussions also tends to place a time constraint on the meeting. An hour to an hour and a half usually is a good time limit for a panel discussion when it is planned as a single event. However, panels are generally planned with a forum to follow. Time limits of less than one hour devoted to the panel discussion and probably not more than forty-five minutes designated for the forum are reasonable guidelines for a panel-forum discussion. Of course, these time limits are only suggested guidelines; the need for more or less time will be dictated by the individual situation.

Earlier, it was noted that panel discussions proceed in an orderly, logical manner, but some planning is necessary to help ensure the desired outcome. The first phase of planning incorporates all the general suggestions made in Chapter Six on problem solving. It may even be a good idea in some situations to end this phase with a brief outline prepared for the problem-solving discussion.

A second phase of preplanning is also necessary for panel discussions. As a member of the panel, you are generally well advised to have a short planning meeting prior to the panel discussion, particularly if your group members have not previously worked together. At this meeting, members of your group should reach agreement on any essential definitional matters and place some limits on the problem to be discussed.

Next, the topic questions or issues to serve as the central focus in the discussion should be agreed upon and ordered as they will be introduced into the discussion. Care should be taken to determine that you can cover the selected topics concisely and efficiently during the panel discussion. Then, to help ensure that the selected topics will be discussed, your group should specify some general guidelines regarding the time allocated for each topic or question. Again, these time limits are merely guidelines, and they will be useful only to the extent that each member observes them within reasonable limits.

Once this procedural outline of the group's plan is completed, the members of your panel are ready to independently think about their individual contributions. Clearly, the development of the procedural outline is not followed by a rehearsal session. There has to be some balance between the preplanning of the panel and the spontaneity desired during the actual panel discussion. Responses from you and other members during the panel discussion should appear to be improvised and extemporaneous, rather than rehearsed. Your actual panel discussion should be characterized by flexibility, with fresh ideas and interactions; it should be well prepared without appearing to be rigid.

The chairperson, or moderator, is the person to whom both the panel and the audience look to get the discussion under way. After quieting the audience, he or she should announce the topic and introduce the members of the panel. The leader should then be seated with the panel, open the discussion with a few introductory sentences, and then involve other members in the panel discussion. The chairperson should operate in the panel discussion as suggested in the chapters on problem solving and leadership, remembering that there are special requirements imposed on the public discussion. Particularly, the chairperson must be sensitive to the audience's needs for summaries, for reiteration of ideas to improve clarity, for transitions between topics, and for emphasis in steps to be followed in the discussion process. After the chairperson gives the final summary for the panel discussion, he or she may turn to the audience, either to make concluding remarks (if only a panel discussion is scheduled) or to follow the procedures stated earlier for the forum (if a panel-forum is scheduled).

This section will conclude by describing an example of a panel discussion in which you might be interested. Assume that some group of faculty and students in your university believes that the role of students in the decision-making processes of the university should be increased, but other groups disagree with this view. Students and faculty have requested that the administration invite several experts to the campus to discuss the matter. The president of the university has complied with this request and has appointed a committee composed of students and faculty members to implement the suggestion. You are appointed to the committee.

After substantial discussion, the committee agrees to invite four experts from outside the university's community to participate in a panel-forum discussion. The topic selected for the panel-forum discussion is "What should be the university's position toward increasing student involvement in decisions concerning the university's affairs?" The committee might then agree upon a list of specialists who could serve effectively as panel members and invite them to participate in the panel-forum discussion. After the chosen individuals accept invitations to participate in the panel-forum, the committee might select from the campus community a person who is knowledgeable about the topic and who possesses group leadership skills to serve as the chairperson. The leader and the panel would then be expected to perform the duties previously described for the panel and the forum.

Principles

1. The panel is a public discussion in which a group of four to eight experts talk about a problem, following the problem-solving format, in front of an audience and under a chairperson's leadership.
2. Experts should participate on the panel and follow the problem-solving format (using its informal style of interaction) for the purpose of sharing with the audience information about a problem and its solution.
3. The conditions of the physical environment should be such that the panel members may see and hear one another easily and so that the panel can be seen and heard by the audience. Ideally, the panel should be seated on a platform.
4. When possible, a panel-forum combination should not run longer than one hour and forty-five minutes.
5. The panel's discussion should be planned in two phases. In the first phase of planning, all the principles for problem solving listed in Chapter Six are considered, and the session is ended with a brief outline for the problem-solving discussion. At the second planning session, the panel should agree on essential definitions, limitations of the problem, topic questions or issues and their order of introduction into the discussion, plans to cover pertinent topics, and time limits for topics.
6. The chairperson for a panel discussion should get the meeting under way, orient the audience to the topic or problem, and introduce the

panel members. In addition, the chairperson should follow many of the principles listed for the forum, because the panel is a public discussion, and follow *all* of them when a panel-forum is employed.

The Colloquium

A *colloquium* is a form of public discussion in which a group of three to six persons discuss a problem among themselves and with the audience under the leadership of a chairperson or moderator. The colloquium, or colloquy, as a form of public discussion is essentially a hybrid in which the panel and forum are combined together (rather than in sequential order). The members of the group are experts on the problem or topic under discussion, and their views may be quite divergent. Sometimes, representatives of the audience may sit with the experts in front of the audience to participate in the forum portion of the discussion, but it is essential that the primary members of the panel have expertise relevant to the problem under consideration.

The purpose of a colloquium is to identify, develop, and work toward the solution(s) of a problem and related subproblems within the problem-solving format for the benefit of the participating audience. Accordingly, a colloquy is a public discussion conducted for the benefit of the audience, in which the audience shares in the deliberations on the problem and its solution(s).

The colloquium has two levels of purpose that are similar to those previously identified for a panel. At one level, the experts on the panel for the colloquium attempt to solve the problem by following the problem-solving format. At another level of purpose, the panel has the objective of informing the audience and stimulating the audience to participate in the problem-solving process—or, at least, to make an effort toward the solution of the problem and its interrelated subproblems.

Because the colloquium is a combination of the panel and the forum, it possesses a number of characteristics that we have previously discussed. Panel members would undoubtedly wish to proceed through the preplanning phases detailed previously to help ensure an effective outcome for the colloquium (see pp. 184). The chairperson opens the discussion, quiets the audience, makes a few comments about the occasion, announces and introduces the topic or problem, introduces the panel, and gets the problem-solving discussion under way.

You will find at this point in the colloquium that there is a departure from the procedures typically employed in the pure panel discussion. When either the chairperson or the panel members determine that some matter is hindering the pursuit of a satisfactory solution to the problem or subproblems, the audience is invited to participate by asking questions or making remarks (see Figure 10.3). For example, as a chairperson you might observe

FIGURE 10.3 *The Colloquium*

that two panel members disagree on a matter; that a salient issue, subproblem, or solution is being omitted or ignored in the discussion; or that a questionable point is not being challenged. At this point, you would shift from the panel discussion to the forum discussion until the matter is settled. Then you would shift back to the panel discussion until the next opportunity for the audience's participation occurs. This process continues until the discussion is concluded, either by the time limit or by arrival at an agreed-upon solution to the problem and interrelated subproblems.

You might already have surmised from the brief description of the colloquium that there are no set speeches. As in the panel discussion, individuals, either on the panel or in the audience, do not speak in any set order. Interaction among panelists and between panelists and the audience is informal. At a colloquium, you would expect substantial give and take and interruptions under the flexible guidance of the chairperson. The systems analysis must be ongoing.

However, a skillful leader alone is not enough to ensure the effective operation of a colloquium. Panelists must also assist the chairperson in performing his or her responsibilities. Moreover, the chairperson and the panelists must perform all the functions while still following the systematic inquiry explicit in the problem-solving format.

The environment, an external variable, can contribute significantly to the outcome of the event. Ideally, the leader and members of the panel are seated on a platform at the front of the room. Seating should be arranged so that the panel members can see one another, the chairperson, and the audience. Of course, it is also important that everyone be able to hear what is being said. Panelists, as well as members of the audience, should speak loudly enough to be heard by all in the room.

The length of time may not be a constraint for some small group discussions, but it is an important matter for public discussions. Usually an hour and a half is a reasonable time limit for a colloquium. Some colloquies may run slightly longer or shorter depending on the audience's interest in the topic and its commitment to becoming involved in the deliberations.

For an example of a colloquium, the illustration used earlier for the forum dealing with the task force on student publications will be continued. As a result of the forum described previously, your task force has obtained the divergent views of various constituencies on the campus concerning matters relevant to student publications. However, your task force has not yet received the advice of experts on the topic of what the university's policy should be concerning the support of student publications.

In an effort to obtain such advice and at the same time to involve the university community in the deliberations on the problems, your task force decides to hold a colloquium. Your task force agrees to invite three experts from outside and two experts from inside the university to participate in the colloquium discussion. Of course, the experts are selected from a priority-based list of specialists with divergent views and on the basis of their ability to assist the chairperson in performing his or her responsibilities. The chosen individuals accept the invitations to participate in the colloquium. Next, a leader from the campus community who has group leadership skills and is knowledgeable about the problem is selected to serve as the chairperson. The panelists meet in advance to plan the portion of the colloquium dealing with the panel discussion. The panelists and chairperson then conduct the colloquium according to the procedures we have suggested.

Principles
1. The colloquium is a form of public discussion in which a group of three to six experts, selected for their divergent views, talk about a problem, following the problem-solving format, in front of an audience and under a chairperson's leadership.
2. The purpose of the colloquium is to identify, develop, and work toward the solution(s) to a problem and related subproblems for the benefit of the participating audience.

3. The chairperson should plan for the colloquium by following the two-phase planning operations described previously for the panel (see pp. 183–184).
4. The principles for the problem-solving format and its related informal style of interaction as listed in the earlier chapter on problem solving should be followed.
5. The environmental conditions should be such that the discussion group of the colloquium is on a platform, can see and hear one another easily, and can be seen and heard by the audience/participants.
6. A colloquium should last no longer than an hour and a half.
7. The chairperson for a colloquium should open the meeting, introduce the problem, introduce the discussion group, and follow the general principles for a moderator specified in the earlier chapter on leadership. However, he or she should extend these principles by inviting the audience to participate by asking questions or making comments whenever the experts' discussion is deterred from the pursuit of a satisfactory solution; thus the leader should shift from the public group discussion to the audience and back again throughout the colloquium. The chairperson should also implement the principles listed for the forum, because the colloquium is really a hybrid in which the panel and forum are combined.

The Symposium

A *symposium* is a series of brief speeches on various aspects of a particular problem presented to an audience. The number of people involved in a symposium ranges from two to six speakers plus a chairperson (see Figure 10.4). The speakers are expected to be knowledgeable about the topic, and they prepare their speeches in advance. Unlike the panel discussion or the informal discussion held in private, the speakers are uninterrupted during their presentations. A symposium, therefore, generally lacks some of the spontaneity and immediacy present in panel discussions. A symposium is slightly more formal than a forum, a panel, or a colloquium.

The primary purpose of a symposium is to present information to an audience. As a form of public discussion, a symposium is probably less suited to problem solving than is a panel discussion. However, like a panel, a symposium is frequently combined with a forum to create a symposium-forum discussion. A symposium may lead to a panel discussion or a combination of symposium and panel-forum discussion. In rare instances, a symposium may be used to persuade the audience, but its principal function is to inform.

Arrangements are usually made for the chairperson and speakers to meet for a short planning session prior to the symposium. In this planning

FIGURE 10.4   *The Symposium*

session, the members should conduct a brief systems analysis. They should especially examine their purposes, the audience, and the environment. On the basis of this analysis, specific plans for the symposium can be made. The plans made at this meeting are typically not as involved or as complete as those made for panel discussions. Nevertheless, a planning session helps to ensure that the symposium will accomplish its purpose. The participating speakers determine in advance how the topic or problem will be divided. The problem may be divided on the basis of divergent positions relevant to the problem, particular interests of individuals concerning the problem, or significant solutions to the problem. However, all aspects or phases of the divided topics should relate directly to the single problem under examination. The specific order in which speakers will make their presentations may also be determined at the planning session.

In addition, the speakers will generally agree in advance on the time to be allocated for each speech. The time periods are usually divided equally among speakers, and they generally range from a little less than ten minutes to not more than twenty minutes per speaker. Of course, the amount of time per speaker will depend on the number of speeches to be given and the time available for the symposium. When the symposium is planned as a separate event, it should usually not run longer than one hour and fifteen minutes. As mentioned earlier, plans are frequently made for a panel discussion, forum discussion, or a combination of the two to follow a symposium. When a symposium is to be used in combination with another type of public discussion, the symposium itself should run for less than one hour, with not more than a total of one hour and forty-five minutes devoted to the combined forms of public discussion.

Generally, after the planning meeting, each speaker prepares his or her speech, following the general procedures taught in public speaking classes. Between the initial planning session and the symposium, substantial individual work is required by speakers to develop and practice effective speeches. It is important that the speakers for a symposium be knowledgeable about their subject matter, but it is equally important that they be competent speakers. You have undoubtedly had the opportunity to hear a speech given by an outstanding expert that was presented very poorly. If the audience is to become and remain involved in the speeches given at a symposium, then the speaker's competence must be considered when selecting participants for the symposium.

The speeches for a symposium are presented from a stage, a raised platform, or the floor in the front of a room. As with other forms of public discussion, it is important that the speakers be heard and seen by all members of the audience. Before and after speaking, the speakers sit on chairs in the front of the room. Sometimes they sit behind a table, but this may not be necessary if the symposium is to be presented as a separate event. What is important is that the seated participants be seen by the audience; this is particularly important when a panel or panel-forum discussion is to follow the symposium. Of course, speakers usually stand behind a lectern, rostrum, or a table to deliver their speeches.

As with other forms of public discussion, the chairperson is responsible for getting the symposium started and for making sure that it moves along smoothly. The chairperson's first task is to bring the audience members under control by quieting them with a few comments. He or she next begins the introductory remarks, which probably will include commenting on the occasion, announcing the topic or problem, stressing the problem's importance for the audience, and stating how the problem is to be divided among the speakers. The chairperson then introduces each speaker in succession, and the speeches are presented. If a panel discussion, forum discussion, or a combination of the two is scheduled after the symposium, the chairperson follows the procedures outlined here for these forms of public discussion.

In the earlier discussions of the forum and the colloquium, an example was provided of how each could be used by a task force on student publications on which you might serve as a member. To illustrate an example of a symposium, that example will continue here. Assume that you are still a member of this task force, and assume also that the group has deliberated for several months since holding the forum and the colloquium to provide the campus community with access and input into the task force. The task force has now arrived at a consensus on the tentative recommendations to be made to the president of the university.

In order to inform the campus community about the tentative recommendations, to get feedback on possible problems relevant to them, and to ensure that no worthy suggestion has been overlooked, the task force might now schedule a symposium-forum discussion prior to submitting the final recommendations to the president. The topic for the symposium-forum might be stated as follows: What should be the policy concerning student publications at the university?

The task force's chairperson might serve as the moderator for the symposium-forum, performing the responsibilities identified earlier. Each member of the task force might speak briefly on a particular aspect of student publications and on tentative recommendations. For example, one member might speak on the role of student publications in meeting students' needs, another on the range of student publications needed to meet these needs, still another on financial support for student publications, and so on. After all speeches are concluded, the chairperson is expected to present a summary and then begin the forum discussion, following the procedures discussed previously. Of course, it would be possible for the task force to have scheduled only a symposium in this case, but the advantages of doing so are limited. Generally, symposia are scheduled in conjunction with at least a forum.

Principles
1. The symposium is a form of public discussion in which a series of brief speeches (usually made by two to six speakers) on various aspects of a specified problem are presented uninterrupted to an audience.
2. The purpose of the symposium is to present information to an audience.
3. Persons knowledgeable about the topic and skilled in public speaking should present the speeches.
4. The symposium should be combined with the forum for better audience involvement.
5. A planning session prior to the symposium is used to determine how the speakers will divide the topic, choose the specific order in which the speakers will speak, and determine the time to be allocated to each speech.
6. Speakers should prepare and practice their speeches thoroughly.
7. When scheduled separately, the symposium should run no longer than one hour and fifteen minutes and not longer than one hour and forty-five minutes when it is combined with another form of public discussion.
8. The speakers and chairperson should be on a platform, if possible, and they should be seen and heard by one another and by the audience.

9. A chairperson should quiet the audience, make introductory remarks, stress the importance of the topic and occasion, state how the topic has been divided by the speakers, introduce the speakers, and provide a brief summary at the conclusion of the meeting. (If a forum or a panel discussion is planned in conjunction with the symposium, the principles stated previously for these forms of public discussion should be followed.)

Selected Private Discussions

Private discussions, unlike public discussions, are not held in front of an audience or with audience participation. Yet, just as with public discussions, individuals participating in private discussions need guidelines or procedures to follow. Without guidelines, groups easily develop bad habits, such as redundancy, digression, inefficiency, disorganization, and confusion. Specific private discussion formats that are increasing in popularity are quality circles, self-directed and natural work teams, media-assisted groups, (teleconferencing and computer-mediated communication) and therapy and self-help groups.

Quality Circles

In recent years, quality circles have been used increasingly as a private discussion group alternative. Originally used in Japanese businesses, quality circles are now being implemented by businesses in the United States.

Quality circles consist of six to eight employees who meet voluntarily on a regular basis to generate ideas and to discuss work-related problems of productivity and quality control (Hellweg and Freiberg, 1992). Using problem-solving techniques, these groups present ideas and solutions to management for approval and then monitor the implementation process. Theoretically, performance should improve because the employees have had in-put into the decision-making process and this does seem to be supported by research (Andrews and Herschel, 1996).

The problem with quality circles doesn't seem to be with the concept; it most likely is with the way it is implemented or its extended use. To succeed, quality circle participants must have top management support, a willingness from superiors to accept suggestions and criticism from subordinates, and training in task and social decision-making skills (Smeltzer and Watson, 1984). Since quality circle teams, like individuals, need to be reinforced for their efforts and accomplishments, many companies find continued improvement by meeting with groups individually, expressing renewed enthusiasm for the program, or implementing a reward system (Lawler and Mohrman, 1985).

Because the quality circle group is maintained over long periods of time, it is important to consider how participants relate to one another. Participants should (1) listen to and show respect for other points of view, (2) criticize ideas, not individuals, (3) give equal treatment to group members, and (4) give credit to those who deserve it. Think about how you would feel if the following situation had happened to you. After working for the company for less than a year, Jane was asked if she would like to join a quality circle group in her department. Since she was curious, she did. She was impressed by the openness at the meetings and by the fact that the group's suggestions were actually considered and implemented by top management. After her fourth session, Jane offered a plan for minimizing overtime. Because her suggestion saved the company more than $100,000 in the first year it was implemented, her work group received special recognition and a bonus. Accordingly, because the group's contributions were recognized and rewarded, the group continued to offer ideas and suggestions.

When implementing a quality circle effort, it is important to consider the potential for resistance from middle management. To overcome resistance, after informing the entire organization of the quality circle concept and its objectives, it is a good idea to train middle managers before training any other groups of employees (Napier and Gershenfeld, 1999). When middle managers are trained well, most enthusiastically adopt quality circles as a valuable management tool.

Before training executives, middle managers, supervisors, and employees, and before the first quality circle meeting, each organization should establish its rules. These rules should be in writing in order to minimize the potential for misinterpretation and conflict. Management should consider developing rules in the following categories: circle formation, circle schedules, leading circles, choosing projects, requesting information from outside sources, reporting to management, delivering management presentations, and following up on projects. As you can see, introducing and maintaining a quality circle effort takes a major commitment from upper management. Organizations should weigh the advantages and disadvantages very carefully before using quality circles as a participative management strategy.

Self-Directed and Natural Work Teams

While many companies continue quality-circle efforts, others are embracing the total quality management movement. These companies use self-managing work teams to plan strategies, implement solutions, analyze processes, and make adjustments to improve work initiatives. Self-directed or natural work teams are made up of a small group of employees who are responsible for an entire work process, segment, or activity (Wellins and George, 1991). For example, in a hospital, rather than rotating doctors, nurses, nurses aides, social workers, and technicians from wing to wing, a medical team forms to assist a wing of patients as a team. The medical team always works together and needs little or no outside supervision. Employees who work as teams learn to manage themselves and their work. They form to improve products, assess day-to-day scheduling, set goals, and solve problems. A self-directed work team's goal is to learn how to monitor and lead itself.

Self-directed work teams are different from quality circles. Requiring little or no supervision, these teams are formal, permanent structures of the organization. Keep in mind that not all work groups are teams. Self-directed work teams differ from work groups in that they share leadership roles; have mutual and individual accountability; have a specific purpose; require collective effort; encourage open-ended discussion and active problem-solving; measure performance directly; and discuss, decide, and do real work together (Katzenbach and Smith, 1993).

Team members are expected to learn jobs required of other team members and need ongoing training to function most effectively. Members need to learn new technical skills to perform different tasks, communication skills for working as a team, and quality principles and practices such as problem identification and continuous improvement (Wellins, 1992). The skills that have been discussed in earlier chapters of this book are ones self-directed work teams use on a day-to-day basis.

As with quality circles, the formation of self-directed work teams often meets with resistance. Since teams assume responsibilities once reserved for supervisors or managers (i.e., hiring, performance reviews, purchasing, etc.), many supervisors fear that their jobs will be eliminated. While some positions are lost, most organizations report that supervisor and manager roles are more often redefined. New supervisory role definitions may include eliminating obstacles, coordinating team efforts, training team members, and/or serving as team members themselves. As organizations implement team-based management approaches, employees need help in making the transition from the traditional management model to one that develops individual empowerment through the use of self-directed work teams (Brauchle and Wright, 1993).

Media-Assisted Groups

As you know, participating in group meetings takes time and energy. Business executives are probably more aware than any other group of how much it costs to run meetings. When professionals have to meet with associates out of town, costs include time away from work, transportation, meals, and so on. Because of the expense of out-of-town meetings, a number of organizations have investigated alternatives. Two alternatives that are receiving increased use and attention are teleconferencing and computer mediated communication. There are three types of teleconferencing: audio, video and audiographic.

Audio Conferencing.   The type of teleconferencing that has received the most widespread use is audio conferencing. Audio conferencing allows individuals or groups of people who are located at different sites to hear and be heard, but not to see or be seen, by one another.

The first time individuals are asked to participate in an audio conference, they may think, "No big deal—I talk on the telephone all the time." However, they are likely to respond differently after taking part in such a conference. Audio conferencing is not as simple as one might expect. In fact, inexperienced audio conference participants often find themselves interrupting others, not knowing when to speak, failing to identify themselves, or nodding instead of responding verbally. Talking with three or more people is different from talking with one. The difficulties with conference call meetings include the inability to see nonverbal responses, think well over the telephone, respond to visual cues, see the speaker for audience analysis, and minimize outside distractions. According to Ostendorf (1989), the most common errors when participating in audio conferencing include confusion or delay in beginning the meeting, unclear meeting goals, lack of interaction among group members, difficulty in identifying speakers, and difficulty in obtaining the floor.

In an effort to overcome audio conferencing difficulties, guidelines should be given to all participants. The organizer of the conference should (1) select a moderator/gatekeeper to keep the meeting orderly, (2) notify all attendees in writing of the time and date of the call (using time zone), (3) give calling instructions, including the duration and purpose of the meeting, (4) request that participants identify themselves by name when speaking, and (5) identify the conference's time limits.

It is interesting to note that after a person has participated in one audio conference, he or she is more likely to prepare more completely for the next one. When participants understand the process and structure of audio conferencing, meetings run very effectively.

Video Conferencing.   Because of the constraints of audio conferencing, many people have investigated the possibility of using video conferencing. Unlike watching the one-way communication of television, video conferencing allows the two-way communication among individuals or groups interacting with one another. The video room is usually equipped with two or more cameras so that all members are visible, several microphones, visual aid equipment, several audio speakers, and a large screen. In addition, there is often an isolated control booth with engineers to monitor and control video input/output.

Even though video conferencing has been available for a number of years, costs, until recently, were prohibitive for many organizations and groups. Now, however, advances in technology have made video conferencing more cost effective. Even so, adoption of this communication medium has been slow for two basic reasons. First, most people do not like to see themselves on TV and are afraid to face the camera. Second, face-to-face communication is a more desirable means of communication. Even with multiple cameras and microphones, participants often miss subtle nonverbal cues and are more hesitant to make contributions. Nevertheless, it appears that video conferencing is the medium of the future, because meetings can be reproduced easily and sent to absent participants. It also works easily, participants prepare more completely, and meeting follow-through is more disciplined.

Video conferences do differ from face-to-face meetings, but future video conferences may be more similar to in-person meetings as the technology becomes available to enable participants to view three-dimensional holographic images rather than flat screens.

In an effort to overcome participants' anxiety, some organizations offer training in video conference techniques. In these classes, participants gain experience and confidence by learning how to conduct or moderate video sessions, how to use visual aids, and how to communicate effectively as a participant. To make the best use of the technology available, a conference coordinator should keep the following guidelines in mind (Young, 1989): (1) begin and end on time (leasing hookups are for a predefined time period); (2) appoint site chairpersons to maintain complete participation; and (3) brief and prepare participants with written documents prior to the meeting.

Although this section has discussed video conferencing used in private discussions or closed-circuit formats, video conferences are also used in public discussions or open-channel formats. In the future, you will see increased use of open-channel video conferences for marketing new products, educational seminars and training, sales meetings, stockholder meetings, fund-raising, annual conferences, press conferences, and problem-solving sessions.

Audiographic Conferencing. In order to address the limitations posed by the audio conference's lack of interaction and the video conference's expense, many organizations have introduced audiographic conferencing. One of the newest forms of teleconferencing, the audiographic conference combines audio conferencing with electronically created visual images. Audiographic conferences use telephone lines to transmit oral messages and graphic materials.

Visual images are transmitted using electronic blackboards, facsimile machines, and computer terminals. Although electronic blackboards and tablets have been available for a number of years, they have only recently come into widespread use. As a person at one location uses a special instrument to write on the electronic blackboard, the image begins to appear simultaneously at other locations. Now, in addition to electronic blackboards, audio conferences are using facsimile machines and computers to develop more interactive presentations and programs (Johnstone and Gilcher, 1989). Since visual images can appear at any number of locations, organizations see future potential for audiographic conferences. For example, universities are using audiographics to provide educational opportunities to individuals in remote areas on a limited budget; hospital physicians use audiographics to provide high-resolution emergency consultation to other physicians in rural settings (the video images are presented on a high resolution monitor). Finally, businesses use audiographics to share information and get immediate feedback about new products and services.

Computer-Mediated Communication.   Another alternative to face-to-face meetings is computer conferencing or computer-mediated communication (CMC). Consider the following example. Six managers living in five different cities are participating in an implementation group conducted in Atlanta, GA. These managers are carrying on a lively discussion about the latest virtual reality video game, "Whizbat." Since managers often meet to discuss business issues, this scenario is not too unusual. However, what makes this group unique is that they have never heard each others' voices and have never met face-to-face. Each person is in front of a computer at his or her location. The screen includes small color photographs with a code number for each participant. When a person has something to add, he or she types a message, which is transmitted with his or her code to each location simultaneously. Meetings like this one are taking place regularly across the globe.

Computer-mediated communication (CMC) has changed the dynamics of group work in education and business. But, are these meetings the most effective options for groups? Sproull and Kiesler (1991) found that computer-mediated communication tends to be more open, and it tends to encourage participation by otherwise reticent group members. Another study (Schloss, 1997) found that groups who utilized computer-mediated discussion achieved greater integrative complexity. For creative groups or groups with members who have communication apprehension, computer-mediated groups might prove to be a positive approach to the group process.

There may be some limitations to computer-mediated groups, however. In their study Sproull and Kiesler (1991) also found that communication was more honest or "blunt." In fact, inflammatory messages, or "flaming," occurred more frequently than in face-to-face groups. Additionally, computer-mediated groups had a more difficult time reaching consensus. Although some group members use icons (e.g., "smiley faces") to communicate emotions or change type sizes and fonts in their messages, the nuances of nonverbal behaviors are absent. The end result is that decision making in computer-mediated groups may require more time.

In both face-to-face and computer-mediated groups, member roles emerge and are defined. For example, self-serving, maintenance, and task role comments have been identified in computer-mediated communication as they have in face-to-face groups. But, is participation in computer-mediated groups as satisfying? Apparently not. Studies have found that members may generate more ideas and learn more in computer-mediated groups but they report more satisfaction and enjoyment from participating in face-to-face interactions (Althaus, 1997; Olaniran et al., 1996).

With the development of technology, more group members will be participating in media-assisted groups. The decision to use teleconferencing, computer-mediated communication, or face-to-face meetings should be based on the desired outcome of the meetings. Most likely, a combination will help a group achieve optimum output and cohesion.

Therapy Groups and Self-Help Groups

In Chapter Two, we discussed the family group as the most basic and long-lasting group to which we belong. While families may provide a sense of belonging, the mobility and hectic pace of today's society often doesn't allow families to provide the kind of emotional support some family members need. As family roles change, other groups emerge to fill voids with increasing numbers of therapy and self-help groups forming to meet social and therapeutic needs. These groups use the dynamics of a group to stimulate interaction, personal growth, and self-understanding.

While group therapy or self-help is rarely sought as an initial intervention in times of crisis, it can serve a valuable function. In fact, when a person's family or social network is found inadequate to help that person cope, seeking outside affiliation is necessary. In times of crisis, in particular, individuals may feel pressured to heal quickly and may sometimes try to cope prematurely. Groups can help with crisis management, as well as other social needs.

While both therapy and self-help groups strive to help individuals maintain psychological and physical integrity, each format does it in a different way. Group psychotherapy is a means of altering behavior and emotions (Gladding, 1999; Yalom, 1995). Group therapy, often an offshoot of individual therapy, may be used in combination with individual therapy. A therapist or counselor usually invites his or her patient to join a group. These groups can take different forms, but generally are made up of five to ten people who create a unique social setting. Within the group context, members try new behaviors, and other members are given opportunities to respond under a professional's guidance. While groups may be homogenous or heterogeneous, members usually have some commonality among them. Different issues emerge, for example, when a group of adolescents, couples, divorcees, or incest victims interact.

Therapy groups differ from self-help groups in that a person in therapy strives to alleviate a pathology and develop health. In addition, in therapy groups, personal relationships between professionals and members are forbidden. In self-help groups, members are undergoing normal experiences and join the group voluntarily to help solve mutual problems and to provide ongoing support.

Think of the groups advertised as supportive outlets in your community. Signs invite people to join self-help groups, and newspapers list self-help events such as meetings for battered women, narcotics, sex addicts, diabetics, adult children of alcoholics, or parents without partners. With little or no fees charged, these meetings provide members sincere concern, equal status, continuous support, and opportunities to play roles as both helpers and helpees. In fact, in many self-help groups, such as Alcoholics Anonymous and Overeaters Anonymous, members serve as sponsors to other members and are available to support one another twenty-four hours a day. In the absence of the family, groups serve a valuable function in giving members a sense of belonging and support.

Principles

1. Quality circles consist of six to eight employees who voluntarily meet on a regular basis to generate ideas and to discuss work-related problems.
2. Using problem-solving techniques, these groups present ideas and solutions to management for approval and then monitor the implementation process.
3. Successful quality circles are characterized by top management support, a willingness on the part of superiors to accept suggestions and criticism from subordinates, and training in task and social decision-making skills.
4. If a quality circle effort is to work, organizers must involve and train middle managers first.
5. Participants in quality circles need to:
   a. Listen to and show respect for other points of view.
   b. Criticize ideas, not individuals.
   c. Give equal treatment to group members.
   d. Give credit to those who deserve it.
6. Organizations should establish rules for using quality circles before the first meeting.
7. Self-directed or natural work teams are made up of a small group of employees who are responsible for an entire group process, segment, or activity.
8. Self-directed work teams are different from quality circles in that they require little or no supervision and are formal and permanent structures of the organization.
9. Teleconferencing is an alternative for reducing business-meeting travel costs.
   a. Audio conferencing allows individuals or groups of people who are located at different sites to hear and be heard but not to see or be seen.
      1. The inability to see nonverbal responses, to think well over the phone, to respond to visual cues, to see the speaker for audience analysis, and to minimize outside distractions makes audio conferencing difficult.
      2. The organizer of an audio conference should select a moderator/gatekeeper; notify all attendees in writing of the time and

date of the call; give calling instructions; request that participants identify themselves by name; and identify the conference's
time limitations.

b. Video conferencing allows two-way communication between individuals or groups.

1. Adoption of video conferencing has been slow, because many
people do not like to see themselves on television and because
face-to-face communication is more desirable.

2. In an effort to overcome participants' anxiety, some organizations offer training in video conferencing techniques.

3. Video conferencing can be used in either closed-circuit or open-
channel formats.

c. Audiographic conferencing combines audio conferencing with electronically created visual images.

1. The visual images are transmitted using electronic blackboards,
facsimile machines, and computer terminals.

2. Facsimile machines and computers allow for more interactive
presentations.

3. Audiographic conferences have a wide variety of applications,
and their use is increasing.

10. Computer-mediated groups are both similar to and different from face-
to-face groups.

11. Psychotherapy groups are groups of five to ten individuals who are
attempting to alter their behavior or emotions under professional
guidance.

12. Self-help groups are made up of voluntary members who provide support for each other, while trying to solve mutual personal problems.

13. Psychotherapy groups differ from self-help groups in that therapy
members are trying to alleviate a pathology and achieve good health;
self-help group members are trying to understand and deal with natural, normal experiences.

Small Group Communication Strategies

Chapter Six discussed Dewey's formal problem-solving procedure. Now it is
time to discuss four additional techniques that can be used during public or
private discussions to keep participants involved and on track.

The Buzz Session (Phillips 66)

The *buzz session*, or Phillips 66 technique, bridges the gap between public
and private discussions. Used most often during private discussions, it can
also include the participation of the audience. In fact, the buzz group

method was first associated with J. D. Phillips (1948), who divided large audiences into groups of six for six minutes to perform some task (see Figure 10.5). The groups may be asked to discuss an aspect of a problem, to formulate questions, or to brainstorm an idea.

Buzz sessions are used regularly but are not limited by size or time constraints. The buzz group method is simply the process of dividing a group into smaller units for discussion purposes. After the smaller groups are formed, the leader or moderator assigns a task for the time allowed. After the time is up, a spokesperson for each group reports its results to the larger group. If you are a member of an organization that has committees, you may have seen this technique used. For example, a student government association recently used a variation of the buzz session during its orientation for new members. The president divided the student senators into eight groups of five members. Each group was assigned a committee chairperson, who explained the role of their committee (e.g., student-faculty relations, homecoming, teacher evaluations, and so on). Each group was then given fifteen minutes to come up with goals and ideas for the committee. Afterward, the committee chairpersons presented their information to the total group.

FIGURE 10.5 *Buzz Sessions*

The buzz session technique often helps participants in large meetings to feel more involved. A person who may be uncomfortable expressing his or her opinion or asking a question to a group of thirty might feel less intimidated in a group of four, five, or six. When you decide to use this method, be sure to plan. You must determine the questions you want answered, the group size, the duration of the session, and the type of instructions you need to provide, and you must allow adequate time for each group to report back to the larger group.

Role Playing

Besides task problems, some groups are convened to discuss people problems, or human relations issues. One method of group involvement used during private discussions is *role playing*. During the role play, one or more participants are asked to assume a role based on how they think another person would act or feel. Members present, analyze, and suggest solutions to problems (see Figure 10.6). Role playing allows participants to actually experience dimensions of a problem or sensitive issue that may have been overlooked, not discussed, or approached from a different point of view. (Although role playing can be used during public discussions, individuals may feel more reluctant to participate in front of an audience.)

Role playing is effective when used purposefully during meetings. In fact, the "drama inherent in role playing makes it an excellent device to heighten audience interest and involvement. People playing the roles can relax and act out the part, because the group members know that they are not playing themselves" (Bormann, 1975, p. 328). Role playing can be used during educational, religious, business, and family meetings. For example, role playing may be used by teachers to handle a classroom dispute between two students, or, during a business session, bosses and secretaries may be asked to switch roles while acting out a problem situation.

Although role playing allows participants to have artistic freedom, the role-playing technique involves a structured six-step process. First, a problem involving human relationships must be identified. The problem should be of interest or relevance to the group. Second, members of the group need to come up with a plot, setting, and characters for the problem situation. Third, members should be assigned roles to play. The group should avoid choosing individuals who are emotionally involved in the topic, who are shy or reluctant to play the role, or who are likely to "ham it up." Fourth, the group should get nonplayers involved by asking them to take notes, look for certain responses, and so on. Fifth, the players should be allowed to present their interpretation of the problem. Finally, the group should discuss what occurred during the role-playing situation by using what, how, when, and why questions to elicit responses. If there are differences of opinion about how the situation should have been handled, it may be a good idea to repeat the process.

Role playing can be both enlightening and entertaining, but it is inappropriate to use it with all people or groups. In addition, to maximize its

FIGURE 10.6   *Role Playing*

effect, role playing should be planned, introduced, and led by a person with adequate training and experience.

Resistance to participate in role-playing exercises is often associated with not wanting to be embarrassed or criticized in front of others. Adults, especially, hesitate to take risks in groups. Most people need to warm up to the idea of participating in a role-play. To aid in the process, Swink (1993) advises leaders to establish rapport with the group, create opportunities for members to interact early, integrate each activity to earlier parts of a discussion, break participants into small groups, and design activities that require all group members to get up at the same time.

Listening Teams

At times, discussions take place after another presentation, such as a panel discussion, speech, or film. In these situations, participants are usually asked to base the discussion on the content of the presentation. Unfortunately, if we do not listen effectively, we may miss critical information or forget what we have heard before the next session. In fact, it is estimated that we forget as much as 25 percent of the message after a ten-minute presentation (Wolvin and Coakley, 1996). When participants are likely to miss important details because there is too much information or because the information is poorly presented or too detailed, you can help them retain information by using the listening teams technique (Seibold, 1984).

When this method is used, the leader or moderator divides the group into teams prior to the lecture or presentation and assigns each team a specific listening task. For example, if a panel were discussing abolishing the constitutional amendment that limits the president of the United States to two terms, one listening team might be assigned to listen for the historical background information, another for advantages of abolition, the next for disadvantages of abolition, and perhaps the last team for consequences of abolition. After the presentation, the teams are given adequate time to take notes and organize their thoughts before all the teams form one group. The listening team members then serve as valuable resources during the discussion that follows.

This listening team method encourages participants to take active roles while listening. As you know from your reading in prior chapters, quality information input is a major key to quality group outcomes. Research supports the theory that listeners retain more when they have some incentive or responsibility to recall information later (Smeltzer and Watson, 1984; Zajonc, 1960). With this in mind, it may be to your advantage to consider using the listening team technique in the future.

Nominal Group Technique

One technique that can be used in all phases of discussion is the *nominal group technique* (Delbecq et al., 1975). This technique involves the generation of ideas by all group members. When used effectively, this technique saves time, encourages everyone to participate, and increases the potential for agreement and consensus.

The nominal group technique is used to identify problems, create solutions, and determine plans for implementation. If your group were trying to think of ways to recognize outstanding teachers at your college or university, for example, you could use the nominal group technique by following these four steps:

1. *Idea formation:* Group members silently come up with ideas or concerns during a limited time period (usually three to five minutes). Each person writes down as many ideas/responses as possible. Individual group members might write: have a recognition breakfast; send letters of appreciation; write letters to the faculty member's chair; give monetary awards; or send an article to the local newspaper.

2. *Idea documentation:* The leader asks each group member to present one of his or her ideas orally. All the ideas are listed on a blackboard or flipchart pad. Each idea should be put in the contributor's own words. After each group member has made at least one contribution, the leader asks for points of clarification. (Note: After each person has given an idea, you can go around the group again until as many ideas as possible have been listed.)

3. *Idea ranking:* Group members individually rank the ideas in order of preference or importance. The leader may ask for suggested criteria by which to evaluate the ideas. After discussion, group members anonymously vote on their top three to five choices.

4. *Idea discussion and evaluation:* The top choices are listed separately along with the number of votes per choice. Group members discuss important aspects of each choice and finally rank or rate the ideas and suggestions.

Because individuals work independently in the initial phase of the nominal group technique, one advantage is that equal participation is encouraged of all group members regardless of status or power differences. The views of members who ordinarily might not participate openly are treated the same as the ideas of very vocal group members. In general, group members feel more satisfied and more effective than when no specific procedure is followed (Kramer et al., 1997).

Brainstorming

As we discussed in Chapter Six, brainstorming can be used effectively during problem-solving sessions. Brainstorming is also useful for enhancing creativity. Using the guidelines provided in Chapter Six, brainstorming breaks down rigid thinking and can be used to generate new ideas. Research (McLeod et al., 1996) has found the effectiveness of the process is enhanced when the brainstorming groups are ethnically diverse. Major corporations are now using brainstorming in the guise of creativity sessions or idea teams to help unlock the hidden potential of many of their employees (Smith, 1985). Now more than ever, companies are looking for ways to prevent discouragement of ideas.

Principles
1. The buzz session technique is used in public private discussions.
2. During a buzz session, a large group is divided into smaller units for discussion. After the smaller groups are formed, the leader assigns a task for the time allowed. After the time is up, a spokesperson from each group reports to the larger group.
3. Role playing allows participants to experience dimensions of a problem or a sensitive issue as they present, analyze, and suggest solutions to real problems.
4. The role-playing technique involves a six-step process.
   a. A problem involving human relationships must be identified.
   b. Members of the group need to come up with a plot, setting, and characters for the problem situation.
   c. Members should be assigned roles to play.
   d. Nonplayers need to be involved.
   e. Players present their interpretation of the problem.
   f. Players and nonplayers discuss what occurred in the role-playing situation.
5. Listening teams are used to encourage active participation.
6. Listening teams are formed when a moderator or leader divides a group into teams prior to a lecture or presentation. Each team is then assigned a specific listening task. After the presentation, each team is given time to take notes and organize their thoughts. The team members then serve as resources for the discussions that follow.
7. The nominal group technique involves the four steps of idea formation, idea documentation, idea ranking, and idea discussion and evaluation.
8. The brainstorming technique or creativity session is useful for generating ideas as well as for problem solving.

Summary

This chapter examined several special forms of and techniques for small group communication. Special forms of small group communication were divided into two categories: public and private. Public discussions take place in front of an audience or in some way engage participation from persons who are not members of the group. Private discussions, on the other hand, include those forms of small group communication that are not conducted before an audience or do not involve the participation of nonmembers.

Under the category of public discussions, this chapter examined the form, purposes, and characteristics of the forum, panel, colloquium, and symposium. The forms of private discussions examined were quality circles, self-directed and natural work teams, teleconferences, media-assisted groups, and therapy and self-help groups.

In addition to discussing special forms of small group communication, this chapter also examined techniques to use during group discussion, including how to use buzz sessions, role playing, listening teams, the nominal group technique, and brainstorming. Even though you may not use all the forms of group discussion identified in this chapter, it is likely that you will participate in at least one of the forms or use one of the small group communication techniques.

Ideas for Discussion

1. What are the distinguishing characteristics of the forum, panel, colloquium, and symposium? Which of these forms of public discussion are most and least formal? Which involve the audience the most and least?

2. What are the similar characteristics of the forum, panel, colloquium, and symposium?

3. What are some specific events in which you think it might be appropriate to use a forum, panel, colloquium, and symposium separately? What are some situations in which you think it might be appropriate to use certain combinations of these forms of public discussion? Why did you make these choices for your selected situations?

4. What benefits would an organization find from encouraging its employees to participate in quality circles? Could these benefits be achieved by using other forms of small group communication? Why or why not?

5. In what ways does teleconferencing potentially hinder effective small group communication? How can these obstacles be overcome?

6. Explain the advantages and disadvantages of computer-mediated groups over face-to-face groups.

7. Explain the group formats that would be most appropriate for using buzz sessions, role playing, listening teams, and brainstorming. What are the benefits of each technique?

Suggested Projects and Activities

1. Plan a real forum, panel, colloquium, and symposium in which you would like to participate. Start with the specification of the topic or problem, and list every step you should execute, including principles to follow while the public discussion is in operation.

2. Select and observe a public discussion. Identify the type of discussion the group represents, and write a brief paper analyzing the discussion according to principles in your text.

3. Discuss the feasibility of setting up quality circles at your college or university. By conducting campus interviews, determine whether or not quality circles would receive top administrative support. Identify the procedures you should follow.

4. Work with your university media center to set up an audio or video conference. Plan an actual problem-solving session to use this small group format. Coach participants before the session to maximize each person's effectiveness.

5. Select a human relations problem and apply the six-step process for role playing. Be sure to get everyone involved as either a player or a nonplayer. After the process, evaluate your group's effectiveness.

6. Divide the class into three groups, and assign each a different small group communication technique: buzz session, listening team, brainstorming. Have each group plan an activity using the technique. Afterwards, discuss the effectiveness of the technique.

References _____

Althaus, L. L. Computer-mediated communication in the university classroom: an experiment with on-line discussions. *Communication education,* 1997, *46,* 158–174.

Andrews, P. H., and A. J. Herschel. *Organizational communication: empowerment in a technological society.* Boston: Houghton Mifflin, 1996.

Bormann, E.G. *Discussion and group methods: theory and practice,* 2nd ed., New York: Harper & Row, Pub., 1975.

Brauchle, P.E. and D.W. Wright. Training work teams. *Training & Development Journal,* 1993, *47,* 65–68.

Delbecq, A. L., A. H. Van de Ven, and D. H. Gustafson. *Group techniques for program planning: a guide to nominal groups and delphi processes.* Glenview, ILL: Scott Foresman, 1975.

Gladding, S. T. *Group work: a counseling specialty,* 3rd ed. Upper Saddle River, NJ: Merrill, 1999.

Hellweg, S. A., and K. L. Freiberg. Group process in organizations: the case of quality circles. In R. S. Cathcart and L. A. Samovar, eds. *Small group communication: a reader,* 6th ed. Dubuque, IA: Wm. C. Brown, 1992, 81–85.

Johnstone, S. M., and K. W. Gilcher. Audiographic conferencing: a primer. In K. J. Hansell, ed. *The teleconferencing manager's guide,* White Plaines, NY: Knowledge Industry Publications, Inc., 1989, pp. 59–72.

Katzenbach, J. R. and D. K. Smith. The discipline of teams. *Harvard business review,* 1993, *1,* 111–120.

Kramer, M. W., C. L. Kuo, and J. C. Dailey. The impact of brainstorming techniques on subsequent group process: beyond generating ideas. *Small group research,* 1997, *28,* 218–242.

Lawler, E. E. III., and S. A. Mohrman. Quality circles after the fad. *Harvard business review,* 1985, *63,* 65–71.

McLeod, P. L., S. A. Lobel, and T. H. Cox, Jr. Ethnic diversity and creativity in small groups. *Small group research,* 1996, *27,* 248–264.

Napier, R. W., and M. K. Gershenfeld. *Groups: theory and experience,* 6th ed. Boston: Houghton Mifflin, 1999.

Olaniran, B. A., G. T. Savage, and R. L. Sorenson. Experimental and experiential approaches to teaching face-to-face and computer-mediated group discussion. *Communication education*, 1996, 45, 244–259.

Ostendorf, V. A. Audio conference with ease. In K. J. Hansell, ed. *The teleconferencing manager's guide*, White Plaines, NY: Knowledge Industry Publications, Inc., 1989, pp. 37–56.

Phillips, J. D. Report on discussion 66. *Adult education journal*, 1948, 7, 181–182.

Schloss, A. *Developing complex group products: idea combination in computer-mediated and face-to-face groups*. 1997. [On-line] Abstract from Ann Schloss Homepage.

Seibold, D. R. Making meetings more successful: plans, formats, and procedures for group problem-solving. In R. S. Cathcart and L. A. Samovar, eds. *Small group communication: a reader*. Dubuque, IA: Wm. C. Brown, 1984, 187–201.

Smeltzer, L. R. and K. W. Watson. Improving listening skills: an empirical comparison of discussion length and level of incentive. *Central states speech journal*, 1984, 35, 166–170.

Smith, E. T. Are you creative? *Business week*, September 30, 1985, 80–84.

Sproull, L., and S. Kiesler. *Connections: new ways of working in the networked organization*. MIT Press, 1991.

Swink, D. F. Role-play your way to learning. *Training & development journal*, 1993, 47, 91–97.

Wagner, R. H., and C. C. Arnold. *Handbook of group discussion*, 2nd ed. Boston: Houghton Mifflin, 1965.

Wellins, R. Building a self-directed work team. *Training & development journal*, 1992, 46, 24–28.

Wellins, R., and J. George. The key to self-directed teams. *Training & development journal*, 1991, 45, 26–31.

Wolvin, A. D., and C. G. Coakley. *Listening*, 5th ed. Dubuque, IA: Brown & Benchmark, 1996.

Yalom, I. D. *The theory and practice of group psychotherapy*, 4th ed. New York: Basic Books, 1995.

Young, I. How to get the best out of video conferencing. In K. J. Hansell, ed. *The teleconferencing manager's guide*. White Plains, NY: Knowledge Industry Publications, Inc., 1989, pp. 105–124.

Zajonc, R. B. The process of cognitive tuning in communication. *Journal of abnormal and social psychology*, 1960, 61, 159–167.

Suggested Readings

DeVito, J. A. *The elements of public speaking*, 7th ed. New York: Longman, 2000. Chapter 9, "Presentation Aids," discusses a variety of visual aids that might be used in either public or private discussions. The chapter explains how to give a computer-assisted presentation using a presentation software package such as PowerPoint, Corel Presentations, or Lotus Freelance.

Hanna, M. S., and G. L. Wilson. *Communicating in business and professional settings*, 4th ed. New York: McGraw-Hill, 1998. Chapter 7, "Technology in the Workplace," discusses the impact of communication technologies on organizations.

Lucas, S. E. *The art of public speaking*, 6th ed. New York: McGraw-Hill, 1998. A popular and very readable text, this text provides the information needed for participating effectively in public discussions.

Schneier, F., and L. Welkowitz. *The hidden face of shyness: Understanding and overcoming social anxiety*. New York: Avon Books, 1996. Ranging from shyness to panic, many individuals experience anxiety when interacting with others. This book provides an excellent overview of shyness (communication apprehension). Chapter 9, "Biological Underpinnings," explains the biological and genetic bases of shyness. Chapter 11, "The Cultural Connection," discusses gender and cultural similarities and differences. The book also presents a variety of techniques and therapies for dealing with shyness.

Planning and
Conducting Meetings

Study Questions

After reading this chapter, you should be able to answer the following questions completely and accurately:

1. Why are many meetings characterized by inefficiency, restlessness, boredom, and frustration?
2. What are the differences between informational and decision-making meetings?
3. What are the three steps to follow when asked to plan a meeting?
4. What are the two purposes for developing a systematic meeting plan?
5. What are the five issues that an organizer should consider when planning a meeting?
6. How do short-term objectives differ from long-term objectives?
7. What elements should be included in an agenda?
8. What are three advantages of having an agenda?
9. What is a bell curve agenda and how does it work?
10. When should a planner select participants of similar or diverse backgrounds?
11. How should demonstrated competencies, experience, availability, and communication style affect participant selection?
12. What are five environmental factors that should be considered before a meeting begins?
13. When should you use formal rather than informal seating arrangements?
14. What special arrangements should you make when using materials and audiovisual equipment?
15. What are five responsibilities of meeting planners or leaders?
16. What is the role of a facilitator during question-and-answer sessions?
17. What are three reasons that people ask questions during meetings?
18. How can you encourage participation during meetings?
19. When using the discussion questioning technique, what eight guidelines should be followed?
20. Why is it important for a moderator to establish and maintain a positive relationship with the audience?
21. What are the important characteristics of effective delivery in formal group settings?
22. What is the most valuable suggestion for creating an effective delivery style?
23. What are two methods of evaluating the success of a meeting?
24. Why doesn't a meeting end when it is adjourned?

Confident that her assistant had handled the minor details in advance, the director walked briskly toward a luncheon, expecting to find five department heads, thirty of the company's highest achievers, and a guest speaker.

She had planned for the session to start at noon and to end promptly at 1:00 P.M., as—based on the participants' $40,000 average salaries—the hour meeting would cost more than $1,500 in salaries alone. When the director entered the room, however, she was greeted by chaos. Her assistant had left to search for additional chairs, the handouts had not arrived, the hotel had forgotten to provide a lectern, the bulb on the overhead projector had blown out, and the caterer had prepared meals for thirty rather than forty participants.

As you can see from this example, meetings can fall apart if they are not planned properly. You, too, have probably attended meetings that you felt were a waste of time. Perhaps a group member was not prepared or arrived late, the room was too crowded, there was no real reason for the meeting, or the leader failed to keep the group on track. Unfortunately, because the people who are responsible for planning and conducting meetings receive little or no training in what to do, many meetings are characterized by restlessness, boredom, frustration, and inefficiency. In fact, even the most well-intentioned meetings can be a waste of time. Consider the following most popular reasons (Yeomans, 1985, pp. 134–135):

1. Participants do not understand the purpose of the meeting.
2. No one is clear about what is to be accomplished.
3. There is no agenda or timetable.
4. Meetings run too long.
5. Meetings are boring.
6. Participants tell "war stories."
7. No one wants to talk about the real problem.
8. The person in charge has already decided on a course of action.
9. Participants attack one another's ideas.
10. Meetings are used when other methods would be better.

More than ever before, dislike for meetings presently seems to be a natural phenomenon. Business managers and technical professionals spend nearly one-fourth of their work lives in meetings and often feel as if they are wasting time. It is estimated that a minimum of twelve million meetings take place in the United States each day. Since meetings are essential for making decisions, disseminating information, and solving problems, experts predict more rather than fewer meetings in the future (Cotton, 1993; Seibold, 1995) Although it may seem that meetings are inevitable, you do have a choice. You can either put up with the status quo or you can learn methods to help meetings run more smoothly and efficiently. Previous chapters have provided you with information about the process of discussion and methods of improving your participation in small groups. This chapter is designed to discuss a systematic process of planning for and conducting meetings by examining steps to follow before, during, and after the meeting.

Types of Meetings

Meetings are held primarily for the purpose of sharing information or making decisions. Before scheduling a meeting, it is important to identify what you want to accomplish. The type of meeting should determine the number of participants, who should attend, the direction of communication, the arrangement of the room, and the preferred leadership style to use. Any number of people may attend an informational meeting, for example, since group discussion is not expected or encouraged (one-way communication). Since the primary goal is to give information, most planners arrange the room in classroom style and use a directive leadership style.

The goals of decision-making meetings are different from those of informational meetings. Planners invite people who will be affected by the decision or who can contribute to the group goals. Since active discussion is necessary to arrive at the best decisions, the size of the group is limited (preferably five to seven participants but no more than twelve). To encourage interaction, participants are usually seated so that each person is visible to the others. During decision-making meetings, the leader acts as a facilitator rather than interjecting his or her own opinions.

Planning the Meeting

Think for a moment about the meetings you have attended during the last week. You may have met to work on a class project, attended a national convention, been asked to serve on the board of a nonprofit organization, or discussed a problem with colleagues in the hallway. Groups come in all shapes and sizes and meet for hundreds of different purposes. Yet meetings are most successful when a systematic plan is followed. A plan serves two purposes. First, it helps ensure that the meeting addresses and meets specific goals. Second, a plan reduces the likelihood of something going wrong. When planning a meeting, the organizer should consider whether or not to have a meeting, the meeting's objectives, agenda preparation, participant selection and notification, and preparing the facilities.

To Have or Not to Have a Meeting. An important question that is frequently overlooked in meeting planning is, "Is there really a need for this meeting?" Too often meetings are scheduled without considering other alternatives (Hackman and Johnson, 1996). Depending on the situation and purpose, a person's objectives can be satisfied more effectively through written reports, letters, memos, telephone conversations, or face-to-face interactions with single individuals rather than through meetings. For example, you may get the same or more candid information by conducting a telephone survey or distributing a questionnaire than you would during a group meeting. If you are in a position to choose whether or not to schedule a meeting, remember to ask yourself, "Is it really necessary for us to get together face to face?"

Short- and Long-Term Objectives.   Meetings are called for a variety of purposes. You may meet to plan a surprise party, decide if your block should join neighborhood watch, figure out how to spend the equipment budget, or share research findings for a term project. Regardless of the specific purpose for a meeting, objectives should be thought out, and in most cases written out, in advance (Pursley and Watson, 1983; Zaremba, 1988). Written objectives help you to structure and organize the meeting, as well as provide a standard by which to evaluate the success of your meeting later.

There are short-term and long-term objectives. *Short-term objectives* refers to the outcomes of the actual meeting; *long-term objectives* refers to the overall goals the group or organization may have. Short-term objectives should specifically state what actions to take or decisions to make. For example, when a group of student leaders convenes to discuss the most effective method of introducing new students to campus activities, they would probably have different short-term and long-term objectives. A short-term objective may be to assign student representatives to a committee, come up with a schedule for the extracurricular activity fair, or decide ways to encourage organizations to be represented. At the same time, long-term objectives may be to reduce student attrition, encourage campus involvement, and develop school spirit.

Preparing an Agenda.   After establishing objectives, meeting planners should develop an agenda for the meeting. The *agenda* serves as a plan or road map to follow during the meeting (see Figure 11.1). Without an agenda, it is difficult to know where to begin; groups often overlook key issues, and little is accomplished. Effective agendas should specify the following (Pursley and Watson, 1982):

1. The purpose of the meeting
2. The date and location
3. A time to begin and end
4. Objectives
5. Topics for discussion with reasonable time frames for each topic
6. Brief minutes from previous meetings when appropriate
7. Announcements
8. Materials necessary to bring to the meeting

It is a good idea to consider the order of agenda items. Tropman and Morningstar (1996) recommend using the "bell curve agenda" with the middle of the meeting reserved for challenging or controversial topics. The meeting begins with relatively simple business such as minutes of previous meetings or easy decisions. Adler and Elmhorst (1999, p. 271) note "Once members have hit their stride and a good climate has developed, the group can move on

SAMPLE AGENDA

Date of Meeting:_____ Time:_____A.M. P.M.

Place of Meeting:_____

Meeting Arranger:_____

Meeting Participants:

_____   _____

_____   _____

_____   _____

_____   _____

Purpose of Meeting: _____

_____

Goals: _____

_____

_____

AGENDA:

Topic	Time	Item Type	Discussant
1.			
2.			
3.			
4.			
5.			
6.			

MINUTES FROM LAST MEETING:

FIGURE 11.1   *Sample Agenda Format*

to the most difficult items." The last part of the meeting can focus on easier items and a summary of actions to be taken before the following meeting.

Using this format maximizes your planning effectiveness, because participants are in attendance for the most important issues (latecomers have arrived and early leavers are still present). In addition, this format gives ample time for discussion of difficult or important items and plans for the discussion of key issues when participants are alert and at their mental peaks.

When participants know what topics are to be discussed, they also get an idea about the meeting's short-term objectives. When a group meets its short-term objectives, then it is usually on the right path to meeting its long-term objectives as well.

Agendas keep meetings on track, thus preventing the tendency for participants to stray off to tangents. Tangents are inherently more interesting than the topics on an agenda but usually do little to achieve meeting goals.

Agendas help maintain direction but should not be so rigid that they prevent discussion of unexpected issues that do pertain to your objectives. You can probably remember a time when a leader or moderator cut off a discussion by saying, "That's all the time we have for this topic—let's vote," or tried to fill time by saying, "Come on, there has got to be more that needs to be discussed; we've talked for only five minutes." Many planners incorporate flexibility into their agendas by using the ten- to twenty-minute range for discussing a topic rather than a fixed fifteen-minute time period. Incorporating flexibility also allows you to move quickly to and from points.

Although most of us understand how important it is for the leader or planner to have an agenda, many people forget how important agendas are for participants. Distributing an agenda lets participants know what to expect. This knowledge usually helps them arrive better prepared. Some people provide agendas at the beginning of the meeting. This is beneficial, but when possible, it is best to have the agenda prepared and distributed prior to the meeting.

Selecting Participants.   Before distributing the agenda, you must know who the participants will be. At times meetings are made up of volunteers, registrants, or those designated by the bylaws. However, many participants are individually selected by one person. Although it is difficult to generalize about the best way to select meeting participants, the following discussion will provide general guidelines for the times when you do have a choice.

Suppose your boss selects you to head a search committee to hire two new employees. He or she suggests that you choose people to work with you. Before deciding whom you want to work with you, as the planner, you have several decisions to make. First, do you want members of similar backgrounds or diverse backgrounds? How many group members do you want?

Members with similar backgrounds can speak a specialized language, complete with technical jargon, abbreviations, and buzz words. In addition, fewer introductory explanations are required when the people are familiar with you, the topic, and one another. On the other hand, groups whose members have similar backgrounds are often limited to using traditional approaches and ideas. Using members with diverse backgrounds usually produces more creative insights and solutions to problems. Unlike a similar group makeup, diverse group memberships do not have the same language and experiences. For this reason, these group members often need more time initially to get to know one another and to clarify terms.

Before selecting members, you must decide how many people you want involved. It is best to choose fewer participants when time is a factor, cohesiveness is important, or immediate decisions are necessary. Including more participants is desirable when a variety of solutions is needed or when you have more time.

When selecting group members, remember to consider what effect group size may have on productivity. Some researchers have found that as group size increases, the effort exerted by group members decreases (Viega, 1991; Weldon and Mustari, 1988). Known as the social loafing effect, this phenomenon occurs when groups become less productive as there are more group members available to share in group responsibilities. It appears as if members of larger groups may feel less compelled to exert maximum effort, because they think that someone else will do it or because individual contributions are unidentifiable. If a larger group is desirable, it may be necessary to identify and discuss individual contributions in an effort to exert pressure for group members to perform to the best of their abilities.

After you have decided how many participants to include and whether or not you want individuals with similar or diverse backgrounds, your selection should be based on *demonstrated competencies, experience, availability,* and *communication style* (Goodall, 1990). First, member selections should be based on *competencies* related to the topic or subject of the meeting. For example, if the problem concerns a drop in automobile sales, you would probably want people from the marketing/advertising area, service, and direct sales. Second, selection should be decided based on actual *experience* related to your objective. If your objective is fund raising for the poor, you will probably look for a person who has worked on similar projects. A third consideration is *availability.* With today's busy schedules, it is often difficult to coordinate group participation. The most experienced people, for example, may not have the time to serve on another committee. Even if people do agree to serve as participants, check their schedules carefully. It may be better to go with second choices rather than have a skeleton group meeting. Finally, your selection should consider each potential member's *communication style*—you want group members to work together easily. Try to find out how the person has worked in groups in the past. Remember that the best predictor of future performance is past behavior.

Analyzing Participants. Once group members have been selected, it is important to analyze the individuals you have chosen so that you can make general predictions about participants' attitudes and reactions. This analysis helps you to structure the pace and mood of each meeting. For example, if you have several people who were forced to attend, you may want to take time to get them involved. At training meetings, for example, some participants view their selection as a form of punishment rather than as a reward. It is the job of the facilitator to explain that organizations do not invest training dollars in employees who are expendable to the organization.

The easiest way to analyze participants is to ask yourself a series of descriptive questions such as the following and to compare the answers with your short-term objectives: What do the participants know about the topic? Do the participants want to attend the meeting or are they required to attend? Are the participants committed to the purpose, organization, or profession? What special skills or training do participants have that will help the group? And how well do the participants get along with the other group members? Considering these and similar questions enhances the probability of your structuring successful meetings.

Once you have analyzed your group, you can begin to identify group roles, assign responsibility, and delegate authority (Kieffer, 1988). Based on a member's experience or expertise, he or she may be asked to take minutes, prepare a report, find an expert presenter, make arrangements, or facilitate the discussion.

Notifying Participants. After you have selected the participants and their roles, it is also important to consider participant notification. All participants should be notified of meetings well in advance; otherwise your meetings will be poorly attended. Depending on the size, location, and importance of the meeting, it is wise to follow up initial notification with a second memo, mailing, or phone call shortly before the meeting date. The follow-up allows you to verify attendance and to answer pre-meeting questions. Tupperware,™ Inc., for example, has learned to use follow-up very successfully. As you may know, Tupperware™ sells products through hosts who have in-home parties. The host receives step-by-step instructions to follow for maximizing attendance, including issuing an initial phone call, written invitation (agenda), follow-up telephone call, and, if possible, reminder card.

Preparing Facilities. Although more attention is given to items for discussion than to the place to meet, meetings often fail because the facilities are not appropriate (Schwarz, 1994). With this in mind, planners need to be conscious of the importance of the environment, equipment, and materials.

As mentioned in Chapter Seven, the environment in which a meeting is held should be considered carefully. Since attention spans and attitudes are strongly influenced by the comfort of the surroundings, planners should make sure that the meeting place is comfortable, pleasant, and as free of distractions as possible. The room should be quiet, without disturbing noises such as those from telephones, computer printers, radios, and other people. In addition, chairs and tables should provide adequate leg and elbow room. This becomes increasingly important as the length of the meeting increases. Rooms should be well lit and well ventilated to funnel out stale air, and the thermostat should be at a comfortable setting. A good rule of thumb is to have the room a little too cool rather than too warm. Cool temperatures promote clear, alert thinking, while warm temperatures increase drowsiness.

Meeting planners should also consider the effect of seating arrangements. Too often planners forget that they can adapt their environment to meet individual needs; instead, they accept what they are given. However, the meeting's effectiveness may be decreased if the room is too large or too small, if there are no tables for participants, or if the drapes have not been pulled. You can arrange the seating in either formal or informal styles (see Figure 11.2). Formal styles are used more often for business or educational meetings and for larger groups. For example, if it is important for participants to see one another, you may want to consider using a horseshoe or round table arrangement. If, on the other hand, it is important for participants to take notes, you may want to consider using a classroom or conference table style.

Preparing Materials and Equipment.   Aside from the physical conditions of the room, it is also important to consider the use of materials and equipment. If it is necessary for participants to take notes, paper and pencils should be provided; as you know, people who are required to attend meetings are not always convinced of the meeting's importance and may show up unprepared. Name cards or badges are also useful when participants are unfamiliar with one another.

Many meetings are delayed because of audiovisual equipment malfunctions. With this in mind, all audiovisual equipment should be prepared and checked in advance Presentation Software (like Powerpoint) can be very effective but it isn't fool proof. Slide, film, and overhead projectors as well as video cassette players are notorious for breaking down, blowing up, and burning out at the worst possible moments. It is a mistake to begin a meeting without having spare bulbs, machines, or at least a contingency plan. If chalkboards, flip charts, or easels are used, be sure to have extra chalk, erasers, thumbtacks, marking pens, and pads on hand. It is also a good idea to double-check all equipment requests. Recently a professional speaker who had asked for an overhead projector and was given a film projector had her meeting delayed for thirty minutes as a result. The best advice to follow when considering audiovisual materials is summed up by Murphy's Law: "Whatever can go wrong will go wrong."

When planning for your next meeting, there are five points you should consider before using visual aids. First, each visual aid should be necessary to emphasize an idea, clarify a thought, or illustrate a point. Second, give group participants plenty of time to see the visuals. At times, presenters are so familiar with their visuals that they forget that others need time to become familiar with them as well. Third, use a variety of visuals to illustrate different points. It may be best to use slides or overheads during a large group meeting. Display models or flip charts may be best for smaller groups. Be sure to use variety in the shapes, sizes, and colors in your visuals. Fourth, speak to your listeners, not to the visual. A good visual can speak for itself. You need to keep your eyes and attention on your meeting participants. Finally, practice using visual aids before the meeting. As was mentioned earlier, just as meetings can be delayed because of equipment difficulties, they can also be delayed because

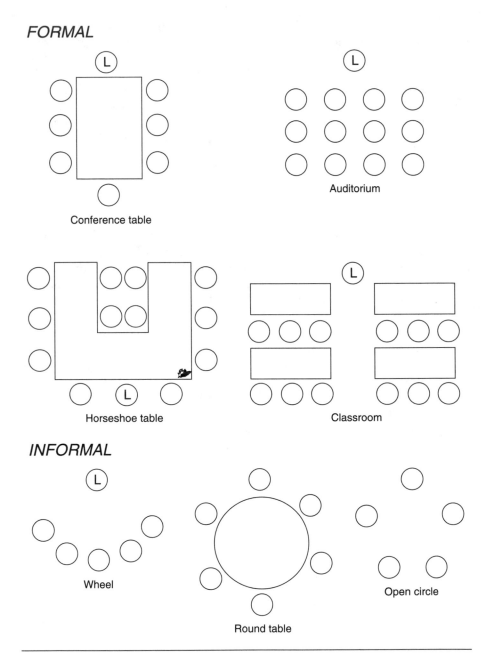

FIGURE 11.2 *Seating Arrangements*

of the presenter's lack of familiarity with the equipment. Find the on/off switch, focus on the projector, number your visuals, locate marking pens, and rehearse with remote control units before the meeting begins.

Principles
  1. People responsible for planning and conducting meetings receive little or no training in what to do.
  2. The two primary purposes of meetings are to share information or to make decisions.
  3. Many meetings are characterized by restlessness, boredom, frustration, and inefficiency.
  4. A meeting plan serves two purposes:
     a. It helps ensure that the meeting addresses and meets specific goals.
     b. It reduces the likelihood of something going wrong.
  5. Many meetings are scheduled without considering such other options as written reports, letters, memos, telephone calls, or face-to-face interactions with one individual.
  6. Written objectives help to structure and organize meetings.
     a. *Short-term objectives* refers to outcomes of the actual meeting.
     b. *Long-term objectives* refers to the overall goals of the group or organization.
  7. The agenda serves as a plan or roadmap for the meeting to follow and keeps the meeting on track.
     a. The bell curve agenda divides the meeting into three parts, with simple business topics coming first, important or difficult issues being considered in the second part, and easy topics included during the last part of the meeting.
     b. Planners should incorporate flexibility into their agendas.
     c. It is just as important for participants to have an agenda as it is for planners.
  8. Planners are responsible for deciding the composition of the meeting group.
     a. Group members with similar backgrounds take less time initially and have common reference points.
     b. Diverse group membership is recommended when more creative insights or solutions are needed.
     c. Fewer participants work better when time is a factor, cohesiveness is important, and immediate decisions are required.
     d. When there is more time and a variety of solutions is desirable, having more participants is recommended.
     e. Selections should also consider demonstrated competencies, experience, availability, and communication style.
  9. Many meetings fail because the environment, equipment, and materials were not given adequate consideration.
     a. Rooms should be comfortable, pleasant, and as free of distractions as possible.
     b. Using formal or informal seating arrangements can maximize a meeting's effectiveness.
     c. Remember that whatever can go wrong with audiovisual equipment probably will.

10. When using visual aids, the presenter should make sure that the visual is necessary, give group members adequate time to see the visual, use various visual formats, speak to the group members and not to the visual aid, and practice using the visual aid in advance.

Conducting the Meeting

When you follow all the steps discussed in the previous section, you will discover that many hours are necessary to effectively organize and plan even a one-hour meeting. Now that you know how to plan an agenda, select participants, and arrange the facilities and materials, you need to prepare yourself to conduct the meeting. Effective planners are aware of their responsibilities as leaders and facilitators.

Responsibilities of Planners/Leaders

Although the behind-the-scenes planning is the biggest contributor to a successful meeting, a meeting planner's responsibilities may not end here. Plan to arrive early to ensure that the meeting gets started on time. Once the participants have arrived, the meeting planner may also have another set of responsibilities as the speaker or moderator. In these situations, ensure that:

1. *You are well prepared.* The previous section discussed methods of preparation. At this point you must also prepare yourself for the issues to be discussed. You don't want to be surprised by your participants' responses or reactions. One method of preparation is to ask group members to submit questions for discussion before the meeting. This enables less vocal participants to voice concerns and allows you to know what issues are of most interest.
2. *You provide structure for the meeting.* After obtaining input from individuals who will participate in the meeting, you need to take responsibility for what will actually happen during the meeting. You should prepare a written agenda that includes both the short- and long-term objectives for the meeting. In addition, as a moderator or leader, you must provide participation rules, introduce a recording system, and manage time.
   a. *You ensure that all of the items on the agenda are discussed.* One of the most frustrating experiences for participants is to be told that something is going to be discussed and then not get to it. Again, failing to follow the agenda can set a precedent for future meetings.
   b. *You ensure that no items not on the agenda are discussed.* It is easy for groups to get sidetracked. If an issue is important, it should be included on the formal agenda or be suggested as an item for the next meeting (unless it is related to an item on the agenda). Without

limitations, important issues may be discussed superficially or meetings may run overtime.

c. *You explain the participation rules.* The rules may be formal or informal. Some moderators choose to use parliamentary procedures (see *Robert's Rules of Order*, Roberts and Evans, 1990) and take a formal approach to meetings. Others choose to have a free-for-all discussion with few formal or informal rules. The planner is responsible for determining which approach is most appropriate for accomplishing meeting goals. For example, if a meeting is designed to generate new ideas, including formal rules with too much structure might hinder creativity.

d. *You introduce a recording system.* Groups need a common memory. Too often, as mentioned in Chapter Five, participants don't listen effectively. A recording system allows for ideas to be written down for future reference. In addition, selecting an individual as a recorder also encourages involvement and participation. Recorders may make notes on flip charts or blackboards so that all group members can see what they have accomplished, or recorders may take notes that are summarized frequently. It is a good idea to send group members a summary of what was recorded to use in future meetings.

e. *You ensure that meetings begin and end on time.* Meetings should start and end on time, but few do. Beginning and ending late can have damaging effects because it sets a poor precedent for subsequent meetings. In addition, if you wait for late-comers, you will get off schedule and not have adequate time to discuss items on the agenda.

f. *You allow meetings to run no longer than necessary.* Many meetings drag on without direction. Using time frames for each item on the agenda helps participants avoid getting bogged down. However, if participants seem especially interested in one issue and the discussion is going well, allow yourself the flexibility of spending more time. When you do, however, remind yourself that some time will have to be made up later in other areas.

Facilitating Discussion. As mentioned in Chapter Eight, leaders have a responsibility to encourage participation. As a planner/leader, keep in mind that the quality of participation is more important than the quantity. You need to remind participants that they have an obligation to contribute to the effectiveness of the meeting. You do this by being sensitive to attempts to participate, reinforcing early attempts to participate, placing hesitant members in favorable communication positions, and regulating destructive participation.

One of the most important responsibilities of a facilitator is his or her role during question-and-answer sessions. Keep in mind that people ask questions for clarification, to seek information, and to challenge others. Your role is to keep questioning on track and to intervene when necessary.

You may also be asked or expected to begin the questioning process. When you do, be sure to ask for ideas, opinions, and suggestions by asking such open-ended, leading questions as "Now that we have heard the problem, what suggestions do you have?" or "I know this is a sensitive issue, but what do you think we have as alternatives?" Avoid using closed questions (like "Did you understand the assignment?"), which encourage "yes" or "no" responses.

The first time you have an opportunity to use the discussion questioning technique, you may feel awkward. In order to feel more at ease, consider the following suggestions (Watson and Barker, 1998):

1. *Prepare questions in advance.* Although it is not your responsibility to ask all questions, you may have to get things started. Because it is best if you are an effective role model for other participants, keep in mind that questions should be worded concisely, require thought, require more than a one-word answer, relate specifically to the topic, and use one of the following words: *why, what, when, who, where,* or *how.*

2. *Take responsibility for asking questions.* Remember: If you want people to talk, you have to ask the right questions. If one question fails to get a response, try another approach.

3. *Wait for answers:* Don't rush participants. When there is silence, you may begin to feel uncomfortable, but participants need time to digest, think about the question, and formulate answers.

4. *Call on participants by name.* You can encourage involvement by asking questions of selected participants. As a rule of thumb, call first on those people who appear most confident; call on more timid participants later.

5. *Listen to all answers.* Follow up on all answers, as listening is a sign of respect and reinforces the person who chooses to respond. When you hear a response you didn't expect, you may tend to rush the participant. Let the group evaluate the appropriateness of the response.

6. *Repeat questions to make sure that all can hear.* Especially in larger groups or when participants can't see one another easily, you may need to repeat the question to ensure that all have heard what was said.

7. *Welcome audience questions and interruptions.* You may initially feel threatened or intimidated by disagreement or open criticism. Keep in mind that your verbal and nonverbal responses will set the stage for further discussion. Acknowledge disagreement by saying, "It looks as if we have two points of view on this topic. Let's take a moment to consider each."

8. *Summarize periodically.* Before launching into a new topic area, summarize what has been discussed up to that point. Be sure to give an unbiased account, including differing points of view.

Delivery in Formal Group Settings

As mentioned earlier, the role of the meeting planner is to make sure meetings run smoothly. Since planners often have the opportunity to serve as moderators and facilitators, it is important to examine the role of verbal and nonverbal delivery during formal group meetings. (Remember to refer to Chapter Seven for additional nonverbal communication considerations during small group interactions.)

As a moderator, your responsibility may be to provide an orientation for the meeting, introduce panelists, provide transitions between presenters, lead the question and answer session, or analyze what has been said. Since you will be evaluated on your delivery skills and abilities, it is important for you to establish and maintain a positive relationship with those in attendance. Variations in your verbal and nonverbal behaviors can build and/or weaken your first and lasting impression (Watson and Barker, 1999).

Vocal delivery is critical for maintaining listener attention and interest. Your speaking rate, inflection, vocal variety, enunciation, and use of pauses influence others' perceptions of you. In most formal settings, presenters should work to have a speaking style that is natural and conversational. Conversational speaking gives the impression that you are talking with each person individually and usually includes more vocal variety. It is also important for you to speak loudly enough so you can be heard in all areas of the room. Before beginning your remarks, check on how well participants can hear.

Physical delivery is also important. When a speaker appears nervous or uncomfortable in front of an audience, he or she may lose credibility and influence with the group. Speakers need to respect the importance of impression management. Think about mannerisms such as your posture, hand gestures, eye contact, facial expressions, and/or dress. Distracting mannerisms can hinder your effectiveness. Decisions should be based on factors such as the number of participants in attendance, how formal or informal the meeting is, the configuration of the room, and your personal preferences.

The two delivery questions asked most frequently by beginning moderators are: "What should I do with my hands?" and "How can I improve my eye contact?" We suggest that you think about what you will do with your hands in advance. While there is no single correct answer, do consider whether or not you will rest them on a lectern, put them in your pockets, hold a pen/pencil, put them behind your back, or dangle them by your sides.

Eye contact is one of the most important aspects of delivery. Moderators need to watch for and acknowledge audience reactions. For example, when you notice participants straining to hear, you need to adapt quickly by speaking more loudly or adjusting the sound system.

Remember to wear comfortable clothing that is appropriate for the audience. If participants dress in businesswear such as suits, be sure to dress similarly. The most valuable suggestion we can offer is to *practice.* Practice in the room in which you will be speaking, and use any audiovisual equipment you will be expected to operate. Find out whether or not a lectern, overhead projector, or microphone will be available. If so, get comfortable with each. This discussion of delivery has been very brief; for additional information, refer to the suggested readings or register for a public speaking course.

Principles
1. Leaders or moderators have a responsibility to be well prepared, to provide structure for the meeting, to explain the participation rules, to make sure that all items on the agenda are discussed, to avoid discussion of items not on the agenda, to introduce a recording system, to hold meetings no longer than necessary, and to begin and end meetings on time.
2. Leaders have a responsibility to encourage and facilitate participation.
3. People ask questions for clarification, to seek information, and to challenge others.
4. A facilitator's questions should be open ended and leading.
5. When using the discussion questioning technique, a facilitator should prepare questions in advance, take responsibility for asking questions, call on participants by name, listen to all answers, repeat questions, welcome questions and interruptions, and summarize periodically.
6. The meeting planner or moderator should establish and maintain a positive relationship with those in attendance.
7. When delivering formal presentations, it is necessary for the moderators to practice:
   a. Vocal delivery
      1. Speaking rate
      2. Voice inflection
      3. Vocal variety
      4. Enunciation
      5. Use of pauses
   b. Conversational speaking style
   c. Physical delivery
      1. Posture
      2. Hand gestures
      3. Eye contact
      4. Facial expressions
      5. Dress style

Evaluating the Meeting

Even with all the preparation and planning, you still need a method to determine how successful your preparations have been. Contrary to popular belief, a meeting doesn't end when it is adjourned. It is afterwards that the real value of the meeting begins to take effect. Only later do the results of what was discussed, said, and decided become apparent. Even so, you need to think of ways to get feedback.

A postmeeting evaluation can be conducted formally with a printed questionnaire or informally through word-of-mouth comments. Evaluations serve two primary purposes. First, they determine whether short-term objectives were met; second, they help planners improve future meetings. In addition to participant evaluations, you also need to conduct a personal inventory or evaluation (see Figure 11.3).

If a meeting has been successful, you need to find out specifically what worked. If it was not successful, you need to carefully analyze the situation to determine what went wrong and how the problems can be corrected for the future. You may discover that you did not prepare as well as you had thought, didn't select compatible or cohesive participants, or failed to get everyone involved. For example, you may have planned well but were nonetheless sabotaged by the meeting hotel. If this were the case, you may decide to use another facility next time. Even though you may find problems that were not critical to the meeting's success, through analysis you can identify weaknesses and increase your planning effectiveness for subsequent meetings.

CHECKLIST

After each meeting, consider the following guidelines and identify areas that you need to improve for future meetings.

_____   1. Begin the meeting on time.
_____   2. Call the meeting to order.
_____   3. Describe the nature of the problem.
_____   4. Begin the discussion of the problem.
_____   5. Follow the agenda.
_____   6. Avoid digressions and small talk.
_____   7. Maintain order.
_____   8. Avoid talking too much.
_____   9. Draw out quiet members.
_____   10. Move to the next point after the issue is discussed completely.
_____   11. Summarize frequently.
_____   12. Play the devil's advocate; feel free to disagree.
_____   13. Ask for questions from the floor.
_____   14. Preside over the question and answer period.
_____   15. Prepare questions of your own.
_____   16. Be sure that everyone can hear.
_____   17. Be open and flexible.
_____   18. Be specific and concrete.
_____   19. End the meeting on time.
_____   20. Prepare a written report when group completes its work.

FIGURE 11.3 *Responsibilities of Discussion Leaders*

Principles
1. A meeting does not end once it is adjourned.
2. Postmeeting evaluations can be conducted formally through question-naires or informally through word-of-mouth feedback.
3. Two purposes of evaluations are to determine whether short-term objectives were met and to help planners improve future meetings.

Summary

This chapter focused on the systematic process of planning for and conduct-ing meetings. Because few people receive training in what to do, considera-tions were given to steps to follow before, during, and after the meeting.

The planning process determines the success of a meeting. A meeting plan ensures that the meeting addresses important goals and reduces the likelihood of something going wrong. When given the responsibility of plan-ning a meeting, the organizer should decide whether a meeting is actually necessary; write out specific short-term and long-term objectives; prepare an agenda; select, analyze, and notify participants; and prepare the facilities. Preparing the facilities includes adapting the environment to the needs of the group and preparing and checking audio-visual equipment and materi-als in advance.

After explaining the numerous steps involved in preparation, the chap-ter then discussed conducting the meeting. Planners have five major respon-sibilities. They must be prepared, begin and end meetings on time, discuss all items included in the agenda, not discuss items not on the agenda, and ensure that meetings last no longer than necessary. In addition, planners often must serve as facilitators. As facilitators, they must remind participants of their responsibilities to participate and encourage active involvement. Facilitators are also asked or expected to begin the questioning or discussion process. Because leading a discussion can be difficult for novices, the fol-lowing guidelines were suggested: prepare questions in advance, take responsibility for asking questions, wait for answers, call on participants by name, listen to all answers, repeat questions to make sure that everyone heard, welcome questions and interruptions, and summarize periodically.

The chapter also emphasized the importance of delivery style for meet-ing planners/moderators in formal group settings. For an effective delivery, they should practice their vocal delivery, conversational speaking style, and physical delivery. Overall, practice is the most valuable recommendation for success in this area.

Finally, even after the participants have gone home, the meeting hasn't ended. The real value of a meeting comes from the results of discussion and participation. Planners need to conduct an evaluation to determine the suc-cess of their efforts. Evaluations can be conducted formally or informally.

Ideas for Discussion

1. Why are some meetings unsuccessful even with planning?

2. What kind of training should meeting planners receive to ensure meeting effectiveness?

3. During meetings you've attended in the past, what contributed most to your evaluating it as successful or unsuccessful?

4. What are the biggest challenges that meeting planners face?

5. Why do you think it may be difficult to work with group members who are volunteers, appointees, and/or elected?

6. From past experience and using information in this chapter, describe how you could help one of your meetings be more successful.

7. Explain what concerns you most about facilitating a discussion, and describe methods of making your attempts more successful.

8. What type of meeting would you most like to plan? Why? Discuss the steps you would follow.

Suggested Projects and Activities

1. As a class, select a community problem that needs a solution. Then plan a meeting to discuss the problem. Be sure to prepare a written agenda complete with short- and long-term objectives and to select participants and a meeting facility.

2. Contact a convention planner or hotel convention salesperson and set up an appointment. By interviewing the person, find out what steps he or she follows. Ask to observe the actual process, if possible, from beginning to end.

3. Select a realistic situation in which you have the responsibility of conducting a meeting. Using the guidelines presented in this chapter, make a list of what your responsibilities should be and prepare questions to use for facilitating a discussion.

4. Attend a meeting with another classmate. Determine what planning was used and observe how the meeting was conducted. Using the form shown in Figure 11.3, evaluate the success of the meeting. Provide suggestions for the future.

References

Adler, R. B., and J. M. Elmhorst. *Communicating at work: principles and practices for business and the professions*, 6th ed. New York: McGraw-Hill, 1999.

Cotton, J. L. *Employee involvement: methods for improving performance and work attitudes.* Newbury Park, CA: Sage, 1993.

Goodall, H. L. *Small group communication in organizations*, 2nd ed. Dubuque, IA: Wm. C. Brown, 1990.

Hackman, M. Z., and C. E. Johnson. *Leadership: a communication perspective*, 2nd ed. Prospect Heights, IL: Waveland, 1996.

Kieffer, G. D. *The strategy of meetings*. New York: Simon and Schuster, 1988.

Pursley, M. G., and K. W. Watson. How to plan and hold a meeting. *CITIBUSINESS*, August 1983, 33–34.

Pursley, M. G., and K. W. Watson. *Meeting planner's manual: a guide for effectively preparing and conducting meetings*. Auburn, AL: SPECTRA, 1982.

Roberts, H. M., and W. J. Evans. *Robert's rules of order*, rev. ed. Glenview, IL: Scott, Foresman, 1990.

Schwarz, R. M. *The skilled facilitator: practical wisdom for developing effective groups*. San Francisco: Jossey-Bass, 1994.

Seibold, D. R. Developing the "team" in a team-managed organization: group facilitation in a new-design plant. In L. R. Frey, ed. *Innovations in group facilitation: applications in natural settings*. Cresskill, NJ: Hampton Press, 1995, 282–298.

Tropman, J. E., and G. C. Morningstar. *Meetings: how to make them work for you*. New York: Van Nostrand Reinhold, 1996.

Viega, J. F. The frequency of self-limiting behavior in groups: a measure and an explanation. *Human relations*, 1991, *44*, 877–895.

Watson, K. W., and L. L. Barker. *Meeting management*. New Orleans: SPECTRA, 1998.

Watson, K. W., and L. L. Barker. *The executive presentation reference guide*, New Orleans: SPECTRA Incorporated Publishers, 1999.

Weldon, E., and E. L. Mustari. Felt dispensability in groups of coactors: the effects of shared responsibility and explicit anonymity on cognitive effort. *Organizational behavior and human decision processes*, 1988, *41*, 330–351.

Yeomans, W. N. *1000 Things you never learned in business school: how to manage your fast-track career*. New York: Signet, 1985.

Zaremba, A. Meetings and frustration: practical methods for structuring group sessions. *Supervision*, 1988, *49*, 7–10.

Suggested Readings

Boehme, A. J. *Planning successful meetings and events: A take-charge assistant book*. New York: American Management Association, 1999. Planning effective meetings is not an easy task. This book is a practical guide to meeting and conference planning from initial planning to contracts, budgets, and promoting the meeting. Chapter 1, "Planning the Meeting," identifies initial questions to be answered and provides a sample timeline. Chapter 9, "Audiovisual Materials," discusses considerations when hiring an audiovisual vendor as well as a variety of room setups.

Gill, L. *How to work with just about anyone: A 3-step solution for getting difficult people to change*. New York: Simon & Schuster, 1999. Many committees seem to have people who frustrate one another. This book reveals a three-step strategy for changing irritating, nonproductive behavior.

Grice, G. L., and J. F. Skinner. *Mastering public speaking*, 3rd ed. Boston: Allyn & Bacon, 1998. Chapter 14, "Using Visual Aids," explains a variety of types of visual aids, factors to consider before using the visual aid, and guidelines to follow while using the visual aid.

Lippincott, S. M. *Meetings: Do's, don'ts and donuts: The complete handbook for successful meetings*, 2nd ed. Pittsburg, PA; Lighthouse Point Press, 1999. Chapter 7, "Managing Multisite Meetings," explores various issues related to the electronic alternatives for multisite meetings. In addition to worksheets for calculating conferencing costs, the chapter provides hints for conducting successful teleconferences. Chapter 8 discusses types of software for managing "virtual meetings" and provides tips for effective use.

Pell, A. R. *The complete idiot's guide ® to team building.* Indianapolis, IN: Alpha Books, 1999. Written by an author of nearly forty books in human resources management, this book is an entertaining and practical guide for getting people to work together harmoniously. Chapter 11, "Maintaining Harmony Within the Team," provides suggestions for creating a collaborative atmosphere.

Glossary

achievement goal The major outcome or product that the group intends to produce or seeks to achieve.

active listening Listening with the total self—including attitudes, beliefs, feelings, and intuitions.

agenda Step-by-step plan to be followed by a group or meeting.

assembly effect Occurs when the group is able to achieve something that could not have been achieved by any member alone or by a combination of individuals' efforts.

attending responses Responses that demonstrate interest and involvement in what others are saying.

attentive silence Silent time in which others can express themselves completely.

audio conferencing Allows individuals or groups of people who are located in different locations to hear and to be heard, but not to see or to be seen.

audiographic conferencing A conferencing method that combines audio conferencing with electronically created visual images.

balance Ensures that the system has more inputs than outputs.

bell curve agenda Technique for planning an agenda that divides a meeting into three parts with simple business items first, important or difficult issues in the second part, and easier items last.

buzz session Technique used to maximize the number of people involved in group discussion.

closed-minded Strong adherence to views that will prevent undertaking or listening to anything that is different, innovative, or new.

closed system One that is isolated from its environment; it does not exchange energy, matter, or information with elements outside the system.

cohesiveness Complex of forces that bind members of a group to one another and to the group as a whole.

colloquium Form of public discussion in which a group of three to six experts, selected for their divergent views, discuss a problem following the problem-solving format in front of an audience and under a chairperson's leadership.

communication channel Type of communication interaction between two individuals.

communication network Communication interaction patterns in a group, whether it be two persons, three persons, or more.

communicative act A transmission of information, consisting of discriminative stimuli, from a source to a recipient.

computer-mediated communication A conferencing method that uses multimedia computer technology to interact with individuals at different locations.

conscious personal goal An awareness of the goal to satisfy a need.

cybernetics The process of adjusting to feedback about inputs.

dampening response A response that helps group members refrain from arguing about opinions and feelings and concentrate instead on listening to and accepting (i.e., dampening) the viewpoint of other members.

decision making The process of selecting among several alternatives.

deductive reasoning Reasoning that begins with a general observation and leads to a specific conclusion.

defensive communication Communication characterized by evaluation, control, and certainty.

delayed feedback A response received after a period of time.

demographic analysis An analysis that considers the age, educational level, socioeconomic status, occupation, sex, and group membership of a target audience.

designated leader A person who is assigned the primary responsibility for guiding a discussion.

digging Behaviors that rely on empathy and attention to nonverbal messages to reduce conflict.

directive feedback A response that involves a value judgment of the speaker's message and usually hinders further interaction.

discussion attitude An individual's mental predisposition toward the topic, group members, and self.

diverting Behaviors that manage conflict by asking questions, restating the message, and providing feedback to clarify the real areas of conflict.

door openers Noncoercive invitations that encourage speakers to begin talking.

educational group A group formed to provide knowledge and instruction.

effective synergy A group characteristic used to help the group achieve its goals.

encounter or therapy group A group formed to help members adjust or make changes in their behavior.

environment The total external conditions and factors that surround us daily and are capable of influencing us as individuals.

equifinality The process whereby a system may reach its final state (equilibrium) from different initial conditions and in different ways.

evidence Facts and perceptions to be used to prove a point in determining problems and developing solutions.

feedback A message transmitted to indicate some level of understanding of and/or agreement with a stimulus or verbal message from another.

field theory Description of group behavior based on positive and negative forces inside and outside the group.

following Responses that encourage speakers to continue talking.

forum Form of public discussion in which the full audience examines a topic or problem by giving impromptu speeches, taking issue with what has been said, asking and answering questions, and responding to comments under a chairperson's leadership.

general feedback A response that gives a broad idea about how a message or comment was interpreted.

goal The objective or end result that a group or an individual seeks to achieve.

group Three or more individuals collectively characterized as sharing reasonably similar attitudes, beliefs, values, and norms; these persons possess defined relationships to one another so that each participant's behavior has consequences for the other members of the group.

group goal The reason for the group's existence; the object or end result.

groupthink Condition resulting in a highly cohesive group when group morale and uniformity of opinion become more important than critical analysis of ideas.

hierarchy Increasing levels of complexity.

immediate feedback Feedback that occurs directly after a group member makes a comment.

individual A single person functioning in a reasonably isolated setting.

inductive reasoning Reasoning that proceeds from a number of specific statements to a general conclusion.

information   Knowledge about objects and events and about the relationships between objects and events.

infrequent questions   Queries that help the listener to better understand the speaker without directing the conversation.

inputs   Energies received from the environment that keep a group functioning and on track.

instrumental cohesiveness   High attraction to the group resulting from satisfaction of achieving goals.

interact   Verbal or nonverbal act of one person followed by a verbal or nonverbal act of another person.

interact system model   Systems theory model that helps analyze interaction within small groups.

interdependence   A characteristic suggesting elements of a system that interrelate and affect individual elements and the system as a whole.

internal structure   Aspects of a group, such as size, member roles, leadership styles, seating arrangements, and interaction patterns.

interpersonal conflict   The disagreement that most people call a "personality clash."

interrupting feedback responses   Responses that break into the words or thoughts of another person.

interview   A one-to-one meeting conducted to solicit information.

irrelevant feedback   A response that does not apply to the situation that is being discussed at the time.

leaderless small group   A group in which all members share the leadership function.

leadership   Communication skills that move a group toward its recognized goal and/or maintain the group in any given situation.

leadershipless small group   A group in which no member provides actions that move the group toward its goal.

lifespace   Physical space in which a group member has activity.

listening   The selective process of attending to, hearing, understanding, and remembering aural (and at times visual) symbols.

listening teams   Subgroups formed when a moderator divides a group into teams prior to a lecture or presentation, with each team assigned a specific listening task. Afterwards, each team serves as a resource for discussions that follow.

long-term objectives   Specific planned outcomes for a meeting.

maintenance goal   A goal designed to maintain, strengthen, and/or ensure the continued existence of the group; refers to the social climate of the group.

maintenance synergy   A characteristic used to establish rapport, overcome conflict, control disruptive participants, and maintain relationships.

masking   Displaying a facial expression that is different from inward beliefs or feelings.

media-assisted groups   Individuals at different locations interact simultaneously with the aid of audio, video, audiographic, or computer electronics.

minimal encouragers   Responses that signal interest in what others are saying, thereby encouraging them to continue talking.

motivation   Force that impels or repels an individual toward or from people or conditions of the group.

need   A perceived discrepancy between perception of the present status and perception of an ideal status.

nominal group technique   A technique that involves the four steps of idea formation, idea documentation, idea ranking, and idea discussion/evaluation.

nondirective feedback   A response that encourages discussion by keeping options open.

nonverbal communication   All communication forms other than the written or spoken word that impart meaning to an individual or group.

open-minded Objective reflection on the ideas presented by others.

open system One that interacts with the environment.

outputs Products, information, and/or services that a system or group sends to its environment.

panel Public discussion in which a group of four to eight experts discuss a problem, following the problem-solving format, in front of an audience and under a chairperson's leadership.

passive listening Absorbing the message without critically evaluating it or trying to understand or remember it.

perception An awareness or process of becoming aware, as a result of sensory stimulation, of objects, events, conditions, and relations that are internal or external to a person.

perception field Composed of all those stimuli that are discriminated collectively at a given time and determines what is perceived, not what is there to perceive.

personal goal An objective or end result that an individual attempts to achieve.

personal space Thought of as an expanding and contracting bubble of air that surrounds a person. (Invasion of personal space may result in withdrawal.)

phillips 66 See *buzz session.*

physical delivery Behaviors and mannerisms (i.e., posture, hand gestures, eye contact, facial expressions, and/or dress) that influence impressions speakers make in front of audiences.

population traits Member characteristics, such as age, educational level, income, values, attitudes, and motivations.

presence of others Unleashes social contingencies and constraints that are not always present when an individual works alone.

primary group Composed of family members or close friends who provide a sense of belonging and support.

principle of least group size Group just large enough to include individuals with all the relevant skills to solve the problem, yet small enough to provide opportunities for individual participation.

private discussions Discussions not held before an audience; they do not involve participation by nonmembers.

problem A question proposed for solution or consideration implying certain obstacles that must be overcome.

procedural conflict Disagreement about the procedures to be followed in accomplishing the group goal.

process The dynamics of small group communication, or the changing nature of the individual and intragroup interactions.

proposition A statement advocating a particular plan or point of view.

public discussions Discussions held before an audience that often encourage participation from the audience members.

purpose That which makes a goal attractive; the objective or end result that a group or an individual seeks to achieve.

purpose-oriented analysis An analysis that gives an idea about how much information an audience has about a particular topic.

quality circle A group consisting of six to eight employees who meet voluntarily on a regular basis to generate ideas and to discuss work-related problems.

reasoning A technique used to demonstrate how the evidence proves a particular point.

reflective responses Responses that restate the feelings and/or content of a communication.

relational competencies Communication skills necessary for managing interpersonal relationships and group climate.

restrictive feedback A response that occurs when group members are concerned about the consequences of being open and honest during a meeting.

role A set of behaviors that are expected of and/or displayed by the individual who occupies a particular position in a group's structure.

role influence Influence of one individual over another by power, authority, or persuasion.

role playing Procedure in which group members are assigned roles relevant to a particular problem under study and then are placed in situations in which they act out, in an impromptu fashion, the implications of the situation.

role skills Characteristics that enable an individual to enact a role effectively.

self-concept A person's attitude about or view of self.

self-directed or natural work teams Small group of employees who are responsible for an entire group process, segment, or activity.

self-help group Voluntary members who provide support for each other while attempting to solve mutual problems and/or deal with normal crisis situations without the guidance of trained professionals.

serious listening Listening to analyze the evidence or ideas of others and making critical judgments about the validity and/or quality of the material presented.

short-term objectives Overall goals or plans for a group or organization.

small group A collection of individuals, from three to fifteen in number, who meet in face-to-face interaction over a period of time—generally with an assigned or assumed leader—who possess at least one common characteristic and who meet with a purpose in mind.

small group communication Process of verbal and nonverbal face-to-face interaction in a small group.

social group Composed of members whose primary goal is to share ideas and conversation.

social listening Employed in informal small group settings, and usually associated with interpersonal conversation and entertainment.

social loafing Condition resulting when there are more group members to share

responsibilities but the members become less productive.

socio-emotional cohesiveness High attraction to the group based on rewarding interpersonal relationships.

solution getting Process of discovering possible solutions to a particular problem.

specific feedback Responses that provide clear-cut comments about how a message or comment was interpreted.

stereotypes Categories individuals are placed in by first impressions and snap judgments from past experience; impressions quickly formed from physical appearance or small details of clothing.

subgoals Implied in the main goal or explicitly stated as subordinate goals by the group after the formulation of the main achievement goal.

supportive communication Occurs when group members listen openly and are more accepting of the opinions of others.

survey Information-gathering technique used to gather a cross-section of information or opinions.

synergy Total amount of energy available to the group to perform its activities.

syntality A group's personality or effect as a totality.

system A complex of interacting elements.

systematic Step-by-step plan for approaching problems in small group discussion.

systems analysis Suggests that one consider information about each element and the interrelationships among the elements to understand and make predictions about the system as a whole.

tangential feedback Responses that tend to sidetrack a conversation and divert the group from the actual purpose of the discussion.

task An act, or its result, that a small group is required to perform, either by itself or with someone else; tasks are performed to accomplish goals.

task competencies Communication skills necessary to perform tasks and to manage group goals.

task conflict Disagreement about the substance of a discussion.

teambuilding Creating a sense of team spirit or group unity.

teleconferencing Audio and/or video techniques that allow individuals at different locations to communicate with one another at the same time.

territory Area over which ownership is felt. (Invasion of territory may result in aggressive behavior.)

theory of group syntality Emphasizes the importance of interrelationships within groups.

therapy group Five to ten individuals who attempt to alter their behavior or emotions under the guidance of a trained professional.

unconscious personal goal A goal pursued without awareness of what one is seeking.

video conferencing Technique that allows two-way communication among individuals or groups interacting with one another in different locations.

vocal delivery Voice qualities (i.e., speaking rate, vocal variety, enunciation, and use of pauses) which influence how speakers come across to an audience.

Index